Textiles *of the* Islamic World

Textiles *of the* Islamic World

John Gillow

With 638 illustrations, 623 in color

Contents

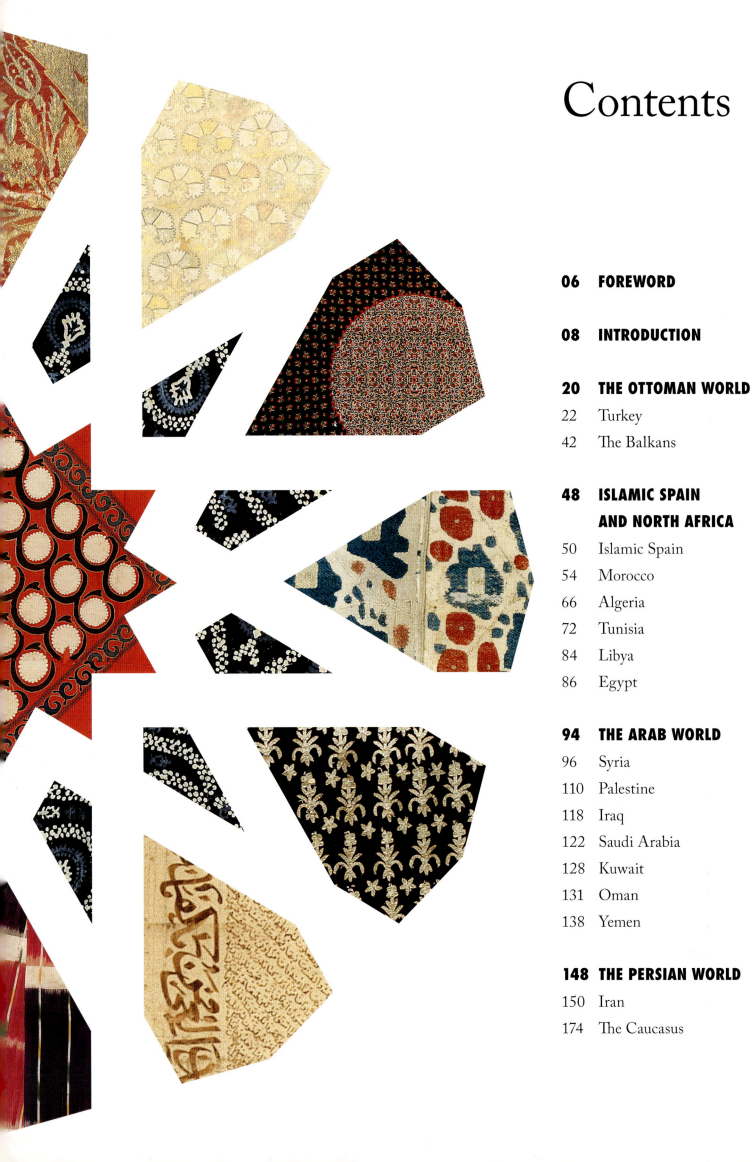

06 FOREWORD

08 INTRODUCTION

20 THE OTTOMAN WORLD
22 Turkey
42 The Balkans

48 ISLAMIC SPAIN AND NORTH AFRICA
50 Islamic Spain
54 Morocco
66 Algeria
72 Tunisia
84 Libya
86 Egypt

94 THE ARAB WORLD
96 Syria
110 Palestine
118 Iraq
122 Saudi Arabia
128 Kuwait
131 Oman
138 Yemen

148 THE PERSIAN WORLD
150 Iran
174 The Caucasus

182 CENTRAL ASIA
184 Uzbekistan
203 Turkmenistan
212 Tajikistan
215 Kyrgyzstan
218 Afghanistan

232 THE MUGHAL WORLD
234 India
247 Pakistan
260 Bangladesh

266 EAST AND SOUTHEAST ASIA
268 China
272 Malaysia
276 Indonesia
290 The Philippines

294 SUB-SAHARAN AFRICA
296 East Africa
300 West Africa

308 GLOSSARY
310 FURTHER READING
312 MUSEUM COLLECTIONS
315 PICTURE CREDITS
316 ACKNOWLEDGMENTS
317 INDEX

Foreword

Forty years ago, as a young schoolboy, I travelled to Istanbul. Wending my way through the still remaining piles of Byzantine ruins, I found myself a cheap place to stay. The next morning I awoke with a start to the call of the muezzin, a sound that was to become increasingly familiar over the decades, as I spent more and more of my time in the Muslim world. That day I went to the Grand Bazaar, looking for an embroidered waistcoat for a schoolfriend. The search was long, only coming to fruition after several increasingly gauche attempts at bargaining. The Istanbulis always had the better of me; in fact they probably do to this day, much as I would like to think otherwise.

As I wandered around the bazaar, I was entranced by carpets, furs, beaten brass, carved wood and exotic silver jewelry, none of which a poor schoolboy's pockets could afford. What I did find were scraps of Ottoman embroidery, which were then very cheap, and which I bought as presents for my sister, girlfriend and doting grandmother. I was hooked – not just on the textiles themselves, but on the lives of the peasants and nomads who had created them. I resolved there and then to lead a life of travel, focused on finding out more about hand-crafted textiles and their origins.

By the late 1970s I was making my living collecting and selling Asian folk textiles. Though I spent much time in India, and later China and Africa, I kept coming back to textiles used and created by Muslims. If I look in retrospect at my travels, my pathways criss-cross the world of Islam like a latter-day Ibn Battutah, only concentrating on fabrics rather than scholarship. In some sense I have become like the archetypal Muslim merchant, buying in one place, selling (hopefully at a profit) in another, and in the meantime absorbing much home-spun philosophy, together with current political gossip, along the way.

Wandering through an oriental bazaar or souk has remained a constant delight. One walks past the mounds of fruit and vegetables, the fish and meat, the neat pyramids of spices, and there, around a corner, is an old man drinking tea with piles of rugs, shelves of textiles and examples of the now-unfashionable local costume hanging up. Textile heaven awaits, and after a getting-to-know-you period, establishing a common language of business, one can start to sort through every pile and cupboard and, with a little gentle haggling, start to purchase. Sometimes the simplicity and line of the textiles will be what impresses, sometimes the complexity; always the style.

On occasion there are working looms, dye-works and embroiderers nearby, but more often than not one has to ask around and arrange interpreter and transport to an outlying village or suburb. Dealers, once you get to know them, can be sources of information, but its reliability is never to be trusted, so one always has to cross-check and cross-reference before something approaching the truth emerges. If you are trying to find out about a particular textile, you will sometimes have to do the basic research yourself, but usually you will find scholarly works that can help you, or give you clues as to where to look next.

This book aims to supply a broad survey of the textiles produced today and in the past in the Islamic world, putting them in their social and historical context. It is the sum of many years spent travelling and collecting, predominantly in Muslim lands. It has been a most enjoyable task, and one in which I have been so generously helped, not least by the mostly unknown creators of the wonderful textiles that illustrate the pages of this book.

OPPOSITE
Egyptian camel litter with elaborate animal trappings.

ABOVE
Women of North Morocco dressed in shawls and baggy pantaloons.

ABOVE AND BELOW
Turkish dancing girls dressed in cotton chemises, metal-thread waistcoats, pantaloons and silk sashes.

LEFT
Kurdish chieftain wearing a tapestry-weave coat (*meshla*).

Introduction

The spread of Islam in the seventh century AD not only propagated one of the great world religions but also produced a vast network of trade based on common values and the shared language of Arabic. The rise of the new religion and the founding of a colossal political and trading empire were accompanied by marked interchanges of population. It was not uncommon, for instance, for soldiers, administrators and merchants in Islamic Spain to be Syrians or Yemenis, and for their counterparts in India to be Turks, Persians or even Moroccans.

Technology spread in a like manner, and among the most vital – and often most complex – technologies were those of weaving and related crafts. There is evidence, for example, that looms were set up in early medieval Syria to weave figured silks, and the essential parts were then exported to Spain with the heddles pre-set and ready to be used. Textiles formed a crucial role in the worldwide Muslim economy, providing trade and employment, profits and taxes.

What is it that distinguishes the textiles of the Muslim world? Broadly, within this text, we understand the term 'Islamic textiles' to mean textiles made or used by those who profess the faith of Islam. Muslims are found from Morocco in the west to China in the far east, and from the Tatar communities of Russia in the north to as far south as Cameroon in Africa and Indonesia in Asia. Though, in some regions, there is a measure of continuity between textiles that preceded the Islamic era and textiles that followed, there are also certain qualities that distinguish Islamic textiles from those made and used in regions altogether untouched by Islam.

In the Muslim world, pre-Islamic styles were pared down over the years to eliminate any representational images, resulting in what is sometimes known as 'aniconic art'. No such stylistic restriction took place in those societies that resisted the spread of Islam. Post-Islamic textiles in the Muslim world are characterized, along with their avoidance of human and animal forms, by the use of abstract designs and rich decoration. The accent is on ornamentation – calligraphy (devout Muslims emphasize the spiritual benefits of the repetition of the names of the One God), plant life or geometric forms.

Calligraphic decoration has always been much in vogue. The Arabic script is of itself very attractive and, as there are numerous ways to represent Arabic letters, an extensive artistic lexicon has become available. The plant motif, or arabesque – an unbroken, curling line – derives from the Mediterranean vine motif of the Romans and the Byzantines. The Arabs took this motif and incorporated it into their art, making it characteristically Islamic and using it to fill in empty spaces. Geometric forms – straight lines, squares, triangles, diamonds, circular motifs and their variants – can all be added to the calligraphy and arabesques as the designer requires. These geometric forms may have a talismanic, even magical, significance.

Throughout this book we shall look at why textiles of the Islamic world hold an enduring fascination. We shall explore where they come from, who makes them and what

OPPOSITE
Detail of an early seventeenth-century Ottoman silk and metal-thread brocade fragment.

they are used for. We shall concentrate not only on what are traditionally regarded as Islamic textiles – the prestige textiles of the Near and Middle East, North Africa, Moorish Spain and Mughal India – but also items from the whole of the Muslim world, places where Muslims are in the majority, or are a substantial and important minority.

THE HISTORY OF THE SPREAD OF ISLAM

After the death of the Prophet Mohammed in AD 632, the newly converted Arabs established their capital in Damascus. Leadership devolved upon the Rashidun, a succession of four 'rightly guided' caliphs (from the Arabic *khalifa*, meaning 'deputy'). Ali, son-in-law and cousin of the Prophet, was chosen as the fourth caliph in AD 656. However, Mu'awiya, the governor of Damascus and a member of the Umayyad family, seized the Caliphate in AD 661, thereby causing a war during the course of which Ali was killed. Thereafter the Caliphate was made hereditary. Those who accepted this became known as 'Sunni' (from the Arabic *sunna*, meaning 'those who follow the right path', i.e. follow the example of the Prophet). Those who had been supporters of Ali were known as 'Shi'at' Ali' (*shi'at* being Arabic for 'party [of]'); they later divided into different sects. The great schism in Islam – enduring to this very day – is between the Sunni and the Shia.

The Arabs took advantage of the internecine wars that had weakened their neighbours and very soon conquered parts, or the whole, of two of the greatest textile-producing empires of the ancient world. The Byzantine empire survived (though it lost the fabled weaving centres of Egypt and Syria), while the whole of Persia was taken. Under the conquering Umayyads, the frontiers of Islam underwent expansion at a scarcely believable pace. The Arabs advanced into Central Asia and to the borders of China. They also expanded their rule westward across North Africa, and by AD 711 had crossed the Straits of Gibraltar to commence the rapid conquest of Spain.

In AD 750, however, the Abbasids took control of the Caliphate (the overthrown Umayyads retained Al-Andalus and set up a separate Western Caliphate at Córdoba in Spain in AD 756). The Abbasids moved their capital to Baghdad. Mesopotamia had long been under Iranian control, and the consequence of the creation of a new capital in the region was the increasing Persianization of the ruling Arab elite.

In the late 800s the Abbasids lost control of Egypt, their richest textile-producing province. First, the Tulunids took it over. Then came the brief dynasty of the Ikhshidids. After that came the Fatimids, Shia invaders from Kairouan in Tunisia, who denoted their dynasty by taking the name of Fatima, the Prophet's daughter and widow of the martyred Ali. In AD 969 the Fatimids established their Caliphate in Cairo. The Abbasids retained their base in Baghdad, but in 1258 the fabled city – site of thousands of looms, and haunt of the legendary caliph Haroun al-Rashid – fell to a new scourge of the world, the Mongols. As with Merv and the other rich cities of Khorasan (the historic region covering parts of modern-day Iran, Turkmenistan, Uzbekistan and Afghanistan), Baghdad was completely destroyed. It was the Mamluks – a militarized dynasty of manumitted slaves of Turkish, and subsequently Circassian, descent – who saved Egypt with all its riches, textile and otherwise. In 1260 they defeated the Mongols at the battle of Ain Jalud in Palestine, and in the process safeguarded the very existence of Islam.

The Mongols, having wreaked immense destruction, eventually converted to Islam and set up an even greater trading system than the one that had existed before, reaching from Russia all the way east to Korea. The Mongols – and their Turko-Mongol descendants, the Timurids – transferred textile artisans from one part of their empire to the other, encouraging a cross-fertilization of skills and styles, especially between China and the Persian world.

In Persia, the Seljuk Turks had been defeated by the Mongols in the thirteenth century, but prior to that they had rapidly become Islamicized and made inroads into Byzantine Anatolia, establishing a capital at Konya. It was the Seljuk Turks who laid the foundation for another Turkic clan to set up an empire centred in Anatolia and the Balkans. This was to become known as the Ottoman empire. While the Shia Safavid dynasty ruled in Persia from 1501 to 1736, and the Mughal emperors (descendants of the Timurids) ruled in India effectively from 1526 to 1707, and in name up until 1858, the Ottoman empire, from 1453 based in Constantinople (transmogrified into Istanbul), lasted from 1299 to 1923.

Down through the centuries – as dynasty succeeded dynasty, lands were conquered, and people travelled and migrated – Islam spread far and wide. Today, in addition to the Islamic heartlands of Arabia, Syria and Mesopotamia, North Africa, Turkey, Iran and Central Asia, there are large bodies of Muslims in the Balkans, the Caucasus, India, China, Southeast Asia, and East and West Africa.

THE HISTORY OF THE TEXTILE TRADE IN THE ISLAMIC WORLD

The spread of Islam explains why textiles may be more important in Muslim lands than they are anywhere else. Islam is, ultimately, the creation of the mobile, fast-moving, mounted, nomadic tribesmen who in the seventh century AD swept out of the harsh environment of Arabia to conquer much of the civilized world in a matter of decades. These Arabs perforce travelled light, and used textiles for tent-making, bedding, furniture, storage and decoration.

Once the world of Islam started to settle down after the initial upheavals of the conquests, and once the Umayyad Caliphate was established at Damascus, the new Muslim rulers adopted the methods of textile production that were already in place. In both Egypt and Persia – then the two dominant centres for the weaving of sophisticated textiles – a system of state textile workshops was long established. Given the vast number of costumes and other textiles made of expensive fabrics such as cloth of gold, it was only the state that possessed the capital to undertake such an enormous enterprise; no private entrepreneur could have commanded the resources.

All over the Muslim world, these state workshops were known as *tiraz*, a Persian-derived word originally meaning

OPPOSITE
Sixteenth-century panel of cut-pile velvet, Bursa, Ottoman Turkey.

BELOW
Italian-influenced eighteenth-century embroidered panel, Azzemour, Morocco.

OPPOSITE
Kaitag embroidery, Daghestan, *c.* 1800.

LEFT
Sufi banner collected in Egypt, but probably made in a Tunisian workshop in the late eighteenth century.

'embroidery'. In pre-Islamic Persia, the Sasanian dynasty (AD 224–651) had customarily presented opulent robes to its nobles and state officials with the name of the ruler embroidered in bands upon the garment. This practice was adopted by the Abbasid caliphs and other medieval Muslim rulers who followed them. The robes – often adorned with statements praising the ruler, and saying when and for whom the robe was made, and sometimes including the maker's name – also became known as *tiraz*, even when the embroidered bands were replaced with woven inscriptions. Eventually the weaving workshops took the name as well, and produced luxurious textiles not only for the court but also for wealthy members of the public. Ultimately this method of utilizing state workshops itself became known as *tiraz*, and the system was used by all the great Muslim empires – in Umayyad Damascus, and by the successive Caliphates of the Abbasids in Baghdad, the Western Caliphate of Córdoba in Moorish Andalusia and the Fatimids in Cairo, and later the Mamluk slave dynasty in Cairo, and finally the last great Muslim empires of the Safavids in Persia, the Mughals in India and the Ottomans at Constantinople.

As the centuries passed, an increasing majority of the populations in these Muslim empires also converted to Islam, though this was by no means true of all textile workers. There were many Christian weavers, as well as Jewish dyers and textile merchants, not to mention the myriad Hindu textile workers in India. Despite this, Muslim mores became overwhelmingly dominant – to such an extent that, by the thirteenth century, the figurative motifs of humans and animals inherited from previous civilizations and tolerated, in fact till then popular, were replaced by the arabesques, geometric patterns and floral motifs that we think of as typical of Islamic art today.

Islam is a religion of the law. Among the Sunni, four schools of law were eventually established – the Hanbali in Saudi Arabia, Shafi'i in Syria and Egypt, Hanafi in Turkey and Central Asia, and Maliki in Africa and Southeast Asia. Each of these differed in geographical influence, and of course in interpretations of the law. Most contentious was the permissibility of the representation of human and animal forms. Under some jurisdictions this was eventually prohibited, but under others – especially in Shia territories – it was not. Iran, for example, was always a centre of Shiism, and under the greatest of its shahs, the Safavid Abbas I, founder of Isfahan, the Shiite rite became the Persian state religion. Under the Safavids, textiles represented all manner of human and animal forms. Over the centuries, in the Sunni lands, however, representational images in textiles were gradually dropped, and decoration was achieved through geometric and calligraphic forms.

The unification of much of the world into one empire under one religion meant that a vast, highly enriching trading system was established, covering Asia from the Mediterranean over to India and beyond. The new Islamic world had a common religion, a common language and a developing but mutually shared cultural heritage, and these facts encouraged great mobility. Craftsmen, merchants, soldiers and scholars could move freely within the Islamic world and be confident of finding secure employment (this sense of cosmopolitanism was further encouraged by the fact that the ruler of any particular area was more than likely to have come from somewhere else himself). North Africa and Muslim Spain developed strong trading relations with Christian Europe on the one hand and

INTRODUCTION

China on the other. Trading routes were also established from North Africa south into sub-Saharan Africa. By value, the most important commodities to be traded were textiles and the dyes and other raw materials needed for their production, and many were the pious Muslims who earned their living as merchants in textile souks and bazaars.

It was on the land route known as the Silk Road that Marco Polo and his father and uncle travelled to farthest Cathay. Although their route pre-dated Islam, it was under Muslim rule that the cities and oases dotted along the various branches developed and prospered. The Silk Road even survived the depredations of the Mongols and their successors, the Timurids. Baghdad, Merv, Herat and later Delhi were destroyed and divested of their weavers, but the Silk Road survived, and new outposts of weaving culture were set up by the Mongols from the thirteenth century onwards.

The silk route of legend had carried a two-way trade, with textile technology going east and sericulture coming west. Trading centres had already been established in Syria, around the Caspian Sea, and in Central Asia and the Tarim Basin to the east. After the Mongols had completed their swift and brutal conquests, they gave new life to the Silk Road by establishing and giving tax incentives to sophisticated silk and gold weaving centres towards the eastern end of the route on the borders with China. Muslim artisans were taken east to assist with these endeavours. Weavers from West Asia, primarily from Khorasan, were settled in East Asia, fuelling a vibrant exchange of weaving skills with Chinese weavers.

What the first Arab conquerors had done was to establish a common economic market. The Mongols made this market much larger and gave it a greater degree of homogeneity. The West had nothing to compare with these huge trading territories and their textile innovations, prior to the activities of the Italian trading states, though the Crusades had exposed Christian Europe to the products of the Muslim world (the early medieval ladies' fashion for high conical hats and hanging sleeves was but one of the things brought home from Syria and the Holy Land by the Crusaders).

As Islam spread, in the wake of merchant caravans and trading dhows, Muslim dealers acquired reliable trading partners with the same system of ethics in new territories, including West Africa and the East Indies. A Muslim merchant's word was his bond, and this proved essential in a worldwide trading system based more often on mutual trust

ABOVE
Akhnif, man's cloak, Morocco.

BELOW
Bank of the Tigris, Iraq, a conduit of the textile trade for millennia.

OPPOSITE ABOVE
Appliquéd alcove cover, Ganga, Azerbaijan.

OPPOSITE BELOW
Dress from Beit al-Dar, near Jaffa, Palestine.

than on written, but generally unenforceable, contracts. Great cities and ports had already been established – Timbuktu and Kano in West Africa; Malacca, Banda Aceh, Banten, Macassar and Sulu in the East Indies – and some of these continued to flourish. Much of the trading was based on textiles – indigo-dyed cotton in West Africa; Indian woven and printed textiles in the East Indies – though in a rough and ready world this kind of legitimate trade could always be supplemented by slave-running, caravan-raiding and piracy.

The spread of Islam influenced styles of dress, introducing Muslim codes of modesty to tropical regions where clothing requirements were relatively minimal. In sub-Saharan Africa, a whole genre of clothing – the wide-sleeved, all-enveloping Muslim robe – developed. In Southeast Asia, ikat-dyed sarongs became fashionable, most probably in imitation of those worn by Yemeni sailors (examples of their cotton warp ikat are known from the tenth century AD, and Yemenis still run ikat and batik workshops in northeast Java to this day). In both sub-Saharan Africa and Southeast Asia, the sartorial strictures of the new religion proved a great stimulus to the local weaving industry, as well as encouraging imports. Indeed, it is noteworthy that many of the weavers of silk weft ikat in Southeast Asia today are Muslims. This includes not only Indonesia but also countries in which Muslims are a minority, such as Thailand and Cambodia.

As the centuries passed, textiles – a form of merchandise relatively impervious to upset and military disaster – remained the main commodity of the vast interconnected trading system that was available to whomever ruled the Islamic lands.

THE TRADE OF SILK, COTTON, LINEN AND WOOL IN THE ISLAMIC WORLD

Historically, silk was the highest valued textile commodity in the world, and because of its lightness it was the most widely traded. It had, from early times, become a crucial item of trade for both the Byzantine and Sasanian empires, which in their weakness had been so shockingly overcome by the Arab invasions. The developing Islamic culture drew heavily on the art of these two empires, continuing for centuries to use designs whose origins lay within the pre-Islamic era.

Techniques of weaving mulberry silk had been smuggled out of China, at first to Khotan and then to the Ferghana valley, reaching Byzantium by the sixth century AD. The province of Tabaristan, on the Caspian coast of Persia, became the greatest

INTRODUCTION **15**

producer of raw silk in the non-Chinese world, and – until mulberry trees and silkworm-rearing farms were established in such places as Córdoba in Spain in the eighth century – weavers in the Muslim world relied on Persia for supplies of their raw materials. Aleppo in northern Syria became the entrepot through which Persian silk, and also goods from India, reached the Mediterranean world. In consequence, the city became fabulously rich.

Eventually figured silks in complex techniques such as lampas and samite were produced by the weavers of Persia, Egypt, Baghdad and Moorish Spain. These textiles were much desired by the institutions of Europe, and were used to make up vestments for high churchmen and coronation robes for Christian sovereigns, despite the fact that they were often embellished with Arabic calligraphy (Roger II of Sicily's coronation robe, preserved in Vienna, is a famous case in point). The heraldic imagery of hunting scenes and beasts both real and imaginary decorating these Islamic export textiles appealed to the prevailing European aesthetic, which seems to have differed little from that of the Muslims.

Meanwhile, Indian cotton had long been traded to Yemen and the rest of the Arabian peninsula, though an indigenous or domesticated cotton plant was also to be found there. At the earliest stage of trade, during the time of the seventh-century Muslim conquests of Persia, Syria and Egypt, cotton was still only known as an exotic import, and then probably solely as a finished product. The English word 'cotton' is, however, derived from the Arabic *qutn* – a tribute to the Arab role in establishing the fibre as a highly desirable medium for cloth and in spreading cotton cultivation throughout Asia and parts of Africa.

Linen was in common use in the Mediterranean Classical and post-Classical worlds. It had been the fabric of the pharaohs and, along with wool, was much favoured in the world-renowned weavings of the Egyptian Christian Copts.

Wool husbandry had emerged out of Anatolia and Mesopotamia in millennia past, from which spinning and weaving had developed. Because of its perceived naturalness and simplicity, it was always deemed eminently suitable for the *ulema*, the Muslim law-givers and de facto clergy.

Throughout the centuries, materials and techniques continued to spread from place to place, carried by traders, migrants and missionaries. In some locations, new forms were adopted wholesale; in others, they were adapted to local needs or aesthetic tastes.

OPPOSITE
Embroidered detail of a late eighteenth-century double-panelled bedcover, Chefchaouen, northern Morocco.

BELOW
Late nineteenth-century tapestry-woven strip, Syria.

THE LAST GREAT MUSLIM EMPIRES

When the Ottoman Turks under Selim the Grim took Egypt in 1517, they inherited, along with the Caliphate, Egypt's fabulously wealthy textile industry, based in the Nile delta towns of Tinnis and Damietta, and in Fayoum and other parts of Middle and Upper Egypt. The Turks adapted the existing *tiraz* system to their own ends, though by this time they were beginning to suffer competition from the new silk industries of Italy and a newly re-Christianized Spain. Ottoman weavers produced for court use silk and precious-metal brocades and *cetma* (velvets), often voided, with distinctive, dramatic, uncluttered, floral patterns influenced by the newly fashionable Italian silks. Centres of production were Bursa, Istanbul and the Aegean island of Chios, the latter being under Venetian rule for some considerable time during the Ottoman years.

Ottoman silks were dependent on raw silk imported from Persia and, when commercial rivalry with Persia descended, as it often did, into war in the time of Sulaiman the Magnificent, the cessation of the vital supply of raw yarn crippled the Ottoman silk industry. Safavid Persia under Shah Abbas became a world-renowned supplier of figured silk and velvets. The velvets, in particular, with images of beautifully drawn hunting scenes, picnics and drinking parties set against a golden yellow, were world-famous and highly valued when they were received as diplomatic gifts, whether in Europe, Russia, Japan or Siam.

Mughal India, whose territory for much of its duration included Kabul in Afghanistan (famous for its indigo dyeing), was at first influenced by the Safavids in all its arts, including

INTRODUCTION 17

textiles, but later the influence flowed the other way. Mughal India was renowned, as India always has been, for its weaving and dyeing. The Mughal aesthetic – most probably influenced by the new botanical drawings brought into India from Europe at the beginning of the seventeenth century – favoured flowers standing alone, or in rows of two or three. It was this Mughal fashion that was to influence later Safavid brocades and velvets. The outstanding Mughal textile was the *patka*, a girdle that hung stiffly from a man's and on occasion a woman's waist, clearly displaying silk and metal-thread brocade images of freestanding flowers (the weaving of this kind of brocade lived on in India with the Paithani saris of central India, which were woven well into the twentieth century). The Mughals were also famed for their delicate muslins, the products of the Bengali looms around Dacca and in parts of northern India around Lucknow and Benares. Fine brocades known as *kinkhab* were also woven in Gujarat. It was in the middle years of Mughal rule that the European sea powers began to take all manner of Indian textiles to the East Indies to trade for the spices that were so highly desired in Europe.

By the eighteenth century, the Muslim world was in decline, unable to compete with Europe and its accelerating Industrial Revolution. Though India still exported its chintzes and block prints, European import restrictions and overproduction had killed off the weaving of fine muslins in Bengal. Production of fine textiles in both the Ottoman world and Persia was also dwindling. The glory of Egyptian weaving had long faded, and the fabulous figured silks of Moorish Spain were a distant memory. What remained, however, was a lively weaving industry for local consumers in wool, linen, cotton and silk, dyeing in indigo and turkey red, and much domestic and professional embroidery. Draw-loom weavers in Moroccan Fez continued the traditions of Nasrid Granada by weaving silk lampas; in Aleppo and Damascus, complex tapestry weaves were still being created; and in Central Asia, particularly in the khanates of Bokhara and Khiva, stunning warp-ikat silks and silk/cotton mixes were still being made.

Muslim influence continues to be profound, with traditions ultimately derived from the strict Wahhabis of Saudi Arabia now affecting everyday dress. There are women in Southeast Asia, India and Africa who are adopting the head- and face-veil today, where their mothers and grandmothers would have gone unveiled as a matter of course. Textiles, whether handmade or mill-manufactured, continue to be big business and keep Muslim merchants in the markets of the Islamic world busy. They, like their forefathers before them, make a steady living from the cloth trade. Meanwhile, the ingenuity and skill of their fellow Muslim artisans remain the envy of the world, and long may it remain so.

ABOVE
Tie-dyed shawl, Mauritania.

OPPOSITE
Map showing key Islamic regions.

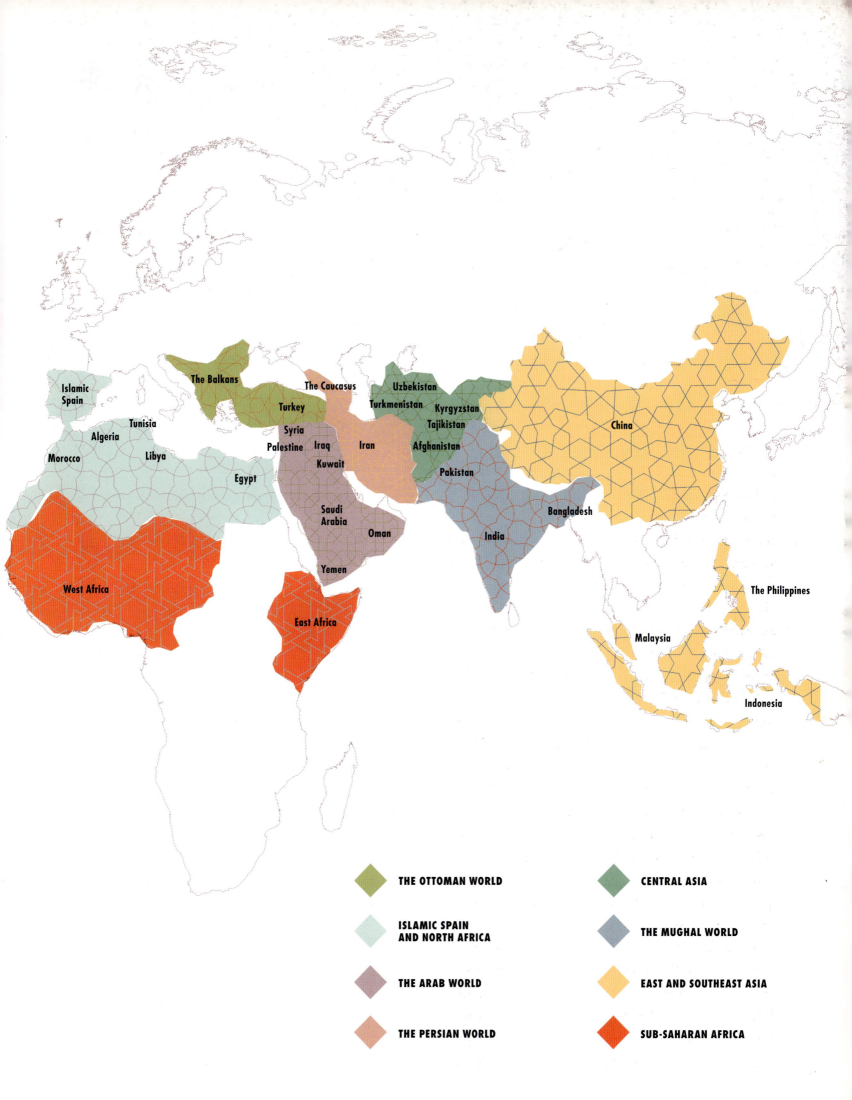

The Ottoman World

Turkey

The Ottoman empire lasted from the turn of the fourteenth century to the beginning of the twentieth century. At its greatest extent, it stretched from the frontiers of Morocco in the west to Persia in the east, and from the gates of Vienna in the north to Aden in the south. It was founded in Anatolia in AD 1299 by Osman I, after whom it was named. The Osmanlis, or Ottomans, were a Turkish tribe who had arrived in Asia Minor in the wake of their fellow Turks, the Seljuks, and carved out a minor principality around Ankara. Gradually taking power from the Seljuks in Anatolia, they expanded into the Balkans, conquering Christian Serbia and Bulgaria before finally extinguishing the Eastern Roman empire – Byzantium, or Constantinople – with the taking of the city by Mehmet II in 1453. Renaming it Istanbul and moving the capital there from Bursa, the Ottomans built a society that combined Central Asian traditions with customs from earlier civilizations.

It was from the time of the fall of Constantinople that the Ottomans became known to Christendom as the 'Turks', a name previously applied only to nomads of Central Asian origin. The Ottomans, having long intermarried with local Christians, absorbed much of the existing Byzantine textile tradition, along with its skilled workforce (the Byzantines were particularly noted for using draw-looms to fabricate complex silk lampas weaves).

The Ottoman court became famous for its fabulous wealth and for the highly decorative nature of its artifacts, especially its textiles. This preference for decoration was to filter down to every level of society and was to be a hallmark of the Ottomans throughout their empire, absorbed by Muslim and non-Muslim subjects alike.

The Seljuks, as they converted to Islam, had brought with them from the Caliphate in Baghdad the Muslim custom of presenting sumptuous robes as marks of imperial favour (less than sumptuous robes could be interpreted as disfavour). The Ottomans continued this practice. Robe-giving was known as *hilat*, and required the Sultan at the Sublime Porte (the Hall of Audience at Topkapi Palace on the Bosphorus) to keep with him a vast stock of robes of costly fabric to reward favoured sons, ministers, generals and visiting ambassadors. High officials also kept stocks of robes for the same purpose. These requirements maintained in employment a large array of weavers specializing in different types of fabric. The three main categories of prestige cloth were: *kadife* (velvet); *kemha* (brocade), in a type of lampas weave; and *seraser* (cloths of gold and silver), in a type of weave known by the French term 'taqueté'.

A more common fabric was *atlas*, a warp-faced silk, sometimes with a cotton weft in a satin weave, often decorated in the ikat technique. There was also an abundance of textiles woven in cotton, of which there was an endless supply from the Ottoman province of Syria. In addition, textiles were frequently made out of Angora goat hair, from around modern Ankara in Anatolia (the original Roman/Byzantine name for Ankara was Angora). In fact, the English word 'mohair' derives from an Arabic word, *mukhayyar* (meaning 'choice'). Sheep's wool was always abundantly used by commoners. The Muslim clergy dressed in plain-coloured garments made from unostentatious fabric, usually wool, which was esteemed for its perceived purity.

PAGES 20–21
Contemporary *mashru* cloth, Gaziantep;
eighteenth-century embroidered cover,
Istanbul; woman's sleeveless *mashru* coat,

OPPOSITE
Ottoman officials in typical attire,
Turkey, mid-nineteenth century.

MATERIALS

Wool

Wool has always been available in great quantities in Anatolia due to the abundant grazing grounds that sustain vast flocks of sheep. Wool, valued for its insulation properties, is used to weave blankets. In the past, much of the rural population's clothing was also hand-woven from hand-spun wool. Felting further increases the fibre's insulation properties, so much of the region's second-grade wool was traditionally made into felt for mats and such essential items as shepherds' cloaks.

Camel hair

As recently as fifty years ago, Anatolia was home to tens of thousands of camels. These were used for transporting goods between the mountain villages and local towns, and for moving heavy merchandise such as coal from Turkey's mines to harbour. Perhaps because camel hair is surprisingly soft, it became an expensive, prestige material, woven into clothes and floor coverings for the wealthy urban elite. It was also mixed with other fibres: it was not uncommon for a fabric to have a section of camel hair woven next to a band of white Angora. Today there are virtually no camels in Anatolia and camel hair is unobtainable.

Angora

True Angora 'wool' comes from the hair of a small goat found in central Anatolia. Angora (modern Ankara) was the main trading centre for this material, and hence it acquired its name. It is exceptionally silky and fluffy, and is warmer than other wools. Because it was always a costly fibre, it was sometimes mixed with sheep's wool. A few Angora goats are bred commercially today, but real Angora of the quality of the past is now unavailable.

Other goat hair

All goat hair expands when wet, which gives it inherent waterproofing qualities. It is also believed by rural people – peasant and Yörük nomad alike – to have certain magical properties. The superstition is that goat hair repels scorpions and snakes. Black goat hair was traditionally used for tents and floor coverings.

ABOVE
Imitation Kashmir tapestry-weave woollen cloth, Sivas.

BELOW
Turkmen nomad woman's coat of *mashru* silk and cotton fabric, West Anatolia.

OPPOSITE
Cotton and woollen indigo double-weave cloth, Mersin.

Hemp

Hemp was grown in central and northern Anatolia until its cultivation was forbidden in the 1970s, as it is the base material for the production of marijuana and hashish. Hemp fibre was particularly valued because it facilitated good air circulation and was therefore used for clothing, wheat sacks and containers for storing fruit and vegetables through the winter. It is also very strong and was used for making rope. It was considered to have magical properties, perhaps because of its dual purpose as a drug source. In the intense heat of an Anatolian summer, when most rural people like to sleep outdoors, many still prefer to sleep on fabric woven out of hemp for its coolness. Today hempen material is imported from India, but it lacks the beauty of colour and suppleness of the old Anatolian-grown fibre.

Linen

Hemp and flax were grown in the same areas. Both were processed and then woven locally. As linen was strong, light, durable and hard-wearing, with the additional property of being cool to wear in hot summers, it was used to make fine-quality clothing for wealthy merchant and well-to-do peasant alike. It was also the ground material for much Ottoman embroidery, as its even weave made the craft of counted threadwork easy. In Ottoman times, much linen fabric was also sourced from Egypt, linen's historical home.

Cotton

Traditionally, cotton was grown in western and southern Anatolia, both for domestic and industrial use, but production was only on a small scale. It was used for clothing, grain bags and mats for sun-drying fruit such as apricots or tomatoes. Like hemp, it allows good air circulation. Old cotton cloth is sometimes unpicked and the unravelled yarn used for kelims, pile rugs, upholstery, bags and curtains. Today, cotton is grown in southeast Turkey, in the newly irrigated area below the Atatürk Dam. It is used to supply Turkey's $20 million-a-year textile industry, which is devoted in large measure to the production of towelling.

Silk

The bulk of the raw silk for the Ottoman silk-weaving industry was imported from Persia, or else obtained from within Anatolia or the Greek islands. The city of Bursa was a renowned centre of manufacture from before the conquest of Constantinople. Typical motifs and techniques were much influenced by Italy, and to a lesser extent other parts of the Mediterranean, resulting in a fusion of European and Islamic designs. Floral and vegetal motifs were popular, often set in ogivals, and with great purity of line. Bursa textiles eschewed the complexity of the contemporary Safavid and Mughal fabrics of Persia and India, and for their impact placed as much reliance on voids as on in-fillings. Italian silks and velvets were also worn – often in conjunction with Ottoman fabrics of the same type – until at least the end of the eighteenth century, and these always influenced Ottoman designs.

Despite periodic injunctions forbidding the export of precious metals, brocaded cloth woven of silk wrapped with either gold or silver, and decorated with images of Christ and Christian symbols, was also exported for church use to the Orthodox treasuries and monasteries of the Balkans and Russia, where examples remain to this day.

TECHNIQUES

Embroidery

Throughout the Ottoman empire, embroidery was the most common method of decorating textiles – in earlier centuries on a ground of hand-woven cloth; in the late nineteenth and early twentieth centuries on both hand- and machine-woven cloth. Production was divided between the domestic sphere (exclusively the work of women for home consumption) and the professional sphere (work for sale, made by men in small workshops or the home). Textile scholar Roddy Taylor states that, although women were responsible for the bulk of embroidering, men made virtually all the larger pieces and all the metal-thread work. Of the examples of Ottoman embroidery that survive today, much is from the professional sphere, as domestic items would have been well used and tended to wear out with time.

Ottoman costume, with its many layers for both men and women, was held together by embroidered cloth sashes. The short sash for women was the *uckur*; the longer sash for men, the *kusak*. These sashes could be plain or striped. They were worn twisted in a coil around the waist, though narrow sashes of fine cotton or linen were worn uncoiled. The two ends were always arranged to hang down from the waist at the front, and were beautifully embroidered with largely floral patterns. As the ends could be seen from both sides, the embroidery was always double-faced. A large motif, floral or otherwise, was commonly set in a pair or in smaller patterns repeated in vertical rows. The ends of the sashes were either hemmed or given a fringe.

Another embroidered item of clothing was the baggy *salvar* (trousers), worn by both men and women. These were of different cuts and materials, but the *salvar* of both sexes had a baggy crotch and were tied with a drawstring around the waist. A woman's *salvar* were the most likely to be embroidered: the only decorated areas would be the two outer panels from ankle- or mid-calf-level up to the edge of the loose chemise that was the woman's upper garment. As with embroidery across the

OPPOSITE LEFT
Seventeenth-century Ottoman embroidered panel.

OPPOSITE RIGHT
Ottoman panel made up of eighteenth-century embroidered fragments.

ABOVE
Eighteenth-century embroidered cover, Istanbul.

RIGHT
Eighteenth-century embroidered turban cover fragment, Istanbul.

OPPOSITE
Early twentieth-century man's striped silk sash, Izmir district.

ABOVE
Silk *mashru salvar*, Bursa.

OPPOSITE ABOVE
Eighteenth-century professionally embroidered silk panel.

OPPOSITE BELOW
Eighteenth-century Ottoman embroidered panel in the Persian style.

ABOVE LEFT
Composite panel made up of trouser embroidery, Salonika or Kavala.

ABOVE RIGHT
Professionally worked towel, embroidered with garden scenes, Istanbul or West Anatolia.

BELOW
Early twentieth-century peasant woman's embroidered smock, West Anatolia.

world, there was no point in embroidering what could not be seen. The style of embroidery worked in Anatolia (Asia Minor) differed from that worked in European Turkey, the latter known as 'Rumeli' embroidery. The Anatolian style is akin to the embroidery found on sash ends, with the same single or repeated motifs, often floral. The Rumeli style, on the other hand, shows vertical rows of flowers worked in brick or chain stitch, interspersed with needle weaving and/or drawn thread work. Very few *salvar* have survived intact, but embroidered panels have been preserved, especially of the Rumeli type.

A Turkish Muslim woman's clothes were supposed to be gathered together upon her death and burned. In practice, many embroidered items were sold to merchants (often Jews and non-Muslim Armenians), who disassembled them and made them into composite and saleable rectangular shapes. The then-cosmopolitan Ottoman city of Salonika (modern Thessaloniki in Greece) was a centre of this trade, as was Kavala (also in Greece). Many of their customers were from Western Europe.

Beautiful cloths with either embroidered or woven decoration were also used to wrap gifts or to store household items. Known as *bohca*, these were large and square and

TURKEY 31

TOP
Man's embroidered trouser tie, West Anatolia.

ABOVE
Patchwork of old embroidery made into a woman's prayer cloth indicating *qibla*, or direction of prayer, Kavala.

ABOVE RIGHT
Turkmen woman's embroidered back apron, West Anatolia.

RIGHT
Silk *salvar*, decorated with couched cording, West Anatolia.

decorated in the typical Ottoman manner with floral patterns. They were always treasured, and many have survived the rigours of time.

Other important cloths that were adorned with embroidery were covers for turbans, quilts, cushions and mirrors. Aprons were even embroidered for extremely affluent men to wear while being shaved.

Oya

One of the most distinctive forms of Turkish textile art is *oya*, or needle-woven braid (also sometimes known as *bebilla*). This is used as a border for men's and women's headscarves, though in recent decades it has also been used to edge kerchiefs that have simple, floral, two- or three-colour patterns block-printed on them either in Istanbul or in smaller centres in Anatolia. Izmir and the Anatolian shore of the Bosphorus are great centres for *oya*. It is worked in the hand, without a frame, just using needle and thread. Simple decorative rows can be built up of two-dimensional flowers or leaves in a single colour. The more ambitious *oya*-maker will create three-dimensional flowers, trees, birds or animals, and introduce one or more contrasting colours. In former times, the thread most commonly used was silk or linen; in more recent times, this has been replaced with artificial fibre, even plastic. Cheaper edgings in the same style can be made with a crochet hook or by using the technique of tatting.

Beadwork

The craft of beadwork has long been practised in Turkey – in years past, using beads from Murano in the Venetian lagoon (it is possible that the craft began when the Ottomans established trading links with the state of Venice); in more recent times, using beads from Bohemia (modern Czech Republic). The main beadwork technique is that of bead-knitting, which is used to make highly decorative bags and purses. As in Syria and Albania, beadwork was often a craft for prisoners, who made tightly worked, wallet-like purses and cigarette pouches. During the First World War, Turkish prisoners-of-war in India made beadwork snakes to while away the hours – a craft that was soon imitated by the Indians themselves.

Block Printing

Turkish printing workshops used wooden blocks to produce simple cotton prints in two, three or four colours. The main

TOP
Block-printed kerchief with *oya* edging, Bursa.

ABOVE LEFT
Early twentieth-century beaded 'jail purse'.

ABOVE RIGHT
Beadwork snake made by a Turkish prisoner-of-war in India, 1919.

TURKEY 33

ABOVE
Block-printed shawl, Bursa.

BELOW
Block-printed headscarf, Istanbul.

BELOW RIGHT
Block-printed prayer cloth, Istanbul.

OPPOSITE
Cotton warp-ikat towel, Trabzon.

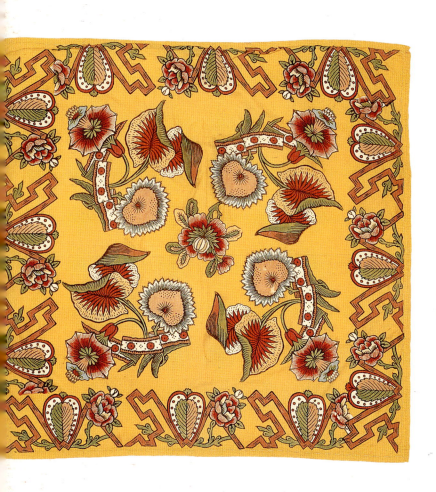

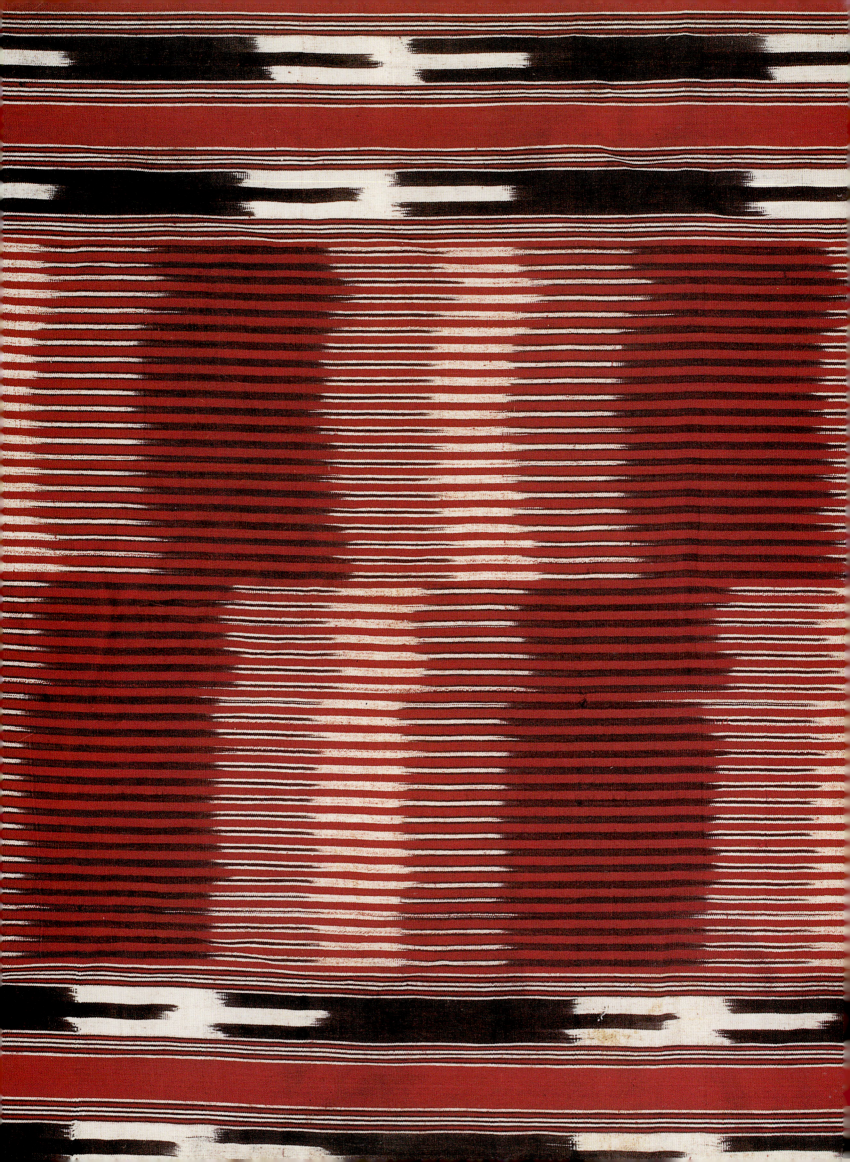

focus was the printing of women's headscarves, though interesting work is also found on prayer mats with decorative floral *mihrabs*. The workshops, often owned by Armenians, were predominantly located in Istanbul, but Bursa was another regional centre, and formerly block prints were made in many places in western Anatolia. One can speculate that the technique of block printing originated in India, becoming cruder as it moved westwards through Persia to Turkey.

Ikat and Tie-Dye

The technique of warp ikat – whereby a pattern is achieved by tying resists onto warp threads in a pre-determined pattern, then dyeing the fibres and untying the resists before the actual weaving process takes place – used to be practised in many parts of Turkey. Today, the technique, which produces cloth with characteristic fuzzy edges where one part of the design merges into another, is limited to the Black Sea port of Trabzon and the city of Gaziantep in eastern Anatolia. Weavers in and around Trabzon produce simple cotton bath towels and wraps in three colours that are in a similar style to the warp-ikat towels of Aleppo and Damascus in Syria. Gaziantep, meanwhile, is famous for its production of warp-ikat *mashru*, a warp-faced silk satin with a cotton weft. These products all have a steady market right across Turkey. Gaziantep *mashru*, whose most famous design is repeated rows of yellow arrowhead motifs, was always used to make Ottoman women's robes. The fabric also has a strong export market in nearby Syria, where it is used as a material for women's coats and as an edging and lining for plainer female garments. Tie-dyed woollen fabric is made up into women's aprons in the hills above Bursa. Silk is tie-dyed for women's headscarves inland from Izmir.

ABOVE
Woman's faux-ikat jacket, Black Sea coast, Anatolia.

BELOW
Tie-dyed woollen apron, Keles.

OPPOSITE
Woman's *mashru* coat, Gaziantep.

36 THE OTTOMAN WORLD

TOP LEFT
Early twentieth-century striped silk bedcover, Bursa.

TOP RIGHT
Woman's *mashru* waistcoat, Bursa.

ABOVE
Tie-dyed silk kerchief, Izmir district.

RIGHT
Woman's sleeveless *mashru* coat, Gaziantep.

ABOVE
Woman's knitted socks, West Anatolia.

BELOW
Shepherd's felt cape, Konya.

Knitting

Rural Anatolia, with its harsh winter climate and its verdant pasturage allowing for abundant flocks of sheep, has a strong tradition of knitting. Farm girls traditionally knitted colourful, hard-wearing socks for both themselves and their menfolk. Men wore long stockings up to the knee, with the ends of their short trousers tucked into the stocking tops. Each region has a different style, and within a given region differently patterned socks are knitted depending on the status of the wearer. A young unmarried man in the Sivas area, for example, will wear patterned socks known as *küçük ağa*, and after marriage socks known as *büyük ağa* – terms that, respectively, mean 'young gentleman' and 'old gentleman'. Other designs abound. Throughout rural Turkey, socks in patterns known as 'corporal' or 'sergeant' were given to men who had attained these ranks in the Turkish army. Men's socks tend to be more decorative than women's. Women's socks, as well as being plainer, are also generally much shorter, designed to be seen just below the wearer's *salvar* or skirt.

There was also an urban tradition of knitting in silk. Floral patterned purses and bags of a sometimes astonishing fineness were produced using this technique.

Felting

Among the most famous felted garments made by women in rural Anatolia are the large capes designed to protect shepherds from the elements. Wherever felt is made, the same basic method is practised. Sheep are washed in a river or stream, then shorn, and the resulting fleece is beaten with sticks to remove grit and burrs (spiny seed heads, or any unwanted particles of vegetable matter). To separate the fibres further, the wool may be combed or carded. If coloured felt is required, some or all of the wool may be dyed at this point. Next the wool is spread evenly on a reed mat that has been sprinkled with hot water. Then the whole is rolled up and tied into a bundle. This bundle is rolled backwards and forwards for several hours, usually under the forearms of a group of kneeling women. When the bundle is unwrapped and dried, the result is a densely intermeshed fabric that can be cut, stitched or moulded. Capes, mats and other felted items are made all over Anatolia, but in recent years Konya has specialized in making decorative coloured felt hats and mats for the tourist market.

OPPOSITE
Krim Tatar tapestry-weave cotton shawl, West Anatolia.

ABOVE
Eighteenth-century embroidered Ottoman panel.

ABOVE
Krim Tatar tapestry-weave cotton cushion, West Anatolia.

THE PRESENT

Modern Turkey was formed from the wreckage of the Ottoman empire at the end of the First World War, largely through the efforts of one man, Mustapha Kemal Atatürk. By 1925, despite invasion, internecine strife and a massive exchange of population with Greece – over one million Christians moved to Greece, in exchange for roughly half that number of Muslims coming into Turkey – the country had settled down within fixed borders (problems continue with the Kurdish minority in eastern Turkey, but they have at no stage threatened the overall stability of the state). The exodus of Christians and the influx of Muslims has been an ongoing process for over two centuries: Crimean ('Krim') Tatars and Circassians from the Caucasus came to Anatolia, prompted by the expansion of the Russian empire, at the end of the eighteenth century and in the mid-nineteenth century, and the last migration of Greeks out of Turkey was as late as the 1950s, while the immigration of 'Turks' from Thrace and Macedonia in the 1920s was mirrored by the arrival of Bulgarian 'Turks' in the 1990s, after the fall of Communism.

As in many countries that have seen great movements of population but a few generations ago, it is difficult to pin down who did what in the textile world. What precisely was the role of the Greeks and the Armenians in the textile trade? It is easier to work out what the incoming Muslim groups are doing now. The Krim Tatars, for instance, produce beautiful tapestry-woven cotton items in the towns of inland western Anatolia. More recent migrants bring with them traditions such as the making of highly decorative socks. All in all, however, the fineness of Ottoman textiles has been lost with the great social upheavals, the loss of court and aristocratic patronage, and the secularization and Europeanization of Turkish society at the behest of Atatürk. With the large-scale movement of peasants into towns has come large-scale industrialization and a change in clothing habits. The modern-day Turkish man or woman will be wearing factory-made clothes, often of synthetic materials, rather than the heavy woollen garments of their forebears. Turkey's abundant supplies of cotton and wool are now used to support a large, innovative textile industry, producing yardage, furnishings and towelling. What is left of the Turkish hand-made textile tradition is embroidery, both professional and domestic; a certain amount of hand-weaving and block printing; the crafts intrinsic to rural Anatolia, such as felt-making; and the weaving of rugs by both settled and nomadic peoples.

The Balkans

The Balkans are the range of mountains that stretch from the Adriatic to the Black Sea. They are the dominant geographical feature of the lands that lie between modern Austria and Greece, and they give their name to the whole region.

Islam arrived relatively early here, establishing itself with the Ottoman defeat of the Serb army at the battle of the Field of Blackbirds in Kosovo in 1389. By the early 1400s, Albania had fallen, and the Ottoman Turks were to dominate the area until the end of the nineteenth century. Despite transfers of population and the vicious wars of the nineteenth and twentieth centuries, Islam remains an appreciable presence, particularly in Bosnia and parts of Bulgaria, and among a majority of the Albanians of Kosovo and Albania proper.

The Ottomans and their adherents formed the ruling class and, although large sections of the population remained Christian (both Orthodox and Catholic), Muslim mores dominated in many fields, including that of textiles. Albania, the most Muslim of the Ottoman Balkan provinces, was one of the most productive textile areas. Its embroidery and couched cording of outer garments for both men and women were famed throughout the Ottoman domains. The intrepid Edith Durham, doyenne of Balkan textile collecting, was so impressed by the quality of the fabrics that she wrote: 'The gold embroidery is not to be surpassed anywhere; the tailors' shops are a blaze of gorgeous colours and designs. Had it not been for difficulties of transport, I should have ruined myself.'

COSTUMES

Men's Dress

Men of the Albanian highlands wore tight trousers of naturally coloured felted wool, often decorated with couched cording. In the south, the Muslim mountain-dwellers wore the *fustanella*, the white kilt akin to but slightly longer than that worn by their neighbours in Greek Epirus. This was worn over tight white trousers, with a short-sleeved white cotton blouse. The outfit was completed by leather slippers with red pom-poms on the toes, a silver embroidered waistcoat, a grand silver embroidered belt with a pouch for keeping guns, and a white felt fez-like cap with a little stalk on top.

Women's Dress

Women in the towns of Albania wore long, full, flounced pantaloons. In the town of Gjirokastër the Muslim women wore silk brocaded pantaloons of imported fabric, a diaphanous blouse with wide sleeves embellished with silver-edged pulled work, and a metal-thread-embroidered waistcoat, all topped by a red *tarbush* cap decorated with metal tassels and sequins.

ABOVE
Balkan Muslim at prayer, *c.* 1900.

OPPOSITE
Swaddling cloth, woven at Kruja or Preza, Albania.

RIGHT AND BELOW
Front and back of woman's corded *mashru* jacket, central Albania.

BELOW LEFT
Embroidered trouser decoration, Skhodra, northern Albania.

BELOW RIGHT
Beaded socks, Kosovo.

TECHNIQUES

Weaving

Fabrics were locally woven. Skhodra, Kruja and Preza were centres for a striped cotton cloth used for clothing, towels, tablecloths and babies' swaddling wraps. Cotton imitations of the famous striped silk bedsheets of Bursa were also woven at Skhodra. Such typically Ottoman fabrics as warp-ikat *mashru*, however, were most likely imported from Anatolia.

Embroidery

Workshops in Gjirokastër, Berat and later the capital Tirana produced extremely fine metal-thread embroidery, while the technique of couched cording was practised by professional tailors in many parts of the country. The sleeves, back and opening of the tight, short-waisted, long-sleeved jackets worn by both men and women were highly decorated in looped motifs in both these techniques. The jackets were often worn over similarly decorated waistcoats. Wealthy urban women wore richly embroidered, usually sleeveless coats. Above full, white, flounced pantaloons, a Muslim bride from Kruja, Elbasani, Tirana or Skhodra would wear a thin white silk and cotton chemise adorned with pulled work, edged with silver at the sleeves and neck. A shawl of the same work is worn over the head and as a waist-tie.

Beadwork

Beadwork in Albania generally lies within the Ottoman tradition. Such decorative beaded items as purses, belts and decorative trims are reasonably common. Albania lies very close to Italy and, having suffered a short period of occupation from 1939 to 1943, there are distinct Italian influences. The use of applied glass and silver beads to decorate the wedding boleros of the women of Kruja and Skhodra may well be a case in point.

RIGHT
Woman's corded jacket, Kukes, northeastern Albania.

BELOW LEFT
Woman's metal-thread-embroidered jacket, Tirana hills.

BELOW RIGHT
Silver-embroidered panel, Bosnia.

BOTTOM LEFT
Woman's headscarf with beaded and be-coined fringe, Tirana hills.

BOTTOM RIGHT
Man's corded and felted wool waistcoat, Tirana hills.

THE BALKANS 45

THE PRESENT

Albanian costume fell into disuse during Enver Hoxha's Marxist rule, which lasted for forty years after the Second World War. During that time, Hoxha isolated the country from the rest of the world, declared it an atheist state, tore down nearly all the mosques and churches, and had priests and imams murdered.

Similar factors – though not as extreme – affected the use of traditional costume throughout the Balkans. In Bosnia, Bulgaria, Romania and Thrace, Muslims once wore variants of Ottoman costume in a manner similar to that of Albania. After 1945, however, Communist rule signified, in effect, Westernization. Partial industrialization meant that many peasants left the land, and, though the remaining peasants were encouraged to keep their costume for morale-boosting folk performances, it has become less and less used in everyday life.

ABOVE LEFT AND RIGHT
Women's forehead decorations, Tirana hills.

BELOW LEFT
Woman's glass-pearl-embroidered waistcoat, Kruja.

BELOW RIGHT
Man's corded waistcoat, Tirana.

OPPOSITE ABOVE
Woman's kerchief with coins and miniature shoes, Kruja hills.

OPPOSITE CENTRE
Corded cuffs, Kruja.

OPPOSITE BELOW
Woven panel for trouser cuffs, Kosovo.

Islamic Spain and North Africa

Islamic Spain

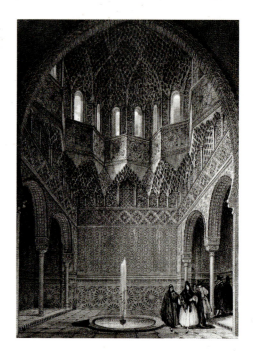

In the early eighth century, the Umayyad Caliphate commissioned an army to conquer the Iberian peninsula. Musa bin Nusair, ruler of Ifriqiya (the Muslim provinces of North Africa), directed the conquest. His deputy, Tarik ibn Ziyad, led Muslim troops across the Straits of Gibraltar in AD 711. Musa himself then joined the campaign, which included the crucial defeat of the Christian Visigoths in the storming of Merida in AD 713. The Muslim invaders continued onwards, capturing the whole of the Iberian peninsula, and were only stopped in southern France by Charles 'The Hammer' Martel.

In their conquered territory, the Muslims built a magnificent civilization, with cool palaces, stately mosques and lush gardens. Though Berbers predominated in the original invasion force, there were also Syrians and Yemenis and many other Arabs to be found among them. With the coming of peace, news of the ample opportunities to be had in colonizing a new and fertile land attracted many craftsmen from the Muslim heartlands. Masons, architects and carpenters came to build the new Andalusia, gardeners and agriculturists to irrigate and farm the new lands, and of course weavers to clothe the new colonists. In AD 756 a new Caliphate was founded at Córdoba, which proceeded to institute the same *tiraz* system of state-owned textile workshops as found in the Muslim lands to the east.

The heartland of Muslim Spain was always to be found in the south, in Andalusia. Córdoba, Seville, Granada, Almeria: these were the cities which even today house beautiful mosques (though long since converted to cathedrals). The north and centre of Spain always contained too many Christians to be relied upon, and indeed would ultimately successfully rebel with the aid of neighbouring Christendom. However, the influence of Islam over a large part of Spain was profound, and was to continue for eight centuries.

TECHNIQUES

Silk Weaving

From earliest times, the Muslim weavers of Spain started producing figured silks, with designs of animals set in roundels in the Persian manner. Initially they used silk thread imported from Persia, but by the 800s mulberry trees and silkworms had been imported and an indigenous silk-rearing industry established. Steady demand, due to the growing prosperity of both Muslim Spain and nearby Christian Europe, helped produce an industry with much vitality. In the 800s weavers were attracted from all over the Muslim world, and elephant designs – perhaps of local manufacture but possibly imports from Persia – enjoyed wide circulation in tenth-century Spain.

Early Muslim textiles in the region were embellished using the angular form of Arabic script known as 'Kufic'. These inscriptions, however, took on a decorative aspect with embellishments of flowers, scrolls or palmettes. By the twelfth century, Naskhi – a more cursive script – was becoming popular, and was incorporated into complex silks.

At the end of the twelfth century, silk patterns began to change. Roundels were superseded by ovals and hexagonal frames, and set within these were animals and birds, both real and mythical, in either addorsed or confronted pairs. This was a style not just confined to Islamic Spain, but prevalent all across the Muslim Mediterranean lands.

Muslim Valencia was long famous for the quality of its silk weaving. When the city fell to James I of Aragon in the mid-1200s, he acted swiftly to preserve its weaving capacity, granting Muslim workers houses and textile workshops under the condition that they remained there for ten years. By the fourteenth century, the main weaving centres in Spain were Valencia, Almeria and Granada, all of which depended on Muslims for their workforce. Chinese influences were by now beginning to be found in the weavings of the peninsula, though they may well have come through Egypt, as there is no evidence of direct contact with the Chinese or their woven goods. By the end of the fourteenth century, silk patterns all over the Mediterranean and beyond had become so mixed that it is difficult to attribute them just to one place. In the fifteenth century, Mudejar (Muslims living under Christian rule) weavers favoured pomegranates (the symbol of Granada), palmettes and lotuses as textile motifs, often used in combination with animals and birds.

Like their Christian counterparts, Muslim weavers were organized into guilds. By this era, they were no longer solely dependent on royal patronage. Spain was undergoing a new epoch of prosperity, due in the main to the commercial activities of the Catalans, whose mercantile network stretched right across the Mediterranean. Many early medieval Islamic silks have survived, due to the contemporary practice of wrapping the embalmed bodies of notable prelates in them before burial. Bodies have also been disinterred and re-buried, allowing fragments of silks – often in the complex weaves such as lampas and samite for which Muslim Spain was famous – to be uncovered, then preserved in clerical institutions and museums.

REGIONS

Granada

As the Christian re-conquest proceeded apace during the fifteenth century, many Muslim weavers moved further south to the mountain kingdom of Granada to avoid infidel rule and in the process to recoup their fortunes. Under the Nasrid dynasty of Granada (the last Muslim dynasty in Spain), there was a great revival of the arts, especially silk weaving, and Granada became one of the greatest textile centres in all Spain. The Nasrid emirs had a vast store of textiles, into which they dipped at frequent intervals to make presentations to worthy subjects and visiting dignitaries. Granadine silks from this era were usually inscribed with the invocation 'Glory to

PAGES 48–49
Embroidered strip, Chefchaouen; embroidered furniture cover, Chefchaouen; curtain, Rabat; embroidered panel, Chefchaouen; all Morocco.

PAGE 50
Hall of the Abencerrages, Alhambra.

PAGE 51
Nasrid silk lampas hanging, Granada, c. AD 1400.

OPPOSITE ABOVE AND BELOW
Eighteenth-century Hispano-Moorish silver brocades, Fez or possibly Tunisia.

our Lord the Sultan'. Fifteenth-century silk lampas textiles from Granada exhibit the classic Nasrid layout of interlacing and decorative band designs that had come to the fore during the fourteenth century.

By the fifteenth century, Granada was also producing the complex, recently introduced fabric of velvet, which was beloved by women for its warmth and subtle sheen and by the nobility for its use as drapes in cold and draughty castles. Velvet was also woven at Valencia, Toledo, Córdoba and Seville.

Philip the Handsome, Prince of the House of Burgundy, visited Granada in 1502, ten years after the final defeat and exile of the last Islamic ruler of Granada, Emir Boabdil. Philip found the city to be strongly commercial, dealing especially in silk yarn to be exported to Italy. He recounts walking through the great shopping arcade known as 'Zacatin', looking at the sumptuous silks for sale and then moving on to the *alcaiceria*, or exchange for raw silk, where he saw yet more silken fabrics woven in the Muslim style. These were on sale in great quantities and the prince noted that they were of great beauty, in a wide variety of colours and patterns.

Fifteenth- and early sixteenth-century silks from Granada – patterned in a series of bars reminiscent of certain tiled mosaics from the Alhambra palace – are known as 'Alhambra silks'. They were also made in Málaga, by Mudejar weavers. Gold thread, which no doubt had become rare and expensive, was used sparingly, if at all, in these fabrics, and was replaced by yellow silk. A common design was rows of stars made up of interlacing.

Hispano-Moresque North Africa
Alhambra silks were also woven at Tunis, Fez, Rabat and Marrakesh. Many Muslim weavers had anticipated changing times and preceded Boabdil into exile years before he surrendered the keys of Granada to Ferdinand and Isabella in January 1492. These weavers continued to make Alhambra silks in North Africa long after the final expulsion of the Moors from Spain by Charles V in 1520.

Many North African towns were founded by immigrants from Muslim Spain. Oran was founded by Andalusian sailors, and the population of Tunis is mainly descended from natives of eastern Spain. In Fez, weavers of Andalusian origin were still weaving *hizam* – silk lampas wedding girdles – with the same patterns as classic Nasrid Granadan textiles, well into the twentieth century.

ISLAMIC SPAIN

Morocco

The Arabic term 'Maghreb al-Aqsa' means 'furthest west', and it is the name applied to what is broadly known in Western Europe as 'Morocco'. This is the furthest west that the tides of Islam reached. Morocco has, however, always been different from the rest of the lands of Islam and the other countries of North Africa. It owed little allegiance to the Ottoman sultans and was always ruled by its own dynasties, whether their capitals were in Fez, Meknes, Rabat or further south in Marrakesh. It only suffered a relatively short period of European colonization in the first half of the twentieth century – by the Spanish in the north (both on the coast and in the Rif mountains), and by the French in the rest of the country, though coastal ports such as Tangier, Casablanca, Azzemour and Mogador were often in European hands. Even today, Spain holds the ancient coastal enclaves of Ceuta and Melilla, as it has since the fifteenth century.

These different influences are apparent in Moroccan textiles, which in turn reflect a vibrant culture that, although it lies so close to industrialized Europe, has remained gloriously intact and largely unaffected by Western mores. To descend the winding streets of the ancient city of Fez, dodging laden donkeys and importunate guides, is one of a traveller's great experiences. Fez must be one of the very few extant examples of a city with a fully functioning medieval economy. Saddlers, cobblers, leather-dyers, brass- and copper-founders jostle with weavers and dyers of silk, cotton and wool. In the towns of Tetouan and Chefchaouen, highlanders from the Rif mountains descend onto the streets to sell the vegetables and sheep that are the products of their farms and pastures. The women of the Rif wear broad-brimmed straw hats decorated with blue tassels or cording, and red-and-white striped shawls and aprons woven in cotton by local male weavers.

ABOVE
Woman of Tangier, wearing a *hizam* girdle.

OPPOSITE
Detail of an embroidered panel from a late eighteenth-century double-panelled bedcover, Chefchaouen.

The great medieval traveller Ibn Khaldoun was known to have remarked upon the quality of Moroccan silk brocades, and the large towns of the north – Tetouan, Fez, Meknes, Rabat and Salé, with their Arab and Andalusian influences – were once great centres of fine silk embroidery. This tradition has long faded except as a cottage industry with a primarily tourist focus. The Berber women of the High, Middle and Anti-Atlas mountains still weave prolifically in wool on their vertical looms, and in the small towns of the Anti-Atlas, such as Igherm, you can even still find women making headbands in cotton on a hand-held frame, utilizing the archaic technique of 'sprang'.

ISLAMIC SPAIN AND NORTH AFRICA

ABOVE LEFT
Sampler, northern Morocco.

ABOVE RIGHT
Embroidered curtain, Salé.

LEFT
Zemmour man's hat, Middle Atlas.

OPPOSITE
Nineteenth-century Rabat curtain embroidered on imported Indian cotton.

56 ISLAMIC SPAIN AND NORTH AFRICA

MOROCCO 57

TECHNIQUES

Embroidery

Fez, Meknes, Rabat and Salé all share a tradition of fine silk embroidery on cotton that is much influenced by southern European embroidery. Cross stitch in an orangey-red, green, black or indigo blue is typical of Fez, and chain, darning and a form of buttonhole are the main stitches used in Rabat. Customarily, the main products are cushions, curtains, bed valances and other furnishings.

The north of Morocco has its own traditions, with that of Tetouan concentrating on Ottoman-derived floral satin stitch in silk on silk satin. Mirror covers and curtains are popular in this work. In Chefchaouen, much-prized covers embroidered in silk on cotton were draped over chests and other pieces of furniture, and were used to cover the edges of the bench-like seat that line three of the walls of the public reception room in an important house. This style of embroidery is of Andalusian origin and is known as *bouchaki*.

A Chefchaouen girl would also prepare a trousseau, known as a *chouar*, which consisted of jewelry, especially necklaces, but also textiles that she had patiently embroidered, including cushions, bedcovers and tablecloths. During the wedding ceremony, the *chouar* is arranged on or around a beautiful chest, along with gifts offered by the husband, such as *babouches* (slippers), silk fabrics, milk, dates and henna. A big celebration is organized soon afterwards, and the items of the *chouar* are shown to those invited and then carried in the procession to the bride's new home. The bride is carried in an often gaudily painted wooden litter that is covered in silk scarves and flowers, screened by a veil and mounted on a mule, accompanied by musicians blowing trumpets and banging tambourines.

Lampas Weaving

Moroccan brides once wore a long silk lampas-woven girdle, known as a *hizam*, bound tightly around the waist. After the wedding ceremony, this would be taken off to symbolize the fact that the bride was now ready to conceive. *Hizam* were generally worn folded in two lengthways; only Sayeed women (those claiming descent from the Prophet) wore them at their full width. The main centre of production was Fez, but the girdles were also made in Tetouan and possibly other towns in northern Morocco.

Lampas weaving is a highly complex technique, requiring a cartoon for guidance. Two people were needed to weave the

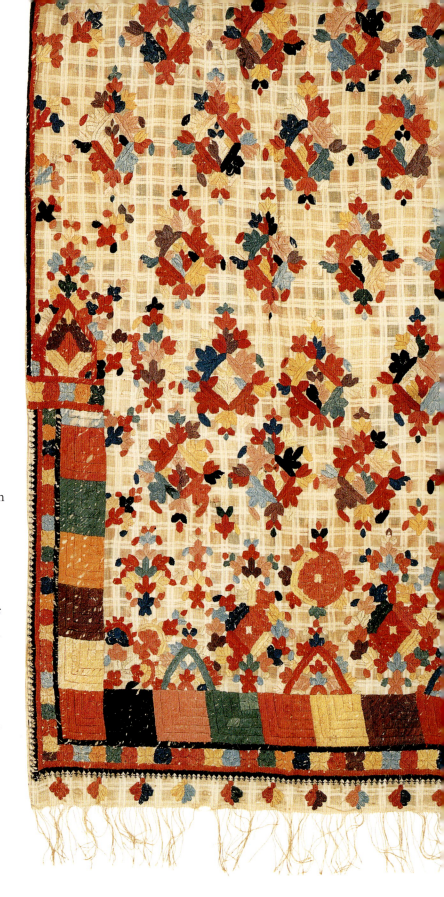

OPPOSITE ABOVE
Rabat curtain embroidered on a silk bedcover from Bursa in Turkey.

OPPOSITE BELOW
Embroidered panel, Azzemour.

ABOVE
Embroidered shawl, Fez.

RIGHT
Embroidered brocade kaftan, Ouija.

BELOW
Tablet-woven braids on jacket cuffs, northern Morocco.

OPPOSITE
Nineteenth-century lampas-woven *hizam* bridal girdles from Fez and Tetouan.

LEFT
Tahendirt, Berber woman's striped woollen shawl, High Atlas.

BELOW
Eighteenth-century silk brocade shawl, possibly from Fez, dyed a typical deep red.

girdles, which were made with both a supplementary warp and weft. The weaver operated the draw-loom, while a boy under his direction sat above the heddles and drew up the main and supplementary heddles in the correct sequence as required. When the pattern on the face of the belt was multicoloured, the effect on the underside was akin to silk weft ikat.

The girdles were of direct Andalusian influence, and were woven by weavers of Andalusian descent. Patterns were mostly drawn from the fabled silk lampas textiles of Moorish Spain, most notably the textiles woven for the Nasrids, the last Muslim rulers of Granada. Patterns in later examples also incorporated motifs from the French textile lexicon. Floral and architectural designs were common, and the ends were often decorated with the auspicious eight-pointed star and the *hamsa* (Hand of Fatima). Complex *hizam* were still being woven in Fez at the end of the nineteenth century, but the fashion began to wane at about that time. They survived in provincial Tetouan and Chefchaouen into the early decades of the twentieth century.

Weaving with Wool

Woven pile rugs, kelims and kelim-work cushions can be found in abundance among the tribes of the Middle Atlas, particularly among prolific weavers such as the Zemmour. In the High Atlas, the Berbers weave the same manner of products but concentrate on their women's cloaks, which are often decorated with a profusion of sequins. Though naturally coloured wool is prevalent in Berber weaving, weft stripes of dyed wool are popular for these cloaks in the High and Middle Atlas. In the High Atlas, complex men's cloaks known as *akhnif* are also woven, with a large inset eye, often in red, to ward off the effect of the evil eye.

The Berber vertical single-heddle loom is widespread in Morocco, and is used as far east as Libya and Siwa in Egypt. It is principally used for weaving wool, but Berber women also use it to weave a wide variety of items, including knotted carpets, kelims, rag rugs and items of clothing. The loom has several useful properties: it is versatile, it takes up little space in the house, tent or courtyard, and it can be easily moved. Women tend to carry out their weaving either intermittently, as and when convenient during the day, or intensively, when there are quiet periods during the agricultural season.

Dyeing

Among the sights of Morocco are the tanneries of Tetouan and Fez. These are set apart, on the edge of the town or down by a water course. Here the workers soak skins amid a vast array of pits, taking off the wool and hair, tanning and often dyeing the hides. Morocco used to be full of similar establishments for dyeing cotton, wool and silk with a range of natural colourants, but now most dyeing is done with chemicals, and threads and fabrics are bought ready-dyed. Nevertheless there are still interesting examples of the 'dyeing art'.

In the dry Anti-Atlas mountains, Berber women wear long woollen body-wraps pinned at the shoulder by ornate

OPPOSITE AND ABOVE
Early nineteenth-century furniture cover, embroidered in silk on cotton in the *bouchaki* style, Chefchaouen (detail shown opposite).

silver fibula brooches. These are known as *haik* or *houli*, and, along with the women's square headscarves, are decorated in dyed motifs of henna brown or with small sections of woollen embroidery in contrasting colours.

Women of the Ida ou Nadif and the Ida ou Kensous Berbers decorate their garments with dyed prophylactic devices that take the same form as the protective tattoos adorning their throats and other parts of their body deemed to be vulnerable to malign influences.

Women of the other Berber communities of the Anti-Atlas mountains, such as the Aït Abdallah, also wear woollen *haik* and veils with henna patterning, but they use it in block form. The henna leaves are mashed up, then the compress is applied to the areas of wool to be dyed. After a couple of days, the compress is scraped off, leaving a red-brown design on the white woollen ground. To deepen the colour, the process may be repeated.

Tie-Dye

Tie-dyed articles of hand-woven wool are used as belts and headscarves in different parts of Morocco. Women's sashes of sheep's wool woven in twill were once made in the urban centres of the Rif region in northern Morocco, notably in Tetouan. Relatively large-scale starburst motifs were placed all along the length of these sashes, achieved by folding and pleating the fabric into cones, then tying the cones. Decorations in tie-dyed brown and yellow and black and red were favoured combinations.

As with textiles popular all over Berber North Africa, simple circular motifs appear on the woollen portions and disappear on the cotton portions. Overall tie-dye patterning is achieved by the unique Berber technique of weaving in occasional cotton weft strips that only faintly absorb dye, if at all. The colour does not take, or bleaches out of the cotton strips, causing the tie-dyed pattern to disappear in the cotton areas, then reappear in the woollen areas. The result is a striped, whitish pattern against a dyed ground. Wide tie-dyed sashes woven in woollen twill with lateral cotton stripes and worn by women on festive occasions can be bought in the souks of Tetouan and Chefchaouen.

For festive wear, women of the Aït Atta of the High Atlas, around Immelt, tie-dye square woollen headscarves decorated in sunburst circles in typical Berber colours of yellow and brown. A single tie produces a great brown sun motif against

a yellow ground, taking up nearly all of the area of the square field. The headscarves are first dyed yellow, then the whole material (apart from small areas left over at each corner) is tied and dipped into the brown dye bath. The traditional dyes used are henna for brown, pomegranate for yellow, henna with ferrous sulphate for black, and madder for red.

THE PRESENT

Morocco has, as elsewhere, been affected by the economic winds sweeping through the world at the turn of the twenty-first century, bringing much change and a prosperity that is real but very unevenly distributed. The lives of many rural Moroccans have, however, altered but little. The shepherd still tends his flocks, the farmer tills his fields, and the small nomadic groups clamber across the barren mountains and valleys in search of fresh pastures. Births, marriages and circumcisions are celebrated with just the same gusto. In many places, the rural economy is dependent on sheep-rearing – all that the land will bear. This means there will always be an abundance of wool that is woven – domestically by women on their upright looms, professionally by men on treadle-looms – into the cloaks, shawls, aprons and *jellabas* worn to keep out the chill of the mountain air. People of the urban centres, as elsewhere in the world, are largely clad in the products of the mechanized mills. For the foreseeable future, country people will keep the weavers, dyers and embroiderers busy, and the booming tourist industry will provide a steady market for hand-woven bags, cushions, rugs, blankets and embroidered clothing.

OPPOSITE
Rif Mountain woollen girdles, tie-dyed in an urban centre such as Tetouan or Chefchaouen.

ABOVE LEFT
Embroidered furnishings, Tetouan.

LEFT
Woman embroidering in silk on silk, using a frame, Tetouan.

Algeria

This vast, rich land – one of the most beautiful in all North Africa, and holding a commanding position over the Mediterranean Sea – has long been fought over. Carthage, Rome and Byzantium once held sway here, then the Arab conquest swept over and rapidly Islamicized the indigenous tribes and enrolled them in the jihad that took them through Morocco and on through Spain until they were halted in southern France. The great coastal ports of Algiers and Oran boasted some of the most daring sailors in the Mediterranean; they gained notoriety as the 'Barbary corsairs'. The governing Deys of these cities, while nominally acknowledging the suzerainty of the Sublime Porte in Istanbul, took a substantial cut of the corsairs' profits from slavery and piracy, and thus Algeria grew wealthy. The country exhibits the same eclectic mix of races as much of coastal North Africa – Berber and Arab, Muslim, Christian and Jew, Ottoman Turk and a mix of African and European slaves. It was heavily colonized by the French between 1830 and 1962, and the mélange of cultures has also had a pronounced effect on the nation's textiles.

COSTUMES

Men's and Women's Dress

The great agricultural wealth accrued from the fertile lands of coastal Algeria, combined with the riches garnered from the sea by trade and pillage, was expressed in a tradition of highly decorative costume for both men and women. Indoors, women wore a full-sleeved, often diaphanous blouse of cotton

ABOVE
Ouled Nail woman displaying her embroidery.

OPPOSITE
Eighteenth-century embroidered scarf or headcloth, Algiers.

or cotton/silk over baggy pantaloons of silk or cotton bound at the waist with a sash or belt, usually of silk, and gathered at the ankle. Younger women donned a short, tight, Ottoman-influenced corselet decorated with metal-thread embroidery and passementerie buttons, worn in such a manner as to accentuate the bosom. Out of doors, urban women of all ages would wear an all-enveloping cloak, often of wool, and a veil covering the lower face. Men wore certain articles of clothing worked in metal thread by professional male embroiderers. Long-sleeved, short-waisted jackets or sleeveless waistcoats were particularly popular with young men.

The long period of intense French colonization destroyed most of the local textile industry, and hand-made products were largely replaced by those of the mills of Lyons and other great centres of French textile manufacture. The partial Europeanization of Algerians – the inevitable reflection of such a colonization – drastically reduced the demand for decorative articles of traditional clothing, and in the cities it is only for ceremonies such as marriage and circumcision that there is any demand at all. The rural people of the Algerian littoral may still wear certain items of traditional costume, but these are also now made up of mill-woven cloth. Only in the isolated oases of the far south, with their populations of a conservative bent, is there any appreciable production of hand-made textiles.

TECHNIQUES

Embroidery

Though urban weaving is traditionally a male profession, embroidery – with the exception of metal-thread work – is a female skill. Metal-thread embroidery in the Ottoman style was practised in all the major towns until the first half of the twentieth century.

Algiers is famous for its floral embroidery, often on net used for women's scarves, chemises, bath towels, hangings and curtains and the long flowing trains that hung down from the *b'niqa* caps that women wore after bathing at the hammam. Embroidery was also worked on finely woven linen or cotton. After Algiers was incorporated into the Ottoman empire in the early 1500s, its embroidery began to show many similarities to that of Istanbul and Smyrna. Its floral motifs, in particular, are similar to the pomegranate or artichoke patterns found in Turkish embroidery, but the Algerian style was also influenced by Persian, Syrian and Italian work. Tulips, carnations, hyacinths and wild roses were all recurrent motifs, and the delicate floral style continued to be popular until the early twentieth century.

Classic Algiers work consisted of counted-thread work on fine, loosely woven linen, carried out by professional female embroiderers, who traditionally worked seated on the floor. They used a frame of Turkish origin, known as a *gourgaf*. Designs were outlined in black silk or sometimes gold thread in double running stitch, enclosing areas decorated mainly in a form of brick stitch and some satin stitch in blue, red or purple silk. The use of eyelet stitch, giving a chequerboard effect, is also characteristic of Algiers work.

Metal-Thread Embroidery

Oran, the bustling northwestern port with its partly Spanish heritage, was the centre for the making of women's woollen capes in fine, soft, white wool decorated with applied metallic braid inset with semi-precious blue stones. Bône (modern Annaba) and Constantine to the northeast had their own styles, reflecting Ottoman influences, but with regional differences incorporating elements from neighbouring Tunisia. Constantine also produced net scarves decorated with metallic strip in the manner of the shawls of Assyut in Upper Egypt.

BELOW
Algiers-work embroidered panel.

RIGHT
Eighteenth-century Algiers-work for use as a coif.

OPPOSITE
Woven woollen blanket, northeastern Algeria.

Weaving

The Berber regions of Grande Kabylie and Petite Kabylie to the east of Algiers were once great weaving centres for pile rugs and kelims. The women also had a strong tradition of using the upright Berber loom to weave woollen chequerboard-patterned *haik* (women's body-wraps; the Kabylie name is *axellal*). The back of the garment was highly decorative, with very fine extra weft patterning. A smaller cloak, the *ddil*, woven in the same pattern, was worn over the back and shoulders, often with a weft-striped silk scarf pinned with fibula brooches. However, as in general throughout northern Algeria, and as with all other crafts, these weaving centres are now in severe decline.

Still prospering, however, in the realm of hand-made textiles are the woollen weavings of the Mzab region of central Algeria – five oases clustered around an underground river that waters the palmeries to give an abundance of dates. The Mozabites are conservative in dress and manner, and follow the Abadi sect of Islam, whose main followers are to be found among the Omanis of southeast Arabia. The isolation of the place and the conservatism of the people have meant that they have retained some of their textile traditions. Plain white woollen curtains with broad end-stripes in wine and green are woven on vertical looms in Ghardaïa and the other oases. In Ghardaïa, women also made striking tapestry-weave marriage shirts in wool for young bridegrooms, using a weaving technique known as *gandoura*. These shirts are still woven but using synthetic dyes, though there are now moves back to naturally obtained dyes. At El Golea, to the south of Ghardaïa, are woven woollen blankets for the trans-Sahara trade, decorated with the same patterns as those of Malian *kassa*, though here woven of a piece on a broad loom rather than made up of strips as in Mali. It is intriguing to ask whether the Algerian blankets were trade goods made in imitation of *kassa*, or whether they were the originals of which *kassa* are a local variant. The ebbs and flows of influences back and forth across the Sahara are worthy of a major study.

Dyeing

Mendil – couscous covers or carrying cloths – are made out of loosely woven woollen squares decorated with either stripes or tie-dye patterns. In the latter case, the patterns are of yellow circles and half circles set against a red-brown ground. The yellow is from pomegranate rind and the red-brown most probably madder.

THE PRESENT

At one time Algeria had just as vibrant a hand-weaving tradition as its neighbours Morocco and Tunisia. Much has been lost, whether as a result of the terrible war of liberation fought against the French in the 1950s or as a by-product of the Socialist industrialization policies enforced by the post-independence FLN government. Recent attempts to revive traditional craft processes throughout the country have come to nothing because of Algeria's ongoing political troubles. Efforts are, however, currently underway, under the auspices of the oil company BP, to reintroduce hand-weaving and vegetable dyeing in El Golea.

OPPOSITE ABOVE
Kelim-weave fragment, Laghouat, central Algeria.

OPPOSITE BELOW
Tie-dyed woollen couscous cover, Ghardaïa.

TOP
Woven woollen curtain, Mzab.

ABOVE LEFT
Shepherd in woollen *jellaba*, Ghardaïa.

ABOVE RIGHT
Metal-thread-embroidered jackets in a bridal shop window, Algiers.

Tunisia

Tunisia is the smallest of all the states of the North African littoral, but it possesses the most magnificent textile tradition of the whole of the Maghreb, and one that is still vibrant today. No doubt this is due to the historical legacy of an influx of a wide variety of peoples over the last two thousand years. Added to a base of longstanding indigenous North African Berbers have come Phoenicians from the Lebanon, Romans, Byzantines, Arabs, Moors and Jews from Andalusia, Turks, French colonists, and slaves from Africa and Europe. This influx has resulted in one of the most eclectic mixes of any nation on earth.

The ethnic diversity of Tunisia is reflected in its textiles. On the northern coast there are Andalusian influences, such as those seen in the intricately embroidered wedding costumes of Raf-Raf, Nabeul, Hammamet and Monastir. Further south along the coast, the weaving town of Mahdia and the island of Djerba produce the long wedding wraps known as *r'da* and the chequered sashes that were also woven in other parts of the Ottoman empire. In the small central-eastern coastal towns of the area known as the Sahel were worked some of the finest and most vibrant metal-thread embroideries to be found anywhere. In the far south of Tunisia, the Berber women living till the 1950s in their hilltop villages of fortified granaries wove woollen shawls on vertical looms. The shawls, decorated with complex motifs in white cotton thread along their borders against a plain field in natural wool, were dyed blue, red, aubergine and black, using natural dyes such as indigo and cochineal, often over a pomegranate-rind yellow dye. Many of these garments, and the sprang headbands of the local mountain women, are tie-dyed in the rough and ready manner of North African Berber woollen textiles. Chenini de Gabès is one of the still extant centres for this kind of work. Similar types of shawl with the same kinds of motif – diamond shapes for eyes, with sharp weaving combs to pierce them, worn as prophylactics to ward off the evil eye – were woven in many of the villages to the south of Gabès and Gafsa.

Tunis was one of the centres of sophisticated weaving in silk. One of its prize products was the rich urban woman's veil known as the *ajar* and consisting of a central see-through mesh with two long ends decorated in bands of supplementary-weft silk in floral and geometric patterns. The decorative ends were designed to hang down on both sides of the woman's face to below waist-level. Initially, the veils were woven in the village of Testour by families of Andalusian origin. This kind of weaving is the direct descendant of the Hispano-Moorish textiles produced in Islamic Spain, the production of which came to a halt soon after the fall of Granada to Ferdinand and Isabella in 1492, and was finally extinguished with the expulsion of the Moors and the Jews from Spain in the sixteenth century. The Moors took with them their sophisticated weaving techniques. The Jews, while practising various crafts such as dyeing, would often set themselves up as gold- and silversmiths. They provided the gold and silver thread utilized in the magnificent metal-thread embroidery of the Sahel, until they left en masse for Israel in 1956. Links with Andalusia are still to be found, both as a folk memory and in the kind of harlequin woman's costume found in Nabeul and Hammamet.

TECHNIQUES

Embroidery

There is a modicum of quite crude embroidery in wool used as an overlay on the woven garments of the southern Berbers, but it is the professional metal-thread embroidery of Tunis and the Sahel that is breathtaking. The best examples are some of the finest to be found not only in North Africa, but the world. The *ma'allema*, or professional female embroiderer, adorned marriage costumes to order and taught young girls between the ages of six and fifteen the rudiments of embroidery, as well as something of the etiquette required of a future young bride. Her evocative and very fine silver- and gold-thread embroidery used metal thread made by the local Jewish silversmith. Many of the motifs used hark back to the Classical world. Such European designs as stylized birds, vases and flowers were common. The best embroidery came from Moknine, Mahdia, Djerba, Hammamet and Sousse, though Tunis had a distinctive style, with flat silver thread being used to embroider onto silk with much use of buttonhole stitch – a style that was also to be found in the Sahel. The quality of embroidery in northern Tunisia has suffered a marked deterioration in modern times. One of the factors has been the lack of fine-quality metal thread after the exodus of most of the Jewish silversmiths in 1956, but the general modernization of Tunisia and the introduction of widespread female education have also had their effect.

Urban Weaving

Tunisia still possesses weaving workshops that produce the silk textiles that a sophisticated urban clientele demands. In the Sahel, *hashiya* (figured ribbons) are used to embellish costumes and curtains. They are woven on draw-looms around Mahdia and Djerba, but the technique is reckoned to have been brought from Tripoli in Libya by Jewish weavers in the nineteenth century. Mahdia has over a thousand looms, producing everything from figured ribbon to the patterned silk and metal-thread *r'da* wraps. Black *r'da ahmar* are woven on horizontal treadle-looms and have equal-sized pattern areas at each end. Similar wraps are known as *r'da biskri* in Djerba, but they have a large patterned area only at one end, and are woven in red as well as black. In both Mahdia and Djerba, the motifs are worked in by hand in metal thread. Older *r'da* borders from Djerba often feature the Star of David, a tribute to the island's once-numerous Jewish weavers and dyers.

PAGE 72 LEFT
Tunisian women wearing *haik* body-wraps.

PAGE 72 RIGHT
Tunisian women wearing *ajar* veils.

PAGE 73
Curtain made up of brocaded silk strips woven on draw-looms, Djerba.

74 ISLAMIC SPAIN AND NORTH AFRICA

OPPOSITE ABOVE
Metal-thread embroidery decorating the neckline of a Moknine bridal blouse.

OPPOSITE CENTRE
Metal-thread-embroidered Moknine bridal headband.

OPPOSITE BELOW
Back of metal-thread-embroidered Moknine bridal waistcoat.

ABOVE
Silk and woollen embroidery on a Raf-Raf bride's dress.

LEFT
Raf-Raf waistcoat.

TOP
Sahel gold-thread wedding chemise.

ABOVE
Moknine coif.

ABOVE
Nineteenth-century silk brocade weave, Tunis or Testour.

ABOVE RIGHT
Wedding dress, Nabeul or Hammamet.

RIGHT
Nineteenth-century silk-brocade-weave *ajar* veil, Tunis or Testour.

TUNISIA

RIGHT
Moknine bridal cap, 1930s.

BELOW
Nineteenth-century silk-brocade-weave *ajar* veils, Tunis or Testour.

RIGHT
Wedding blouse from Tunis, incorporating strips of brocaded silk ribbon woven at Testour.

OPPOSITE
Silver brocade *r'da* wrap, Djerba.

78 ISLAMIC SPAIN AND NORTH AFRICA

Men weave on their horizontal looms, each workspace containing one to ten looms. Both warp and weft are often of silk. Silk yarn is imported from Japan, Italy or China and the metallic thread from Lyons in France. The looms are generally semi-automatic. More complex weaves require jacquard devices or are woven on draw-looms.

Woollen fabrics are produced in the Sahel, as well as silks. Horizontal looms at El Djem and Jembiana produce hard-wearing woollen cloth, often in brown, and used for making up countrymen's *jellaba*. These looms are also used for the manufacture of countrywomen's *shamla* (sashes) in a twill weave, often with lateral stripes; so too the complex patterned woman's *mouchtiya* (woollen shawl), with geometric motifs worked in cotton supplementary weft, and the shawl then tie-dyed with seemingly random dots in two or three colours.

Berber Weaving and Dyeing

Berber women use upright looms to weave woollen shawls with supplementary cotton details in motifs that mirror the patterns of their tattoos and jewelry. After weaving, the shawls are dip-dyed in successive dye baths, with pomegranate rind giving a base of yellow on which other hues can be built up. Other natural dyes used are henna, madder and cochineal; indigo was formerly used, but the indigo workshops of Tunisia are now a thing of the past. The weavers cleverly exploit the dye-absorbing properties of different fibres. Wool takes up dyes readily and permanently, but cotton is less successful. The total effect is also only revealed in the long term. When the shawls are first woven, they have a relatively thick nap, and the cotton details initially, though not permanently, hold some of the colour of the dye bath. It is only after long wear and continual

washing and pounding that the nap wears down and the dye is bleached out of the cotton details, leaving a dramatic design of white motifs against a red, blue, black or brown ground. The cotton thread may be waxed before weaving to help it resist the dye, or it may rely on an extra strong twist to the same effect.

Formerly, the Berbers lived high on the hills (*jebel*) of southern Tunisia, in their fortified granaries (*ksar*). After independence from the colonizing French in 1956, new villages were built down by the new roads, and the old way of life changed forever. Fortunately, some craft skills persisted, and regional styles still prevailed. Around Gafsa, a central arrangement of lozenges and triangles is favoured; around Douiret a plain field with fine details along the border. Three main articles of clothing are woven: the *bakhnug*, a large rectangular shawl; the *tajira*, a square or rectangular shawl; and the *katfiya*, a small rectangular cloth worn over the shoulders to protect the dress underneath from hair oil. On rare occasions a much longer, wrapped and pinned garment called a *houli* was also woven. A young girl still wears a white shawl, a bride or newly married woman a red shawl, and an older woman a blue, black or brown shawl.

Although all these cloths are no longer woven in most southern Berber villages, at Bou Said and other villages around Gafsa, new *bakhnug* are woven that are chemically dyed, then pounded and bleached. These are sold, along with the products of a healthy kelim-weaving industry, to the many tourists who flock to Tunisia.

OPPOSITE ABOVE
Silk and metal-thread woven *r'da* wrap, Mahdia.

OPPOSITE BELOW
Berber woman's *tajira* shawl, southern Tunisia.

ABOVE
Woven and embroidered *bakhnug* shawl, Medenine.

RIGHT
Henna-dyed *bakhnug* shawl, southern Tunisia.

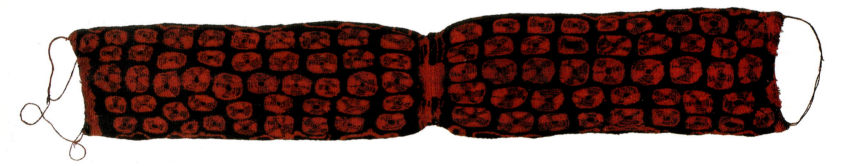

Tie-Dye

The technique of tie-and-dye is often used to decorate the woollen textiles of southern Tunisia, sometimes just the borders, occasionally the whole textile. An often random pattern of green, red, brown or yellow spots forms a counterpoint to embroidery or to a regular pattern of supplementary weft. As in other parts of Berber North Africa, tying can be done on either face of the fabric and is most usually worked on the ends of veils, headscarves and shawls. Apart from this, the method used here shows little variation from that employed in the rest of the world. The undyed fabric is tied with thread and then dip-dyed in the background colour. As often the case with Berber dyed textiles, narrow cotton weft stripes woven into the woollen textile do not take the dye and interrupt the tie-dyed pattern. Contemporary dyes are, in the main, chemical, but to give a reddish-brown hue henna is still popular and, as it is used as a cosmetic, readily available in the market. Tie-dyeing was a speciality of the villages around Gabès such as Matmata, Chenini de Gabès and Gourmessa. Chenini de Gabès is the main contemporary centre of the craft.

THE PRESENT

Though the true glories of Tunisian textiles are gone, weaving of both woollen and silk cloth – particularly in the Sahel – is still in a remarkably healthy state. The domestic market continues to be strong, and the tourists who congregate at Tunisia's beach resorts pay ready cash, injecting a healthy liquidity into the weavers' coffers. Embroidery, unfortunately, is in a much less healthy state. The materials are either unavailable or of low quality, and what few professional practitioners are left are unable to command the prices that their labour and skills deserve.

OPPOSITE ABOVE
Henna-dyed *bakhnug* shawl, southern Tunisia.

OPPOSITE BELOW
Assaba, sprang headband, southern Tunisia.

ABOVE LEFT
Woman's waistcoat, Sahel or Tunis.

ABOVE RIGHT
Striped satin vest with watch pocket, Tunis.

BELOW
Man weaving on a treadle-loom, Mahdia.

TUNISIA

Libya

767 - Une confidence.
Una confindencia.

Libya lies on the southern shores of the Mediterranean, sandwiched between Tunisia and Algeria on one side and Egypt on the other. It is a large country, stretching south into sub-Saharan Africa, but the majority of the population live on the coastal plain in small towns and villages or in the two major cities of Tripoli and Benghazi. This area, like most of North Africa, has historically benefitted from being fertile and agriculturally rich. Cyrenaica – the eastern half of Libya, centred on Benghazi – is particularly green, and affords abundant pasturage to herds of cattle.

Cyrenaica was colonized by the Phoenicians in the seventh century BC. The western half of Libya – Tripolitania – was colonized by the Greeks, and later the Carthaginians. Both Cyrenaica and Tripolitania eventually became part of the Roman empire, but Tripolitania was sacked by the Vandals in AD 435 and then the Byzantines took over. Impressive Greek and Roman ruins can still be seen there today. In the mid-seventh century AD, Arab forces conquered the region, and over the centuries most of the indigenous Berbers converted to Islam and adopted the Arabic language and culture. By the fifteenth century, however, Tripolitania had become an outpost for the Barbary corsairs, who raided Mediterranean merchant ships or required them to pay tribute, leading to the region becoming part of 'the Barbary Coast'. In the sixteenth century, the Ottomans took control and they remained in power until Italian troops occupied Tripoli in 1911. Italy united Cyrenaica and Tripolitania in 1934, and in 1951 Libya gained independence.

The coastal population today reflects the typical Maghrebi mix: Arab, Berber and Ottoman, with remnants of European and Jewish elements. Arab Bedouin tribes are to be found in the desert, while the oases are still predominantly Berber.

PEOPLES

The Berbers

Berbers of the oasis of Gharyan, south of Tripoli, work tie-dye on wool in a pattern of yellow dots against a black or madder-brown ground. The oldest extant examples seem to be dyed naturally with pomegranate rind for yellow and madder root for a red-brown. Square cloths of over 3 ft in dimension (1 m^2) were used for the carrying of couscous pots. In the 1990s these could still be found in the Tripoli souk, impregnated with grease from the pot. Also to be found in the Tripoli souk were blue *bakhnug* shawls in the style of those from the Berber communities of southern Tunisia, though less fine and with embroidered cotton rather than woven details.

OPPOSITE
Bedouin couple from the Libyan desert, early twentieth century.

ABOVE LEFT AND RIGHT
Tie-dyed woollen couscous covers, Gharyan.

BELOW
Embroidered *bakhnug* shawl for a Berber woman, southwestern Libya.

The Jews

Tripoli was a major weaving centre in medieval times, with a large Jewish community that could date its migration to Libya from the Holy Land to Roman times. The Jews specialized in both weaving and dyeing, but in the late nineteenth century they moved en masse to Tunisia, predominantly to the island of Djerba, taking their skills with them. What remained of Libyan textile manufacturing was largely restricted to the Berber hinterland.

THE PRESENT

Libya, with its sparse population, has been much affected by both the discovery of oil in the region and the advent of state control of much of the country's industry and commerce. Many aspects of the old way of life have gone. Nomad and peasant alike have drifted to the towns and taken up employment there. The weaving that Libya was once famous for – the products of the urban hand-loom operated by men and the nomadic ground-loom and Berber vertical loom worked by women – are largely things of the past. That being said, there is still a limited amount of nomadic weaving practised in the way of decorative bags and blanket bags, and, at the southern oasis of Ghadames, simple striped woollen kilims are woven on the vertical loom. Attempts have been made in the southern oases to set up a carpet industry, utilizing local wool, but it remains to be seen whether the current liberalization of the economy and attempts to encourage tourism will result in the revival of weaving as a cottage industry to provide beautiful textiles for both locals and visitors.

Egypt

ABOVE
Sinai Bedouin man dressed in a robe of hand-woven Egyptian cotton.

From the times of the ancient Pharaohs, the Nile valley has been the centre of a succession of civilizations that have been of great and abiding influence not only on Egypt's neighbouring countries but also, through trade, on the world in general. The mighty river Nile has for millennia fed the land of Egypt with highly fertile mud. This effluvium, drawn from the highlands of the countries to the south, was, until the building of the High Dam at Aswan in 1956, Egypt's lifeblood. It renewed and fertilized the relatively meagre arable land, enabling it to feed a much larger population than it could have sustained under normal circumstances.

Flax was one of the crops grown in the fields along the Nile, and Pharaonic Egypt became famous for its linen weaves (cotton was as yet unknown, and wool only rarely used). The linen, worn for the most part undyed, was woven on vertical looms, the warps tensioned with weights. The Egypt of the Ptolemaic Greeks and then the Byzantines continued to weave in linen, but in addition used wool. Egypt, both as a province of Rome in the early centuries of the Christian era, and under its Christian successor Byzantium, maintained its renown as a textile centre, specializing in fine cloths of linen and wool embellished with polychromatic, highly figurative, tapestry-woven details depicting scenes from Classical and rural life, and later Christian iconography.

The Arab conquest of AD 639–640 was to have profound effects on the region's textiles, though changes in design were initially rather slow. The earliest Islamic textiles were in all probability made by the same weavers who had been producing the Christian-influenced textiles, and they quite probably continued to produce these for the native Coptic population side by side with those for Islamic use. Early Egyptian Islamic textiles featured much the same tapestry-woven details but this time with an emphasis on the floral, vegetal and animal rather than the human or god-like. Woven or embroidered calligraphic inscriptions were incorporated, but had not yet become the dominant theme. With time, however, the transformed market resulted in new decorative influences and the widespread use of previously rare materials. Islamic rulers put the profitable textile industry under direct government control. Many surviving pieces from this system were found during excavations at Fostat, Egypt's first capital under Arab rule; the pieces were mainly woven in Egypt, though some came from Persia and Transoxiana.

ABOVE
Zagazig mosque curtain decorated with metal-thread embroidery on velvet, Nile delta.

88 ISLAMIC SPAIN AND NORTH AFRICA

The Abbasid caliphs of Baghdad ruled Egypt from AD 750 to 868, and again from AD 905 to 969. Textiles were the Abbasid art form *par excellence*. A visiting Byzantine ambassador describes seeing 38,000 precious hangings displayed or stored at the palace in Baghdad (these were seen as liquid assets, being both symbols of wealth and highly portable in times of trouble). Many of them, mainly worked in linen, would have been woven in Egypt.

Ahmed bin Tulun broke away from the Abbasids to form the short-lived independent Tulunid dynasty that ruled Egypt from AD 868 to 905. Existing state-owned *tiraz* workshops were maintained, and new workshops at Fayoum in Middle Egypt were opened to cater for both royal and public demand. The decoration of fabrics produced at these workshops included inscriptions in Kufic script, but expressed a strong local Coptic pictorial background as well as a decided Persian influence. During this period, Egyptian textiles were considered among the best in the world. The linen was unequalled, and in particular the towns of Tinnis and Damietta in the Nile delta produced linen textiles in abundance. Textile commerce was by now one of the mainstays of the state economy, and Egyptian textiles reached as far as the Byzantine emperors and the ladies of the European courts. New techniques of weaving luxury fabrics were also introduced. Silk at this period seemed to be in generous supply, and the use of cotton later became widespread.

In AD 969 the Shia Fatimids conquered Egypt. During the Fatimid period, the manufacture and decoration of textiles changed considerably. Many Fatimid textiles show influence from Baghdad, especially in the use of decorative bands with inscriptions, although the original local Egyptian tradition persisted in the frequent use of animal and human figures. Expensive textiles were both a statement of status and a capital investment for both royalty and nobles. The royal wardrobe of the Fatimids was kept in two storerooms and cared for by thirty attendants supervised by high-ranking officials. Inventories of wealthy households also listed thousands of garments. Egypt by this time was the major manufacturing centre for textiles for the whole of the Islamic world. Numerous government-controlled workshops produced cloth for domestic consumption as well as for export. Some of these workshops produced luxury fabrics, like the gold *boqlomon* cloth that changed colour in different lighting. Other workshops supplied fabrics to the general public. Fatimid textiles were often decorated with pictures of rulers and nobles – caliphs in splendour, court receptions, hunting scenes, grape harvests and celebrations, menageries of real and imaginary animals – accompanied by names and inscriptions.

After the fall of the Fatimids came the Mamluk Turkic slave dynasty, who ruled Egypt from 1250 to 1517. Their domains included Syria and Palestine. Highly profitable trade routes between Europe and the East had to pass through Mamluk lands. As a result, Cairo became fabulously wealthy and a major artistic and cultural centre. The largest body of extant late medieval Islamic textiles comes from the Mamluks. Their textiles were produced in Cairo, Alexandria, Assyut in Upper Egypt and Damascus in Syria, among other centres. Under the Mamluks, fine textiles were used as signs of office. Different cloths were hung behind each amir on the Council

OPPOSITE
Bedouin woman's henna-dyed veil, Sinai.

ABOVE
Veiled woman of Cairo, nineteenth century.

of State, and promotion within the Mamluk hierarchy was marked by the royal gift of a new set of garments. Rank was expressed by the new device of a blazon indicating an amir's office at court, and this appeared on textiles as well as in other media. Elaborate ceremonies celebrating the beginnings of spring and autumn also involved a complete change of wardrobe. Long inscription bands on Mamluk textiles skilfully used Arabic letters to create grand rhythmical compositions. The Mamluks also used block-printed textiles, a technique most probably introduced from India. Many sophisticated examples found their way into the treasuries of European churches and courts, irrespective of the predominance of Arabic calligraphy. Textiles for the Mamluk market were also made as far away as Yunnan, in southwest China, combining dragons and phoenixes with inscriptions in Arabic. Mamluk textiles dominated the Mediterranean market until the fourteenth century, when they were largely supplanted by Spanish, Italian and Chinese weaves. The Mamluk textile industry consequently went into decline, but its designs were copied by its successors.

The Ottoman Sultan Selim I defeated the Mamluks at the battle of Reydaniyya in 1517. Cairo lost its capital status and reverted to being a provincial centre in a great empire. The Ottomans, however, maintained the production of Egyptian textiles at a very high standard. Workshops were important to the imperial economy and were kept under strict government control. This control extended over the import of raw materials and production and prices. Artisans were organized into guilds and received fixed salaries. Many examples of complete costume from this period survive, as well as kerchiefs, cushions, saddles and magnificently decorated tents. Ottoman designs were executed in bright vibrant colours and ranged from the highly abstract, such as the *chintamani* motif with its wavy lines and three dots, to charmingly naturalistic flowers and leaves. Floral patterns with jagged leaves and spiralling arabesques were very popular.

Vasco da Gama's discovery of the sea route to India, and Europe's new-found New World in the Americas, deprived Egypt of its role as the controlling entrepot of the Eastern luxury trade. Despite this, it remained wealthy and populous.

By the end of the eighteenth century, the textile industry was the biggest industry in Egypt, and textiles were being exported to the other provinces of the Ottoman empire and to Europe. Brocade, damask and cotton dominated the market at this time, and different garments were specified for each layer of the ruling hierarchy and within society generally.

The end of medieval Egypt and the beginning of its modern period came with Napoleon's defeat of Egyptian troops in 1795. The French brought with them Western scientific modes of thought that revolutionized Egypt but provoked a counter-reaction whose effects are still being felt today. The French were quickly superseded by the British, then the Albanian-born Mohammed Ali made himself Pasha, and Egypt entered a period of mechanization and modernization.

REGIONS

Cairo

In the Old City of Cairo lies Khiyammiya, the 'Street of the Tent Makers'. Here, in little cubicles, male tailors and their apprentices sit appliquéing by hand wall hangings, cushions and bedcovers for the domestic and tourist markets. Popular patterns are scenes from ancient Egyptian mythology, arabesques, calligraphy and birds. Main production, however, was always *qanat* – large-scale drapes in cotton, with bold geometric patterns, which made up the screens and canopies at festivities all over Cairo and Lower Egypt. If the panels in use today are studied carefully, it becomes apparent that the majority are screenprinted rather than appliquéd, but in the past they would all have been made in the Street of the Tent Makers. After the excavation of the tomb of Tutankhamun in the 1920s, and the ensuing popularity of all things Egyptian, many hangings on the Tutankhamun theme were made here for sale in Luxor and Port Said, and to supply Liberty's of London. These now often turn up in British antique shops.

Kardassa

Before the advent of motor transport, Kardassa village, near Giza, was the starting point for camel caravans to Siwa oasis. It is still a centre for hand-weaving on the ubiquitous pit-loom found in parts of eastern Africa and all over the Middle East and India. The weavers are by tradition male, though, as in many parts of the world, the differences between the sexes are now less marked, and women are becoming professional weavers. With the pit-loom, all the warp threads are leashed to the heddles. Shed and counter-shed are made by operating foot-treadles, which are set in the pit, with the weaver sitting on its edge. Cotton, silk and frequently nowadays rayon yardage are woven at Kardassa, predominantly to be made up into *milayah* (shawls). Cloth is still woven here for the Siwa market. One of the *milayah* worn by the Berber women of Siwa is made up of two strips of blue-and-white chequered cloth from Kardassa, joined along the selvedges with silk embroidery in black and yellow.

Naqada

Many hand-looms are still to be found in Naqada, a Coptic village just south of Luxor on the west bank of the Nile. It was once famous for the weaving of metal-thread, tapestry-woven garments and hangings in the Syrian style. Silk *aba* (surcoats) were woven here, but never to the same standard as those from Aleppo and other Syrian centres. Until the 1960s, black and dark mauve silk and cotton marriage shawls used in the western oasis of Bahariya were a staple of production, and more recently the village produced quantities of textiles in cotton or synthetic thread for export to Libya and Sudan. Unfortunately, due to

OPPOSITE
Panel from the eighteenth-century undershirt of a Muslim warrior, inscribed with protective calligraphy.

ABOVE
Appliqué from the Street of the Tent Makers, Cairo.

political problems, both these markets have been lost. Most hand-weaving today is of simple plaid cotton cloth for rural use and for the small surviving trade with the western oases.

Siwa

The oasis of Siwa has an ancient history. Inhabited by Berber people, it lies in the Western desert of Egypt on the Libyan border. Alexander the Great consulted the oracle at the temple here before his conquest of half of Asia en route for India. Traditionally, a bride from Siwa would wear seven differently coloured dresses underneath a very large, loose, wide-sleeved, T-shaped wedding smock. The smock is embroidered in silk with motifs of flowers and auspicious symbols, and is embellished with buttons, glitter and even, latterly, bits of coloured plastic. The smock and accompanying baggy trousers are made of either white synthetic damask or inexpensive black cotton. The cuffs of the trousers and the small black voile shawl that completes the wedding costume are embroidered in silk. The embroidery threads are blue, black, green, red, yellow and orange, which, together with the white buttons, make up the seven colours deemed to bring good luck. The central panel of the neckline is embroidered in chain stitch and bordered by blocks of Romanian stitch. Simple cross stitch and a complex combination of stitches are then employed to form the lines that radiate from the breastbone like a sunburst.

Nubia

The Nubians of Upper Egypt are an ancient people of great historical interest. They were formerly based around Wadi Halfa, a place submerged by the building of the High Dam at Aswan. Nubian women wear a long, flimsy, voile dress in the European style, known as a *girgar*. This is worn with a shawl edged with beadwork.

THE PRESENT

By the mid-nineteenth century, Egypt had been planted with vast acres of irrigated cotton fields and the clank of the mechanized cotton mill was to be heard. By the beginning of the twentieth century, the death knell had been sounded for hand-made textiles. The modern Egyptian textile market is now overwhelmingly dominated by mill production.

ABOVE
Wedding dress, Siwa oasis.

BELOW
Metal-thread-embroidered wedding dress, Western desert.

OPPOSITE
Appliqué tent panel from the Street of the Tent Makers, Cairo.

The Arab World

Syria

Syria is the heart of the Levant. Home to peasant, nomad and highly skilled urban artisans, it has one of the world's great, though under-documented, textile cultures. The country has been much fought over since ancient times, and its textile traditions go back through the Ottoman and Byzantine empires to Classical Rome and beyond. Syria was an important province to all of these empires, and was also one of the first prizes of the Arab conquest in AD 687. Its main cities, Damascus and Aleppo, had and still have heterogeneous populations: Muslim, Christian and Jew interact on friendly social and commercial terms.

Syria has enough arable land to support a viable agricultural base, but much of its territory, particularly to the east, is desert. Bedouin nomads graze their camels on desert pasturage, which is also used by sheep-rearing itinerants. There is usually enough rainfall, with the addition of water from wells and the major rivers, to sustain the flocks, though in the harsh winters the Bedouin have been known to migrate with their camels as far afield as Iraq, Jordan and northern Saudi Arabia. Mechanization, changes in political structure, changes in climate and, in the case of the sheep-owning tribes, over-grazing have led to a dramatic decline in the number of active nomads. Now the Bedouin are mainly settled, as farmers in the case of the Shammar of northern Syria, or have moved to the cities, or joined the army, as with the Roualla of the east and south. The virtual extinction of the nomadic way of life has meant that all the beautiful products of the Bedouin ground-loom – bags, tent dividers and blankets – are now very rarely made. The richer Bedouin also constituted an important market for the weavers of the towns, and consequently fine items such as tapestry-woven *meshla* (jackets) are no longer made.

TECHNIQUES

Tie-Dye

The town of Hama was particularly noted for its production of tie-dyed cotton cloth that was tailored into dresses and sashes for Bedouin, peasant and townswoman alike. A dress with long, hanging sleeves of this material was known as a *thob izzi*. The base material was a loosely woven cotton or sometimes silk fabric, made in Hama. The dress was made up, then a swirling pattern was tied into the body and sleeves. Next the garment was dyed, first with yellow, then perhaps red, and finally a dark brown to form the ground colour. The long, hanging sleeves were tied behind the woman's back when she was working. In more recent times, the sleeves have become narrower, and tassels have replaced the hanging portions of the sleeves. The *thob izzi* was worn with trousers and an under-dress.

PAGES 94–95
Bedouin tent divider, Iraq; silk *izar* loincloth, hand-woven in Hyderabad, India, for Oman; wedding shawl, Falujeh, southern plain, Palestine; supplementary-warp cotton bath towel, Syria.

ABOVE LEFT
Rich Bedouin man and boy in town-visiting garb.

ABOVE RIGHT
Street musicians of the Lebanon, the boy wearing a tapestry-woven coat.

OPPOSITE
Tie-dyed cotton dress, Hama.

ABOVE
Thob izzi, tie-dyed dress, Hama.

RIGHT
Cotton warp-ikat bath towel, Aleppo.

BELOW
Man's tapestry-weave coat, central Syria.

Ikat

Cotton warp-ikat bath towels were another widespread product, as most of the population, male and female, had to go to the public bath to bathe. Over most of the Muslim world, the same baths were used by both sexes, but they were segregated by the simple mechanism of allotting different times to men and women. Beautiful light cotton and sometimes silk bath wraps were woven in Aleppo and Damascus in the ikat technique. They were exported widely – to Turkey, Iraq and Iran, even reaching Aceh at the northern tip of the Indonesian island of Sumatra to be copied both by the Acehnese and their highland neighbours, the Batak. The Arabic term for ikat is *tarbit*. Ikat fabric with a silk or rayon warp but cotton weft is known as *qutni*. *Qutni* fabrics are still woven in Aleppo, Hama and Damascus.

Batik

Until the 1940s, Aleppo was a major centre for indigo dyeing, and it is in that city that a form of batik using a lime resist on

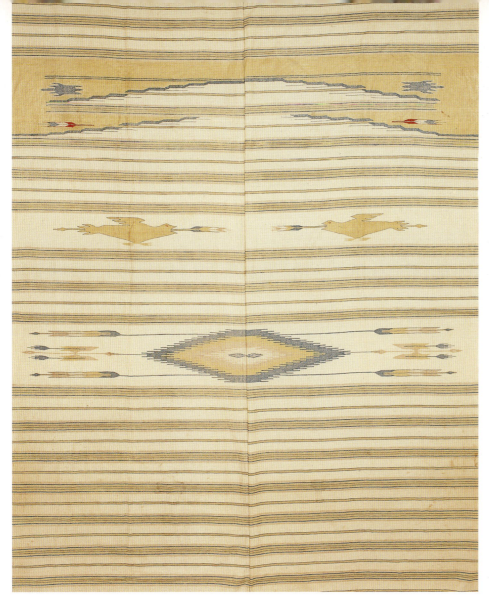 

silk is still practised. The lime resist is printed onto the silk with carved wooden blocks, and then the fabric is dyed black with an aniline dye. An alternative to the traditional technique is to screenprint. The headscarves produced in either technique have a market across Syria and are exported to Iraq, Jordan and Saudi Arabia.

Weaving

In Ottoman times and during the mandate period between the two world wars, Syria had strong export markets in Palestine, Lebanon, Trans-Jordan and Turkey. Aleppo, Damascus and other smaller places were key weaving centres. *Mashru* silk warp-faced satin with a cotton weft was a speciality, often with warp-ikat details. The pride of Syrian weaving, however, was the cotton and metal-thread brocade colloquially known as *zouk*, after Zouk the famous Lebanese weaving centre. It was used for furnishing fabric and also for the geometrically patterned *aba* (open robe) of the Arab gentleman. In the latter case, two strips of *zouk*, often in pastel colours, were sewn together to make up the neck, shoulders and skirt. *Zouk* fabric was also woven in Egypt and Lebanon. Woollen *meshla*, with fine tapestry-woven silk and metal-thread decoration on the collar and back in the *zouk* style, were also woven in central Syria up to the Second World War and exported to neighbouring countries.

Aleppo was the centre for the weaving of woollen scarves in imitation of those of Kashmir and Kerman. Square or rectangular, these were rolled up and used as sashes by prosperous urban men. They were referred to as *ajami*, meaning 'Persian'.

Baalbek in neighbouring Lebanon was historically a centre for cotton weaving and for the making of net scarves decorated with flattened knots of silver metallic strip in the style of Assyut

ABOVE LEFT
Zouk tapestry-weave curtain with cloud and bird and arrow design, central Syria.

ABOVE RIGHT
Resist-printed silk scarf, Aleppo.

OPPOSITE
Supplementary-warp cotton bath towel, Damascus.

ABOVE
Metal-thread and wool brocade woman's headscarf, Hama or Aleppo.

LEFT
Late nineteenth-century tapestry-weave cushions, central Syria.

SYRIA **101**

ABOVE LEFT
Supplementary-weft Ottoman bath towel, Aleppo.

ABOVE RIGHT
Bedouin tent divider, eastern Syria.

RIGHT
Bedouin man's camel-hair *aba*, with metal-thread-embroidered collar and lapels.

FAR RIGHT
Silk and metal-thread tapestry weave used in Ottoman Thrace as a man's sash.

in Egypt. The textile expert Shelagh Weir talks of waste silk being used to weave coarse silk fabric around Mount Lebanon for the Palestinian villagers of Galilee. Square, tasselled headscarves of silk or wool, combined with metal brocade, were woven in Lebanon and also at Homs and Aleppo. Those from the Lebanon were sold into Galilee before 1948.

Tablet Weaving

Syria was once famous for its carmine silk tablet-woven men's belts. There is still a viable silk-rearing industry in the country, but tablet weaving is sadly a thing of the past. Warps were stretched on a long narrow loom or between the weaver and a fixed point. They were not threaded through a system of heddles, but through the corners of tablets lying flat against each other and made out of card, wood or bone. The tablets were most often square, but triangles, hexagons, octagons and other shapes were also used. Depending on the intricacy of the pattern, anything between seven and three hundred tablets might be employed to weave a single band. Each tablet separated the warps threaded through it, lifting some and forcing others down, thus effectively opening a shed through which to pass the weft. By twisting the tablets, individually or in groups, different warps were raised and lowered, and different sheds could be opened. Each time a tablet was rotated, the warp threads twisted around each other. Most tablet weaving can be distinguished by this distinctive warp-twined appearance.

Crochet

Syrian Muslim prayer caps of crocheted silk, worked in a variety of geometric patterns, are famous all over the Near East. They are made as a domestic craft, and are sold by male pedlars in all Syria's souks. Since crochet requires only yarn and a hook, which can be made of wood, metal, bone or plastic, it can be easily carried around and worked on at the maker's convenience. The foundation is a simple chain. First a slip loop is tied, then a loop is pulled through this with the hook. A succession of loops are then worked through each other, one at a time, until the chain has reached the required length. Subsequent rows are added by working a new sequence of loops, each one of which is hooked through the previous loop and also through the previous row. Variations on the basic stitch involve increasing the number of loops carried on the hook or linked together at the same time.

TOP
Man's tablet-woven belt in silk.

ABOVE
Men's crocheted skullcaps.

Embroidery

Embroidered garments, for both men and women, are to be found all over Syria. Professional embroiderers specialize in metal-thread work and all kinds of couching to decorate the short-waisted, long-sleeved jackets worn by women over their dresses. Each area has its own distinct style, to such an extent that older women can tell the village and sometimes even the embroiderer of a particular dress. Fine, delicate, floral embroidery in silk in a wide variety of stitches – particularly satin, herringbone and cross stitch – is to be found on the wedding dresses of Qutaife village in the Qalamoun hills in southern Syria. These dresses are usually of red mill cloth (sometimes also mauve or blue), with a collarless neckline and long, triangular, hanging sleeves. The sleeves, reminiscent of those on early medieval European dresses, may be the result of Crusader influence, or possibly the influence travelled in the opposite direction. The sleeves are decorated with multicoloured faggotting stitchery, in which yellow predominates, and silk tassels are often added at the ends. Embroidered kerchiefs on fine cambric are worked in the same village. Patterns are Ottoman in origin and may well have been influenced by early twentieth-century Muslim refugees from the Balkans.

In the past, the majority of village embroidery was worked on hand-woven, indigo-dyed cloth by counting threads. After the Second World War, with the demise of most hand-weaving, embroiderers switched to cheap black sateen embroidering in cross stitch through waste canvas. After the embroidery is finished, the threads of the waste canvas are pulled away, leaving the embroidered design on the dress. The main exemplars of contemporary canvas work are the two villages of Sukhne and Saraqeb. It is this type of work that can now be found for sale in the souks of Damascus and Aleppo.

Sukhne is about forty miles from the ancient ruins of Palmyra in the east of Syria. Women's dress there consists of coat, blouse and skirt. Coat and skirt are embroidered with stylized floral motifs, often representing cypress or palm trees, formerly using silk threads, now mainly acrylic. Colours are red, or red with purple, sometimes with yellow details, against a black sateen ground. The craft of embroidery is in steep decline in Sukhne, but the same style is still worked in the village of Sfire, which is connected to Sukhne by marriage relations.

Saraqeb is a large agricultural village that lies between Aleppo and Hama in the northwest of Syria. The embroiderers

OPPOSITE ABOVE
Embroidered indigo cotton dress, Qalamoun, southern Syria.

OPPOSITE CENTRE
Hook-work cushion, Aleppo.

OPPOSITE BELOW
Metal-thread-on-velvet embroidery, Damascus.

LEFT
Woman's corded jacket, probably Damascus.

BELOW
Wedding coat, Es-Sechne, near Palmyra.

of Saraqeb and surrounding villages are prolific; they sell any surplus dresses to the shopkeepers of the Damascus souk and further afield. It is not an uncommon sight to see a Saraqeb woman getting off the bus at Damascus bus station with a bundle of new or used dresses for sale. One is supposed to be able to tell the difference between new and second-hand by looking to see if there is a repaired tear to the neckline of the dress. The importunate bridegroom is required to tear the wedding dress just there on the wedding night as proof of his virility. Be that as it may, the dresses, known as *kab*, are embroidered in red – a colour symbolic of fertility – in a V-shape on the back and front, on both cuffs and down one or both sides. The embroidery is canvas work in silk, and the hemline and lines down both side panels are machine-stitched in the same red silk thread. The lines down the side panels are colloquially referred to as 'railway lines', and the stylized floral patterns are probably ultimately derived from Ottoman carnation patterns. Saraqeb women are reputed to turn their dresses inside out when they are working in the fields to save wear and tear. The colour scheme is always red embroidery on a black ground. A similar style – but with the addition of coloured, usually yellow, details – is the work of Maarat al Numan village. These styles of dress are not very old: they go back perhaps some fifty years.

Examples of embroidery in the Syrian style are to be found in parts of Lebanon, but the latter has always been much more open to foreign influences than Syria, which has a more closed

SYRIA 105

economy and has remained remarkably conservative in matters of dress. The twenty years of civil war, roughly 1975–1995, were also not conducive to the production of traditional textiles in Lebanon.

Women's dress in Jordan for both peasant and nomad resembles that of their Syrian cousins, though Jordanian garments are rarely embroidered; if they are, it is only simply. The extremely long dresses of As-Salt, whose trains were brought up to act as the women's headdresses, are alas no longer worn.

Quilting

Syria has an urban tradition of quilting coats for women and girls out of very soft padded cotton to be worn after a bath. These coats are usually white, but they can also come in pastel colours. Modern copies are now made to sell in the Istanbul bazaar. The technique used is very simple. Layers of cloth are laid on top of one another and tacked together, with cotton waste padding incorporated to give warmth. Running stitch or back stitch is then used to sew the layers of the coat together around the edges and at intervals across the central area, holding the filling layers in place and giving a padded effect. Sometimes the rows of stitching are sewn in decorative geometric forms, such as chevrons and zigzags, to give a subtle background pattern.

Block Printing

Block-printed cloths have a history of use in Syria dating back to ancient Rome. Excavations of the desert city of Palmyra have revealed remains of block-printed cloth from India dating back to Queen Zenobia's time (3rd century AD). The patterns on these finds are exactly the same as patterns on contemporary block-printed cloth from Rajasthan. At one time, simple block-printed shawls were made in the souks of Aleppo and Damascus. Now only the manufacture of simple black-on-white cotton bags – given to customers making purchases from cloth shops – continues, though block printing is a cheap and efficient means of producing hard-wearing patterned textiles. To ensure sharp detail, the blocks are carved from the end grain of densely grained hardwoods, such as box, sycamore, ash and pearwood. Different sections of the pattern can be carved onto different blocks in order to avoid excessive weight.

OPPOSITE TOP
Girl's quilted cotton bathrobe, Aleppo or Damascus.

OPPOSITE CENTRE LEFT
Beaded slipper face, Damascus.

OPPOSITE CENTRE RIGHT
Kurdish woman's horned bridal cap, northeastern Syria.

OPPOSITE BELOW
Embroidered cap, southern Syria.

ABOVE
Block-printed shawl, Damascus.

LEFT
Block-printed and appliquéd cushion, southern Syria.

ABOVE
Block-printed cotton shawl, Damascus.

OPPOSITE ABOVE
Block-printed cotton yardage, Damascus.

OPPOSITE BELOW
Contemporary ikat *mashru*, Damascus.

THE PRESENT

The market for many of Syria's fine textiles was lost with the end of the Ottoman empire in 1918, and regional wars post-1948 have lost further markets in Palestine and other neighbouring countries. However, domestic embroidery in a few places such as Saraqeb has continued to flourish. Damascus is also still home to a few jacquard looms on which are woven exquisite silk brocades. The elderly weavers will show you with pride the type of brocade that was specially commissioned for the coronation of Queen Elizabeth II in 1953. But Syria is changing fast. There is an influx of money from the Near and Middle East, which is set fair to change a once-moribund economy. What effect this will have on the production of hand-made textiles is difficult to say. The weaving of *mashru* and other brocades is problematic, and a question of both fashion and price. Will there still be a local market for these fabrics, and will people be able to afford them as the costs of production inevitably rise? And will young weavers be willing to step into the shoes of the old? Syria will always be a country that appreciates fine textiles, but there is a doubt that it will still be a major producer in fifty years' time.

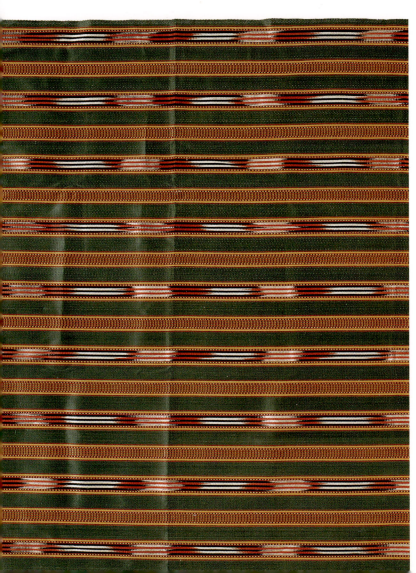

Palestine

Palestine, the Holy Land sacred to three religions, has been much disputed and fought over. Culturally, it was interconnected with Lebanon and Syria to the north and through Sinai to Egypt. Until the foundation of the Jewish state of Israel in 1948, the majority of its population was Muslim, with Christian and Jewish minorities. After 1948 and then the take-over of the rump of the Palestinian lands after the Arab-Israeli war of 1967, the Palestinians were widely dispersed across the Near and Middle East, or became confined to a few areas within historic Palestine – Gaza, in what used to be known as the Gaza Strip; the environs of the towns of Ramallah, Jenin, Nablus, Bethlehem and Hebron; and the old city of Jerusalem and up around Galilee. It is difficult to talk of the production of Palestinian textiles today, as textile production requires peace, and there has been no peace for over two generations. In this section we shall therefore look at the situation before 1948, and the situation before 1967 in the West Bank, and we shall touch upon the situation today.

Palestine was a land of small farmers, often at the beck and call of major landowners, merchants and Bedouin pastoralists who inhabited marginal areas such as the Negev desert. Weaving took place in many locations, though luxury fabrics often created specifically for the Palestinian market were woven at Aleppo, Homs, Hama and Damascus in Syria. There was also the import of other foreign fabrics, notably the tightly woven linen brought by Orthodox Russian pilgrims to Jerusalem before the First World War.

Shelagh Weir, the acknowledged expert on Palestinian textiles, remarks that, though almost every town or village in Palestine had its own weavers, certain towns specialized in the craft. Mejdel, which lay between Ashdod and Gaza was the most important centre, boasting several hundred looms. Weavers there used a form of the Asia-wide pit-loom. There were two types of this loom, a heavy version for weaving wool and mixed woollen and cotton fabrics, and a light version that was for weaving light cottons. After 1948, the Mejdel weavers relocated to Gaza. Other important weaving centres were Safad, Nazareth, Ramallah, Beit Jala, Bethlehem, Gaza and Hebron.

ABOVE
Women of nineteenth-century Bethlehem dressed in traditional attire.

OPPOSITE
Bethlehem dress panel of couched cording and silk embroidery on taffeta.

MATERIALS

Wool and animal hair

The dry climate and hilly terrain of Palestine was ideal for the raising of sheep, goats and camels. There was therefore an abundance of wool and goat and camel hair for usage in textile-making.

Cotton

Cotton was rare. Although it was grown around Safad and Nablus in the nineteenth century, it (and flax) were mainly imported from Egypt, both in the raw state and as yarn. By the end of the nineteenth century, much cotton came from Europe, either as yarn or as finished goods.

Silk

Though raised in small quantities in Palestine to be used as embroidery thread or for weaving, silk came overwhelmingly from Syria.

TECHNIQUE

Embroidery

Palestinian embroidery forms part of a greater Near Eastern tradition, and similarly embroidered garments can be found in Lebanon and Syria and into the Sinai desert. However, embroidery is the Palestinian craft *par excellence* and has become known worldwide as a symbol of the Palestinian people.

Wedding costumes, veils and furnishings were embroidered by Palestinian brides and by the female members of their families, using silk thread on hand-woven cotton or linen. Most of this was of local manufacture and, as the fabric was relatively loosely woven, the embroidery was counted-thread cross stitch. The cloth was either left its natural creamy white colour or dyed indigo blue. As the twentieth century progressed and hand-woven fabric became increasingly unavailable and finally disappeared, it was replaced by mill-made satin and canvas work, in which a fine cotton mesh is laid over the fabric to be embroidered (the cross stitch worked through it replaced counted-thread work). After the canvas-work embroidery is completed, the cotton mesh is carefully snipped away.

Within Palestine, each district had its own style of dress and it was easy to distinguish between them. Countrywomen from the villages wore a style that distinguished them from the Bedouin and the townswomen. Wedding dresses of Ramallah were of red silk worked on a creamy linen or cotton ground.

ABOVE AND BELOW
Embroidered silk on linen dress panels, Ramallah.

112 THE ARAB WORLD

LEFT
Refugee camp embroidered trousers.

BELOW LEFT
Early twentieth-century woman's dress, central Palestine.

BELOW
Gaza dress altered for the post-1967 Western market.

PALESTINE 113

ABOVE
Wedding dress from Jerusalem with DMC-influenced patterns embroidered in silk on linen fabric.

OPPOSITE
Malak, Bethlehem 'Queen' dress.

The dress-fronts of Ramallah dresses were of very high quality, since it was traditional for the bridegroom to commission them from professional female embroiderers (it is for this reason that many more Ramallah dress-fronts turn up at present-day sales than complete dresses). In Gaza, women wore indigo-dyed dresses with long, hanging sleeves, often incorporating into the body of the dress vertical pink silk stripes. In Galilee, the coats were also indigo-dyed but edged with shaped, appliquéd, cotton or satin patches in the Syrian manner. These coats were short and worn over a knee-length white dress, beneath which were worn blue or white cotton trousers.

The style of Galilee wedding costume described above died out in the nineteenth century, but across the villages of southern Palestine women continued to embroider dresses in the same basic style at least until 1948. They had an embroidered chest-piece and long narrow or hanging sleeves. All the dresses were made up after the component pieces had been embroidered, and the shape and size of the mother was taken as a model of what the young girl would grow into after she was married. Not only were highly decorative wedding costumes made, but also much plainer second and third everyday dresses.

The dresses of Bethlehem were slightly different. They were the most complex and the most Ottoman-influenced, with sleeves and breast made up of applied rectangles of couched silk and metallic threads with floral silk embroidered details. The materials often also reflected the wealth that the Christian pilgrim trade brought to Bethlehem. The couching on Ottoman military uniforms and on Christian priests' richly embroidered vestments had a profound impact on Bethlehem work, with cotton and linen often being replaced by a heavy ribbed silk. The wedding garments of Bethlehem were the work of professional embroiderers. Couched panels were commissioned by the bride's family, and more ostentatiously by the bridegroom's, to decorate dresses and the tight jackets that were to be worn in the cooler hills. The bridegroom commissioned a special dress for the bride, known as *malak* ('queen') and made of the richest materials and finest workmanship his family could afford. The metal threads and cords were all imported from Syria. The fashion for this style of couching spread to other villages and was worked at other places, particularly at Beit Dajan, near Jaffa. From the 1920s it was common for panels of couched taffeta to be bought by the bridegroom from Bethlehem or Beit Dajan as a gift to the bride so they could be sewn onto her wedding dress.

The wedding garments of Sam'ua district in the hills to the south of Hebron are some of the most beautiful of old Palestine's products, with floral motifs compressed into a grid of squares against a white, usually linen ground. The dresses of the Bedouin women of the Negev and Sinai are of a comparatively crude cross stitch on a mill-woven black ground. For many years they have used embroidery thread of man-made fibres. A widow will have a dress with blue embroidery, and a married woman with red. When a widow re-marries, her dress may combine both colours. Palestinian women also usually wore a veil, known as a *khirqah*. Fellahin peasant women's veils were of white to distinguish them from the Bedouin women, who wore black. This may reflect the fact that the Fellahin had access to water to wash their clothes and the Bedouin did not.

Palestinian embroidery motifs have many names, which are generally just aide-memoires to distinguish one pattern from another. Nineteenth-century embroidery motifs tended to be stylized representations of natural objects: cypress trees and flowers set into an abstract geometric framework were typical. What distinguishes Palestinian embroidery from that of neighbouring countries is the foreign, Western influence starting with incomers such as the Quakers in the town of Ramallah from the 1870s onwards. It continued with European and American missionaries' educational endeavours introducing Western patterns, and culminated in the 1940s with Palestinian women gaining access to DMC pattern books and Western women's magazines. Silk thread was imported from Syria and was often hand-dyed. If threads were bought at different times, there would be a slight difference in colour, which often led to a pleasingly variegated effect across an embroidered panel. The effect of the introduction of standardized mercerized thread was to eliminate a lot of the variety intrinsic to hand-dyed thread.

THE PRESENT

Regardless of the situation of Palestinians today – whether within Israel, the Occupied Territories, refugee camps or otherwise as part of the diaspora – women still often embroider in the style of their ancestral home, however long they have been separated from it and even when it has long ceased to exist. They will still embroider wedding costume, but are more likely to be producing such items as cushion covers for sale to whatever market is available to them.

OPPOSITE LEFT
Early twentieth-century dress from around Beersheba.

OPPOSITE RIGHT
Wedding shawl, Falujeh, southern plain.

TOP
Kirkah, woman's embroidered shawl, Ramallah.

ABOVE
Wedding shawl of silk and metal-thread embroidery on black crepe, typically embroidered on frames at Bethlehem and Beit Jala.

PALESTINE 117

Iraq

Mesopotamia – the land of the two mighty rivers, the Tigris and the Euphrates – was from time immemorial a great cultural centre. It can trace its lineage back to the ancient Assyrians and Chaldeans. Its capital, Baghdad, was founded as a Muslim city in the eighth century AD, and was from its foundation the capital of the Abbasid Caliphate. This Caliphate lasted till 1258, when the city was sacked by the Mongols, led by Hulugu, grandson of Genghis Khan. The Mongols in turn lost Baghdad when it was captured by the Ottoman Turks in 1534.

Throughout its history, Baghdad was a noted textile centre. Indeed, so famous were the fabrics woven in Iraq that several textile terms derive from the region: 'tabby weave' comes from the Arabic *attabi*, which referred to a textile made in a quarter of Baghdad of that name; 'baudekins', a medieval European name for silk canopies comes from 'Baldec', a corrupt form of Baghdad; and 'muslin', a word still used worldwide, is ultimately derived from a similar fabric famously produced in the northern Iraqi city of Mosul. Baghdad was not only a textile production centre but also one of the greatest trading hubs in the world, through which passed, among other precious goods, textiles, dyes and spices from China, Spain, Africa and Java.

In addition, the Ottoman provinces of Mosul, Baghdad and Basra were famous for their weavings, as were their successors in modern-day Iraq (Mosul was also renowned as a centre for metal-thread embroidery). The Kurds of the north were famous for their weaving in wool.

REGIONS

Southern Iraq

Women by the Euphrates river make brightly coloured rugs with intricate, floral, animal and human designs in woollen chain stitch worked with a hook. They have a preference for orange, red, green and white threads, worked on the tightly woven strips of the apricot-coloured woollen fabric so typical of Iraqi weaving. The strips of cloth are always the same width; the length used depends on the purpose of the article to be made. Arab women of the marshes in southeast Iraq are some of the most famous practitioners of this work, as are the women of the region to the south of Baghdad between the two great rivers which includes Babylon, Al-Hillah and Karbala across the Euphrates; Diwani, Samawa and Nasiriyah (the marshes) on the Euphrates; and the area of Dusaniyah near Kut on the Tigris.

The women choose the wool for the embroidery thread, spin it, then dye it to the required colours. The motifs they work can be laid out in a very ordered manner, or else packed in on top of each other but contained in floral rectangles. Embroidered rugs from the region of Samawa are usually quite regular in

ABOVE LEFT
Bedouin man visiting Baghdad, 1920s.

ABOVE RIGHT
Bedouin woman wearing a silk kaftan, 1920s.

OPPOSITE
Hook-embroidered woollen rug or cover, southern Iraq.

THE ARAB WORLD

their layout. Those of the Babylon area have many small designs closely packed together. Many of the motifs have a symbolic meaning. For instance, a palm tree means longevity, a cypress resurrection, three flowers the unity of a family, a lion strength, a cock victory and glory, and a camel riches and happiness.

Perhaps because the terrain bordering the rivers is flat, monotonous and monochrome, its inhabitants have a deep-seated need for colour, which their textiles more than fulfil. The finished articles are used for a variety of domestic purposes, including as curtains, house dividers or wall decorations.

Kurdish Iraq

The Kurds, traditionally semi-nomadic pastoralists, are to be found over the largely mountainous region that forms the border regions of Turkey, Syria, Iran and Iraq. They are so widespread, however, that they are even to be found in the countries of the former Soviet Union. Speaking an Iranian language and reputedly descended from the ancient Medes, they have never had the political unity to form their own country and appear to be forever doomed to a life of constant rebellion against an alien government and equally constant bloody repression.

Kurdish men and women wear a fringed scarf wound around the head to form a tight turban. The women clothe themselves in dresses or skirts of brightly coloured floral fabric. The men wear baggy, usually black trousers tied with a Kashmir or Paisley scarf as a cummerbund. Until the Second World War, men of some of the Iraqi Kurdish tribes wore a jacket and straight trousers of brocaded silk. The town of Sulaimania was famous for the production of brocaded turbans and sashes woven on pit-looms and sold to the local Kurds. The Iraqi Kurds were also the main market for the silk and metal-thread brocades woven in northeast Syria and made into long-skirted coats.

THE PRESENT

It is very difficult to predict what condition the hand-crafted textile industry will be in, if and when the state of war that began in Iraq in 2003 comes to an end. Surprisingly, some production continues, even under the present catastrophic conditions. Beautiful camel-hair cloth bolts, used to make up an Arab man's *bisht* (robe), are still woven at Najaf both for export and for home consumption. There, by the sacred shrine of Imam Ali, old men weave wool into *agal*, the much prized headrope that binds an Arab's *keffiyah* (headdress). There is also weaving in wool at Mosul and in the Kurdish north.

ABOVE
Kurdish metal-thread brocade coat woven in northeastern Syria for the Iraqi market.

OPPOSITE ABOVE
Bedouin kelim-weave woollen tent divider.

OPPOSITE BELOW
Kurdish man's silk brocade jacket and trousers.

Iraq 121

Saudi Arabia

Saudi Arabia – home to the holy cities of Mecca and Medina – lies at the very core of Islam. The Prophet Mohammed was born in *c.* AD 570 in Mecca, from whence he was forced to flee in AD 622 (this flight is known as 'the Hejira', and is the starting date of the Muslim calendar). The Prophet died in AD 632 in Medina, having established Islam. Newly converted Arab armies then swept out to conquer a large part of the then-known world, taking with them the word of the Prophet and in the process spreading the new religion whose message reverberates across the world to this day.

The epicentre of Islam and its most holy spot is the Ka'bah at Mecca. Although its status as a shrine pre-dates Islam, it – together with nearby Mount Arafat – has always been the focus of the Hajj pilgrimage and the culmination of every Muslim pilgrim's visit to the holy places. The Ka'bah, known as 'Bait Allah' ('The House of God'), is a great cube of black rock. Since historical times it has been given an annual cover, known as the 'Kiswa' (literally, 'robe'), of woven fabric adorned with calligraphic inscriptions in Arabic and embroidered in silver thread with the name of God. This was traditionally the gift of the Caliph, and in Ottoman times was made either in Cairo or Damascus and sent with great ceremony on the annual camel caravan that left both those places with a mass of pilgrims to cross the desert to Mecca and Medina. The Kiswa was once embroidered in special workshops behind Khan Khalil in Cairo, but is now made in the holy city of Mecca itself. A special Kiswa cover with much smaller lettering is made to adorn the interior of the Ka'bah.

Saudi Arabia is vast but mainly arid, and its population is thinly spread across it. Divided by tribe, the Arabs consist of Bedouin nomads, semi-nomadic shepherds, settled farmers and inhabitants of the towns. Although the ever-increasing, oil-based prosperity of the last fifty years, with its concomitant urbanization, has transformed most people's way of life, the feeling of belonging to a certain tribe is still highly important.

The camel-rearing Bedouin and the sheep-herding pastoralists had their traditional grazing domains, known as *dira*. They mainly kept within their own *dira*, except when forced to trespass on a neighbour's in times of drought, which would lead to a bout of intertribal feuding, with raid and counter-raid being staged, the main aim being the rustling of livestock. Casualties were kept to a minimum, however, through a strict code of honour, and women and children were always inviolate. For the nomads, there was an annual cycle of migration. They would live by their wells during the dry season and spread out to the vast grazing grounds during the rainy season, only to return to the same wells in the next dry season.

The women of the tribes wove all the cloth for the tents and the tent and animal trappings out of sheep's wool and goat hair on the single-heddle ground-loom (the workings of this

ABOVE
Rashaidah fringed face-veil, embroidered with silver thread, Hail region.

OPPOSITE
Bani Sa'ad woman's dress, embellished at the neck and sleeves with glass and metal beads, hills south of Taif.

ABOVE
Jahdaly costume with appliquéd bands and metal-bead embroidery, worn with tasselled fabric *ridayah* headdress, Hijaz.

ABOVE
Jahdaly *thobe*, with back panel worn with agate belt, open-seamed sleeves fastening with a button, and *qarqoosh* headcovering, Hijaz.

ABOVE
Thaqeef *muqabar thobe* sewn in alternate bands, with appliquéd hem and embroidered yoke and cuffs, Wadi Mahram.

loom are described in detail in the Kuwait section of this book; see p. 129). The sheep-herders were the most prolific weavers, not only because they had an abundance of raw material, but because their migrations were much less arduous than those of the camel-owning Bedouin, thereby leaving the women more time to weave.

The centre of urban weaving in Saudi Arabia was Al-Hasa in the northeast of the country, where fine camel-hair *bisht* (men's outer robes) were made. These were woven by men on the same kind of pit-looms as in neighbouring Kuwait and Bahrain.

COSTUMES

Men and Women's Urban Dress

Urban dress in the Hijaz – the region that stretches from Medina down to Taif – reflects the cosmopolitan nature of the holy cities of Mecca and Medina. There has long been a constant throng of pilgrims from all over the world, and with them have come all manner of fabrics. Women's dress has often been made up of Indian silks, frequently embroidered in *zari* thread also from India. Urban men in the past would wear a variant of the Ottoman *tarbush* cap, made on a basketry frame, and often worn with a silk headcloth decorated with floral hook-work chain stitch. There were two styles of these headcloths, one embroidered at Calcutta in *muga* or *eri* wild silk, the other in a more colourful and more densely embroidered style, possibly from western India or Iran, or made by Indian or Persian workers based in the Hijaz. These headcloths and the *tarbush* were brought home by the returning pilgrims as religious souvenirs and as visual symbols that their owners had successfully made the arduous journey to the holy cities, had performed the prescribed religious rites, and were worthy of the esteemed title 'Hajji'.

Basic urban costume for both sexes throughout Arabia consists of a robe for the body, tighter for men, looser for women; trouser-like undergarments known as *sirwal* (adopted from Persia after the Arab conquest there in the eighth century AD); and a cloak and/or headcovering. Men wear the classic Arabian dress of the white *dishdashah*, worn underneath the open-fronted *abayah* or *bisht* (robe), topped with a headcloth known as a *ghutra* (the *hatta*, or *kaffiyah*, of the rest of the Arab world) and an *agal* (headrope). Women in many parts of Arabia wear the face-veil, though village women only wear it when coming into town, as it encumbers them in their daily work. The most ancient article of dress is the *izar*, the loincloth that is still basic wear for men in much of south Arabia.

Women's Traditional Dress

Bridal dresses were made by the mother or older female

 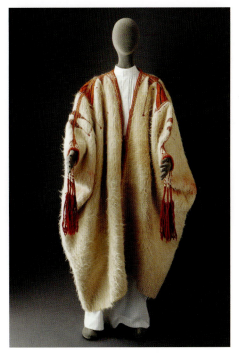 

ABOVE
Bani Sa'ad *thobe*, worn with silver belt, embroidered pantaloons and special-occasion silver *mataweeh* headdress, Taif region.

ABOVE
Man's *bidi aba* cloak made of white goat's wool, embroidered on front and shoulders, and with tasselled sleeves, Al Baha.

ABOVE
Yam *thobe* with wide triangular sleeves, worn with a hand-woven leather belt and woollen headdress, Wadi Najran.

relatives to be worn at both the wedding and subsequent special occasions. Dresses in general are of a basic T-shape, usually with narrow sleeves, but in places that were extremely hot and humid the sleeves could be wide and the dress loose to facilitate a through-flow of air. Some tribes followed the Syrian and Palestinian fashion for hanging sleeves, but in the Peninsula they would have square rather than pointed ends. When the women were working, they'd draw up their sleeves and tie the hanging ends together out of the way behind their back.

The tradition of highly decorative women's costume is especially strong in the Hijaz. The settled pastoralist tribes in the hills around Taif make some of the most richly decorated dresses in the kingdom. The Bani Sa'ad are a well known people who live in the fertile hills to the south of Taif (the Prophet's wet nurse came from this tribe). Their women wear a close-fitting, T-shaped dress that is often lined against the winter cold of the mountains. The dress is decorated with beautifully embroidered triangular side panels in an orangey-yellow silk, and both sleeves and chest are embellished with beads. The beads are either made by the women themselves using silver with a heavy admixture of lead (the holes in the beads are made by pushing a thorn through the hot, still pliable metal) or they are bought glass, of such a colour that at first sight they resemble the metal beads. Beadwork and embroidery also adorn the hems, sleeves and back of the dress, the cuffs of the pantaloons worn underneath it, and the complex headdress, which can be made of up to seven layers.

The Bani Malik live to the south of the Bani Sa'ad and have a similar cut of dress, though the sleeves are shorter to accommodate their silver bracelets. Bani Malik dresses and headdresses are embroidered predominantly in yellow, with small glass beads interspersed with red knots giving body to the embroidery.

The Thaqeef live near Taif, in Wadi Mahram, the place where Yemeni pilgrims traditionally stopped to change into their *ihram* pilgrimage clothing before proceeding to Mecca. The *mubaqar thobe* dress of the Thaqeef of the Shafa area is made up of alternate bands of black and blue cotton, with a hem appliquéd in a grid pattern and an embroidered yoke and cuffs in red and white.

The costume of the noble tribe of Hudheyl, who also live around Taif, is of particular interest. Their dresses are made up of tie-dyed muslin, with patterns of white dots grouped in diamonds against a light blue ground. The women of these settled tribes traditionally went unveiled.

To the north between Mecca and the Red Sea live the Jahdaly. They inhabit the fertile wadis that drain down towards the Tihama, the extremely hot and humid coastal plain. Jahdaly

women are the only tribal group in Saudi Arabia to wear a skirt and blouse, made up of imported muslin dyed locally red or brown. They also wear a more typically Arabian *thobe* in the same materials. Their skirts are often lined with old flower sacks and their headdresses are often adorned with metal beads.

The great nomadic tribe of the Harb dominates the northern Hijaz, around the city of Medina, and in the past ran the caravan trade between central Najd and Mecca, Medina and Jeddah. Harb women's dresses, often of blue cotton, are embroidered along the edges with patchwork hems and adorned with mother-of-pearl buttons. A Harb woman wears a long face-veil, sewn into which are vertical rows of old coins, mainly Ottoman but interspersed with the odd British Indian rupee, French colonial coin or other exotica.

Related to the Harb are the Sulaym, who lead a semi-settled life on the Red Sea coast as fishermen, traders and herders. Sulaym women embroider some of the most beautiful costume in all Arabia. The yokes of their dresses are finely embroidered, the sleeves appliquéd, and the hems made up of fine lines of appliqué interspersed with embroidery. A unique characteristic of Sulaym dresses is the use of cones of metal-thread embroidery decorating the breast and shoulder area. Perhaps they once symbolized fertility. They are fascinating, both in appearance and technique.

The Asir region lies to the south of the Hijaz and runs down to Yemen. It is a hilly farming area of settled tribespeople. Much of their costume relates to that of neighbouring Yemen. Women wear a velvet *thobe*, with embroidered panels in designs – again, like the Yemen – redolent of Africa. As in southern Arabia, when working in the fields they wear straw hats and waist-cloths which cover up their pantaloons.

Wadi Najran lies between the Asir highlands and the desolate, dessicated, uninhabitable 'Empty Quarter'. The main nomadic tribe there are the Yam, whose women traditionally wear an unembroidered indigo blue *thobe* with wide triangular sleeves.

The political and geographical centre of Saudi Arabia is Najd. A land of desert, escarpment and oases, it contains the capital Riyadh and is the homeland of the Saud dynasty who unified the kingdom between 1902 and 1932. Its population was formerly divided between nomad and farmer, with tribal affiliations that often encompassed both. The costume of the urban women of Najd is very Indian-influenced, with a long, loose *thobe* of light Indian silk or chiffon, embroidered with *zari* metal-thread work.

To the north of Najd lie the mountains of Jebel Shammar. The capital of this region is Hail, and it is from round here that the Rashaidah tribe stem, although they are also to be found over much of north Arabia, and branches have long since migrated to coastal Sudan and northern Ethiopia. Rashaidah women wear a dark, often black *thobe* decorated with bright, multicoloured patchwork. They also wear a long face-veil and a headdress decorated with metal beads.

THE PRESENT

Sadly, little embroidery is done today. Life has changed beyond measure, and only a few in the kingdom have a reverence for a past way of life. Though strenuous efforts are being made to collect and preserve costume from the first half of the twentieth century, very little hand-worked costume is being made today, if any. The glories of the textiles of Saudi Arabia are now only to be seen in a museum or online.

OPPOSITE
Early twentieth-century hook-work embroidered headcloth on silk bought in Jeddah.

ABOVE
Thobe of Indian silk, embroidered with sequins and gold, with voluminous sleeves brought round to cover the head, Najd.

ABOVE RIGHT
Harb *thobe* with patchwork shoulders, worn with face-veil in yellow silk embroidered with pearls, Al-Madinah region.

BELOW
Young boy's two-piece embroidered velvet suit, Hijaz, *c.* 1930.

RIGHT
Sulaym *thobe* with elaborate appliqué, embroidery and metal beading, Red Sea coast.

SAUDI ARABIA

Kuwait

Kuwait has for centuries been the marketplace and port for much of northeastern Arabia. As a great seafaring centre, it was involved in pearl diving and commerce both within the Gulf and far into and across the Indian Ocean. It was also the terminus of caravan routes that crossed the north Arabian desert bringing products from Syria and Iraq and the Hijaz. Along these trade routes, cotton from India and Egypt and metallic threads from France and India were imported to supplement locally available wool, goat hair and camel hair.

As well as supporting a population of seafarers and merchants, Kuwait served as the urban focus of a vast desert hinterland that was sparsely inhabited by nomads. It is still within living memory that large tribes from what are now Saudi Arabia and Iraq grazed their flocks and herds here. These nomads are known in Arabic as *al-badu*, from which we derive the English word 'Bedouin'. Sheep-rearing semi-nomads are known as *arabdar*.

Each tribe had its *dira*, or grazing range, and this contained wells around which the tribesmen camped and watered their animals during the extremely hot summer months. The *dira* was fiercely protected, and incursions into another tribe's range without permission often led to warfare. This nomadic way of life has gone, most probably for ever, but the weavings associated with it still exist and some are still being woven, albeit in an urban environment. Traditionally Kuwaitis used many types of locally woven textiles, made either by nomadic Bedouin women on the ground-loom or, up until the 1950s, by men on a commercial basis in Kuwait City, using a double-heddle pit-loom.

TECHNIQUES

Nomadic Ground-Loom Weaving

Until the mid-twentieth century, nomadic tribes practised an annual cycle of migration. They wandered across their vast *dira* in autumn, winter and spring, when the temperature cooled and the annual rains brought pasture to the desert. The Bedouin depended on the camel for transport, food and potable liquid; the *arabdar* depended on their flocks of sheep and goats. The latter were always the more prolific weavers, having ready access to wool. They also had more time on their hands, as their migrations were over lesser distances and they spent a good deal of their time camping by towns, which provided a ready market for their weavings. They also undertook commissions for the Bedouin, who had less opportunity to weave and who regarded finely woven articles as symbols of prestige, wealth and tribal identity.

Weaving comparatively simple items from wool and goat hair was virtually the only decorative craft of the Bedouin; indeed, it was one of the very few luxuries of the extremely frugal life that they led. It was considered a woman's job to make all the coverings, storage bags and animal trappings, and also to provide a place of comfort and shelter from the elements. The largest and most important single item that the Bedouin women wove was the Bedouin tent known as the *beit al-sha'ar* ('house of hair'). These tents are made up of long strips, known as *fiijan*, sewn together selvedge to selvedge. Goat hair, the preferred material, is heat-absorbing, strong, hard-wearing and to an extent waterproof. A Bedouin family's most prized possession is the woven tent divider known as the *ghata* or *rawaq*. This textile divides the public male area at the front of the tent from the private female quarters to the rear. The

OPPOSITE
Detail of a fine *ibjad* tent divider of wool, camel hair and cotton, decorated with horizontal bands of twined weft *ragoom* weaving.

LEFT
Bedouin saddlebag of wool and camel hair, with warp-faced patterning.

PAGE 130 LEFT
Bisht of camel hair, embroidered in Kuwait City.

PAGE 130 RIGHT
Detail of a woollen Bedouin weaving, decorated with lines of complex *shajarah* patterning.

decorative side of the tent divider always faces into the public area. It is here that coffee is offered to guests, and some of the most magnificent hangings forming the backdrop to this ritual are made up by juxtaposing warp-faced and weft-faced strips, then sewing them together.

Nomadic women – both *arabdar* and Bedouin – wove a multiplicity of bags, sacks and blankets. Saddlebags, when not in use, were often used as cushions. From the 1950s, when the *arabdar* started to use large lorries for the transportation of flocks and families to fresh pasture, their women began to weave pieces specifically as cushions. Trappings were once woven to adorn riding camels and the great swaying covered litters in which Bedouin women traditionally travelled. Buttons, metal studs, sequins and even feathers were often added to these decorative weavings. In the woven textiles of the Kuwaiti hinterland, certain geometric motifs recur and are given names such as 'eyes', 'horses' teeth', 'seeds' and 'ribs'. The triangle is also very common, particularly in the decorative tapestry-woven sections. Most patterns are to some extent influenced by the flora and fauna of the desert.

Bedouin women still weave on a single-heddle ground-loom, which in former times they pegged out on a suitable flat piece of ground by the tent. Weaving on the ground-loom is heavy, labour-intensive work, and often two women will work at the loom at the same time if a wider strip than normal is required. The loom is continuously warped around two wooden or iron warp rods, in a figure of eight formation, to create the 'weaver's cross', the layout essential to the formation of shed and counter-shed in this type of loom. The length between the two rods dictates the final length of the weaving. Both the loom and the woven piece are known by the Bedouin as *al-sadu*, a term derived from classical Arabic, meaning 'to reach forward, or towards an object'. The warp rods are tied to wooden warp and breast beams, then pegged securely into the ground. It is very important to keep up an even tension on the warps, although, with a continuous warp, adjustments to keep the tension are easy to make. The warps are separated one from the other, and each alternate warp thread is attached by a leash to a single fixed heddle. This heddle does not move during the formation of shed and counter-shed. The unleashed set of warp threads is manipulated by hand so that it is brought above the fixed heddle for every alternate pass of the weft and below it for the next pass. Thus are shed and counter-shed formed. The weft yarn is passed through by hand with a single stick spool, beaten in with a carved wooden sword-beater, then tightened up with a metal hook or the curved tip of a gazelle horn.

The simplest looms are also the most versatile. The ground-loom has the advantage that it can easily be rolled up and moved or stored at any time during the weaving process without any damage to the work in progress – important when complex supplementary weft and warp patterns are common in most decorative weavings. In such cases, the warp-faced pattern goes lengthwise along the strip in one or two long patterned stripes, whereas weft-faced patterns are introduced in blocks at intervals along the strip. The most complex and prestigious warp-faced, centrally placed, patterned strips are known as *shajarah*, and are only ever attempted by the most experienced weavers.

Urban Pit-Loom Weaving
The weavers of Kuwait City wove on pit-looms. Mainly, they wove wool or camel-hair yardage to make up the *bisht*, the Arab

man's ceremonial, open-fronted, square cloak, embroidered – usually in gold work – at the neck and lapels. The majority of the *bisht* sold in Kuwait today are of machine-made cloth imported from Saudi Arabia and Syria. The best quality, however, are made with hand-woven fabric from Najaf in southern Iraq or Doreg in Iran. In the past, the finest-quality yarn was imported from southern Iraq, but the bulk of the everyday wool used was spun by Kuwaiti Bedouin women. *Bisht* for Bedouin men were always in natural colours of black, brown and white (the ubiquitous female overgarment, the *aba*, was always black). Most weaving in Kuwait City was of this type – plain and unpatterned – though there was a small export trade of finer cloth to Saudi Arabia and Bahrain. There has also always been some demand for camel hair, which, though light and warm, is expensive and has always been the preserve of the rich. *Wuba* (camel hair) is taken from the hump of the animal. It is plucked, not sheared, and comes from Saudi Arabia and Iraq as well as Kuwait. Camel-hair fabric used to be woven in Kuwait City, but the finest quality was most probably always imported.

Pit-loom weavers would sit on a mat placed at ground level, with their legs in a rectangular pit dug into the ground. The wooden loom was made by local carpenters and sized to fit the proportions of the individual weaver. With his feet, the weaver would operate a pair of pedals, which were attached to shafts. The shafts were connected to string heddles slung from 'horses' attached to a beam mounted cross-wise on top of the wooden loom frame. By alternately pressing down on one or other of the pedals, the position of the heddles was altered so as to form shed and counter-shed. Yarn, usually wool, was drawn off from bobbins into a boat shuttle and used as the weft. The weaver then manually threw the shuttle across, beating in each pick by pulling on the centrally located hand-grip of the swivel-mounted comb-beater slung from the top of the loom frame. Woollen warp threads were stretched between square-sectioned warp and breast beams (or 'cloth beams'). The warps were tensioned by torsion on a peg inserted in a hole in the breast beam. This peg was then firmly lashed to a stake that had been hammered into the ground.

THE PRESENT

A weaving revival is underway in Kuwait under the auspices of the cultural society at Al-Sadu House, which provides advice and some training but most vitally has the marketing expertise to sell the products of the loom – generally small items, such as bags and cushions, but also the occasional larger commissioned piece. The tourist market is strong, and there is additional patronage from the big hotels and commercial offices. Ground-loom weaving is still practised, but in the main the loom has been adapted for urban use by shortening it to a length of around 16 feet (5 m) and mounting it in a rigid tubular frame that obviates the need for stakes in the ground – an impossibility when one intends to weave while sitting on a concrete floor. Though the Bedouin are now settled, having moved to the town or taken up work in the oil industry, the police or the military, some of the older women still weave, setting up looms in the courtyards of their urban homes and teaching their skills to their daughters and granddaughters. On the other hand, there has been no pit-loom weaving in Kuwait for two generations, and you have to go as far south in the Gulf as Bahrain to find any hand-weaving on a pit-loom at all.

Oman

ABOVE
Early twentieth-century Omani woman wearing the traditional 'beak'-like face-veil.

Oman occupies a vast area of southeast Arabia, including part of the Rub' al-Khali, the fearsome 'Empty Quarter', which was rarely crossed except by the most intrepid Bedouin, such as the Rashid, and by the European explorers Bertram Thomas, St John Philby and Wilfred Thesiger. The Omanis are followers of the Abadi sect of Islam. This, combined with their relative geographical isolation from the other major centres of Arabia, has meant that they developed a culture and attitude unique on the peninsula. From ports such as Muscat, they established sea-bourne trading routes and an overseas empire encompassing Mombasa, the famed spice islands of Zanzibar and Pemba, and much of present-day Pakistani Baluchistan. The Omanis took with them to Africa the Asian pit-loom, and most of the cloth woven on the East African coast was made on these kinds of looms, or imported directly from Arabia or India.

Most of Oman's own traditional textile industry, be it weaving or dyeing, takes place on or near the coast, but some takes place in the small towns of the historically hostile and rebellious interior, such as Nizwa and Bahala.

COSTUMES

The *Khanjar* Dagger

Every Omani man traditionally wears a curved *khanjar* dagger hung from a belt at his waist. The black and metal-thread braid that decorates the belt was made in the town of Rostaq, but now, as with much else, a cheaper and much less beautiful version is imported from China. Uniquely, the *khanjar*'s leather scabbard is embroidered with silver wire or strips of sheet silver. Nizwa and Sanaw are centres for this work, and Adam is famous for its silver-strip embroidery. The most costly scabbards of silver thread with gold-leaf details are made at Sur. The ordinary *khanjar*, which is attached to the belt by two metal rings, is usually decorated with silver-thread embroidery, but the more prestigious five-ring dagger, worn by Sayeeds (those who claim descent from the Prophet), is decorated with strips of sheet silver.

Men's Dress

An Omani man's costume is simple, consisting of a long, egalitarian *dishdashah* gown of white cotton, a *khanjar* dagger and belt at the waist, and an embroidered cap called a *kummah*, around which is wound a turban consisting of a diagonally folded square shawl of wool or cotton with Kashmiri embroidery (the turban is known as a *mussar*). The Omani *dishdashah* has a tassel at the neck, which can be perfumed. Men's *dishdashah* from Sur are often embroidered on the neck, shoulders and chest, and are loose-fitting as befits men of a seafaring community who would be inhibited by tight-fitting clothing while at sea. The *kummah* is decorated with eyelets edged in buttonhole stitch. Traditionally, these caps were lovingly made by the women of the family, but now they are sold in Muttrah or Muscat souk in their component pieces – a circular top and a rectangular strip to be curved into a circle, then sewn to the crown of the cap. Most hand-embroidery of

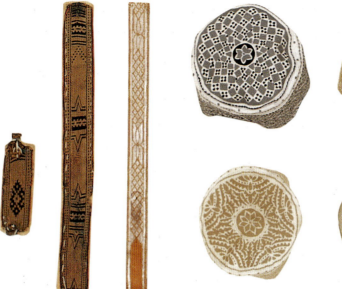

FAR LEFT
Men's braided and metal-thread belts.

LEFT AND BELOW
Men's embroidered caps.

BOTTOM
Bedouin woman's burnished face-veil.

OPPOSITE ABOVE
Wahaybah Bedouin woman's head ornaments.

OPPOSITE BELOW
Woman's *shakbah*, plaited leather and silver-baubled headdress, Wahaybah Sands.

the cap is now done by Bangladeshi workers in Salalah, but caps are also imported from the Philippines already decorated with machine embroidery. (Embroidered *kummah* in the Omani style are also everyday menswear in Zanzibar, confirming the profound influence that Oman has had on the Swahili coast of East Africa.) The universal Arab robe, which opens centrally down the chest – the *bisht*, or *aba*, of brown, cream or black wool – is worn on formal occasions.

Women's Dress
Women dress in a long, loose robe that, like the men's, is known as a *dishdashah*. Traditionally these have been highly colourful but, with today's mood of conservatism in the world of Islam, black has become the favoured colour. Historically, strong variations in women's dress have existed across the country, from region to region and from town to town. In Muscat, women wore a dress to the knee over matching *sarwal* trousers, with a *lahaf* shawl of bright printed cotton similar in style to the famous *kanga* wraps of East Africa. In Al-Dakhla (in the central-northern interior), the women dress very brightly, with the *dishdashah*, *sarwal* and *lahaf* all in contrasting colours. The dresses of the women of Al-Dahirah in the northwestern interior, the Omani enclave of Musandam on the strait of Hormuz and Al-Batinah on the north coast are all decorated with metal-thread embroidery or *talli* work (*talli* are hand-made trims made up of metallic threads, using bobbins on a cushion as in Western bobbin lace). The women of these regions also wear a face-mask. In Jabal Akhdar, dresses are worked with woollen embroidery. In Dhofar, women wear a long, square-cut dress

132 THE ARAB WORLD

of velvet adorned with embroidery, beads and sometimes even gold coins in the manner of neighbouring Yemeni Hadhramaut. This is worn with a light chiffon *lahaf*. The sizeable Baluch community on the Muscat coast wear a variant of the Baluch *pashk* (dress), which is known in Oman as a *balushi*.

Commonly worn in many parts of the interior are veils surrounding the eyes and covering the forehead and nasal areas. They are often made of thin leather dyed either indigo blue or a metallic green.

Another interesting accessory is the woman's headcover of the Wahaybah and Jenaba tribes in the Wahaybah Sands, made out of plaited leather, adorned with silver discs and known as the *shakbah*. These headdresses incorporate silver spacers and small coins into their leatherwork. Women of the more isolated Bataharah and Mahra tribes make a more heavily fringed *shakbah*, unadorned with silver. These pungent items are worn for special occasions covered by a *thob*, a transparent overdress that can be pulled up to go over the head.

TECHNIQUES

Spinning

Omani shepherds and Bedouin women spin wool using the suspended spindle, an ancient method that produces fine, even thread. The shepherds spin with a whorl, usually a stone from a nearby wadi, at the lower end of the spindle shaft. The Bedouin spindle has a whorl at the top. The threads are twisted clockwise to produce a tight, Z-spun, single yarn. Warp yarns bear the tension and take a lot of punishment in the weaving process. The weft yarns, which bear less strain, do not have to be so strong and are spun less tightly, resulting in slightly thicker and softer yarn. In the past Omanis spun cotton in a similar fashion, but no longer. Any cotton thread, as with silk, is now imported. The remaining pit-loom weavers, embroiderers, braiders and bobbin lace-makers all use imported thread. Cotton yarn comes from Pakistan; silk in years past was imported from China and India, but nowadays comes from Japan, as do silver and gold metallic threads for embroidery.

PAGE 134
Cotton *subaiya* waist-cloth from Bombay, bought in Muttrah souk.

PAGE 135
Silk *izar* loincloth, hand-woven in Hyderabad, India.

Dyeing

Powdered madder root was once used to give an orangey-red. Textile expert Gigi Crocker-Jones also noted that on the island of Masirah, off the east coast of Oman, a maroon-red dye was obtained from Murex shells, as at ancient Tyre. Maroon rugs made of wool dyed Murex purple were made on the island until the 1950s. Only white woollen yarn was traditionally dyed, using alum as a mordant in the days when plant dyes were still used. Omani weavers also use undyed goat and camel hair.

Indigo Dyeing

Amoor, the last indigo dyer in Oman, works from a shop in a little side-street off the main souk of the fortress town of Bahala. He uses chips of dried natural indigo to dye mill-woven cotton a light or medium blue (indigo, known here as *udhlam*, was always used to dye cotton and never wool). Historically, indigo dyeing was a lucrative industry for Oman, and flourished in a hot climate with little or no rainfall. The growing season is followed by a period of high ambient temperatures, ideal for dyeing a rich, deep blue. Although synthetic indigo reached Oman in the latter part of the nineteenth century, dyeing with natural indigo thrived in the isolated interior until the mid-twentieth century. Indigo-dyed cotton, often callendered to give it a bright sheen, was used for women's clothing and masks, for men's waist-wraps in the south of the country, and as a colouring for protective tattoos. The dye always had a myth and magic about it, and the Omanis had many superstitions associated with it. Two types – *Indigofera tinctoria* and *Indigofera argentea* – are grown in northern Oman as a commercial crop. The seeds are planted in late March and can be harvested three times over the next five months. The leaves are fermented in large clay jars under an immensely hot desert sun, or else in the dark of the workshop. *Indigofera coerulea* grows wild in the eastern Hajar, and was used to dye cotton yarn green until the late 1970s.

Ground-Loom Weaving

Omani shepherds and Bedouin nomads still use the ground-loom today. In fact, Oman is one of the few places left in the Arabian peninsula where Bedouin women still weave rugs, tent dividers and animal trappings for themselves rather than for a Western-orientated tourist market. They weave in wool, goat hair or camel hair on the single-heddle ground-loom common to nomads all across the Near and Middle East and North Africa. The Bedu woman sits athwart her loom, beating in the new weft pick with the tip of a gazelle horn or an iron pick. It is very arduous work, and for wider pieces two women will often work on the same loom. Prized items are camel blankets and storage bags, and both can be decorated with bands of supplementary-warp work known as *raqma*. The best of these come from the Wahaybah Sands. A favourite dye is madder, *Rubia tinctoria*, the ground-up root of which gives a mellow red with a tinge of brown. Bedouin weavers also make the black *flij* strips which are sewn up to make the black tent that is a nomad's home. The ground-loom can be set up and dismantled as required, and the weaving in progress – together

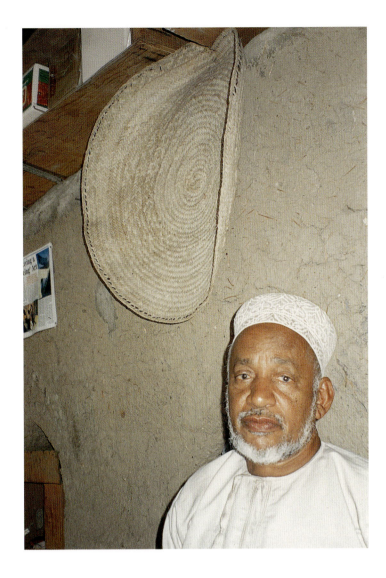

with the loom itself – can be rolled up and moved to a new location. Among the main items woven in Oman are goat-hair windbreaks and camel rugs and trappings, and these are generally warp-faced.

Pit-Loom Weaving

The pit-loom is a loom for settled people and professional male weavers. It usually has a permanent site, although it can also be set up in varying locations, according to the vagaries of the agricultural season. Pit-looms in Oman are almost always of the two-shaft variety. The frame of the loom is made up of palm-tree splits, as in the rest of the Gulf, and the pit that is dug into the ground is nowadays lined with concrete with a mud finish. Only narrow widths are woven in Oman. Any wider length needed is achieved by sewing two or more widths together selvedge to selvedge. Sur on the coast and the oases of Jaalan and Ibra are some of the surviving centres of pit-loom weaving. Though it is men who weave on pit-looms, unusually in parts of Oman they also weave on a type of ground-loom.

THE PRESENT

Though the Bedouin and shepherds weave less and less, the craft still continues. Most of the pit-looms have gone, but they do survive in a few places. What is left replicates the situation that prevails in most of the rest of Arabia, where the increasing prosperity of the last few decades and the newfound ease of communication between previously extremely isolated communities has meant that most clothing is now bought readymade. Tents and animal trappings may still be hand-made, but decorative weavings are now made in smaller sizes to be sold to the expatriate and tourist markets in specialized craft shops.

OPPOSITE
Wahaybah supplementary-warp-decorated storage bag.

ABOVE LEFT
The last Omani indigo dyer, Bahala souk, 2008.

LEFT
Omani metalsmith, wearing embroidered *kummah* cap, 1980s.

Yemen

Yemen has always produced intrepid seamen and hardy mountaineers, being a country with a prodigiously long coastline and much highland terrain (a number of Yemeni place names begin with 'Jebel', meaning 'mountain'). In ancient times, it was one of the sources of frankincense and myrrh, which made southern Arabia a great world trade centre. In the valleys to the south of the capital, Sana'a, Yemen also has the only really fertile land in the whole of the Arabian peninsula. In pre-Islamic times, agricultural prosperity depended on irrigation from the great dam at Marib, but this collapsed in *c.* AD 520, scattering the Qahtan tribes (believed to be the descendants of one of Noah's sons) over the whole of southern Arabia.

Yemen accepted Islam peaceably in the Prophet's lifetime, the Persian governor Badhan converting in AD 628. Archaeological evidence indicates that both warp-ikat textiles and *tiraz* textiles with calligraphic inscriptions in cotton were made in Yemen from the early days of Islam (ninth/tenth centuries AD). Local textiles were already well known for their quality and were exported for use by the Persian nobility, cloth produced in Sana'a and Aden being particularly valuable for East–West trade.

Yemeni textiles also travelled further afield. Local sailors were among the pioneers of the sea route to India, utilizing the monsoon winds that would in season carry them to India's west coast and beyond, and when the season changed carry them back again. Yemenis settled in many places, predominantly on the west coast of India and in what is now Indonesia, and in turn Yemen received immigrants from these places. The culture and architecture of the Hadhramaut coast of southern Arabia, for example, were much influenced by Java, and such noted textile towns as Zabid were home to Indian artisans.

Domestic embroidery was practised by women in many parts of the country to adorn their wedding and everyday dresses (in a country of then-limited resources, these were very often the same thing). The fabric was either of indigo cotton, indigenously dyed and burnished, and often locally woven, or sometimes – especially in the days of the Ottoman empire (1828–1918, though the Ottomans had also ruled Yemen earlier, from 1538 to 1638) – of satin or metal-thread brocade imported from such great weaving centres as Aleppo in Syria. Due to the strong trade links with India, Indian brocade was also often used. Jewish women embroidered decorative trouser cuffs in metal thread on an Indian or Syrian brocade ground for sale to local Muslim women. The metal thread was the product of Jewish silversmiths, but after 1962, when the Yemeni Jews emigrated en masse to Israel, this craft died for lack of practitioners and materials.

COSTUMES

Men's Dress

Typically Yemeni men wear a short waist-cloth to the knees, an embroidered belt to hold a dagger and sheath, a cotton shirt and

ABOVE
Women and children of Sana'a, the women wearing tie-dyed *mamour* veils.

OPPOSITE
Rayon waist-cloth, imported from Hyderabad, India, for Hadhramaut men.

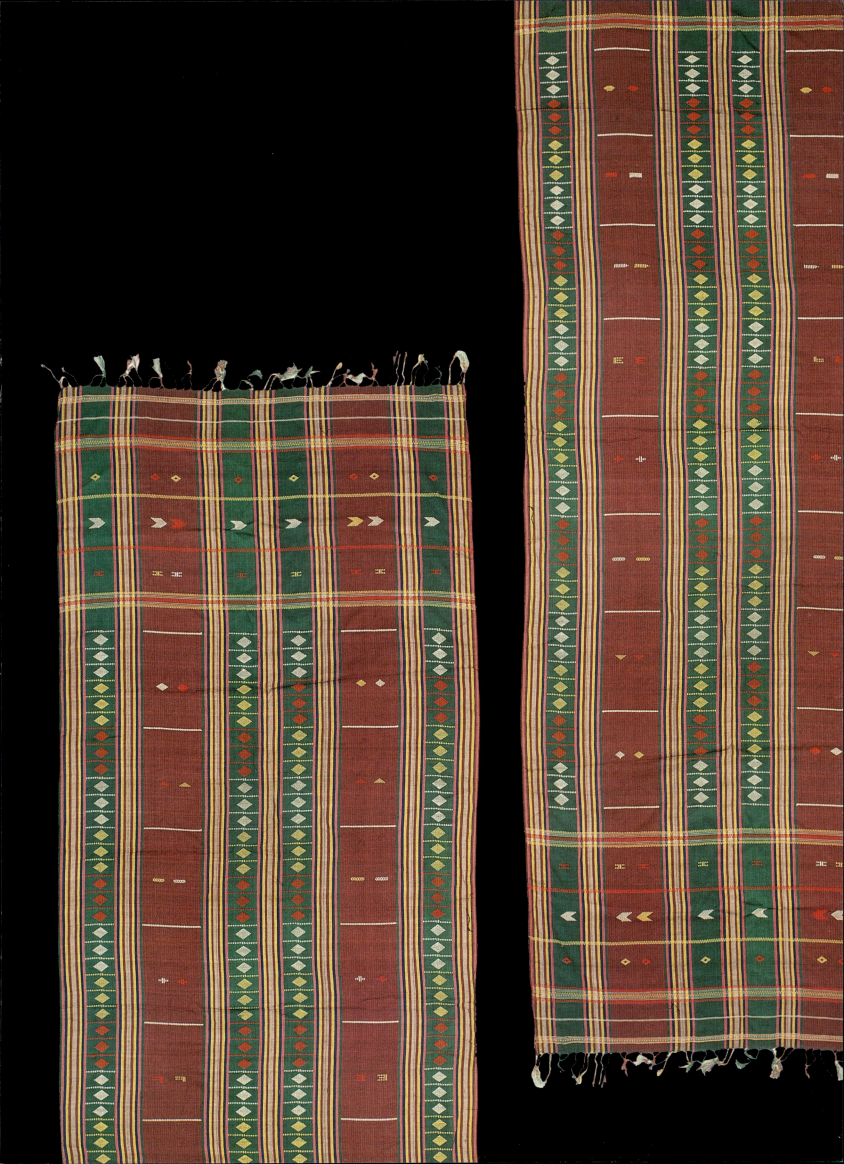

a second-hand jacket of Western tailoring. The waist-cloth may be locally hand-woven in cotton or it may be a synthetic import from India, where there are towns, including Hyderabad, that specialize in weaving textiles for the south Arabian market. The outfit is completed with a turban once made up from a square kerchief adorned with floral motifs in silk chain stitch, but now more usually of white and yellow cotton or synthetic cloth mass-produced in Syria, or is just any conveniently shaped piece of cotton cloth.

Women's Dress

Yemeni codes of female modesty are strict, and a shawl and sometimes face-veil are required. Urban women of Sana'a wear a face-veil of light, finely woven wool, tie-dyed to form a bold pattern of black, white and red circles on a black ground. The veil, produced in local workshops, is called a *mamour*, and it is sewn onto a rectangular panel of professional metal-thread embroidery embellished with red glass beads and a silver chain called a *rsaja*. The *rsaja* is pinned to the woman's hair so that the *mamour* covers her face. The latter can be easily flipped back, as it often is when she needs to have a closer look at the day's shopping in the souk. Yemeni women also wear an all-enveloping dress, often with exaggeratedly wide sleeves for coolness. A Sana'a woman's outfit is completed with a large cotton shawl known as a *sitara*, which is sometimes now locally produced but is more usually a block-printed and burnished import from Ahmedabad in western India. Shawls of imported origin are worn by women all over the country. Often they are block-printed Indian cotton, but sometimes – as in the Red Sea coastal strip known as Tihama – they are tie-dyed with simple bands of gold brocade at the ends, imported from Gujarat. A form of hood, known generally as a *quarqush*, is also worn by both girls and grown women. The *quarqush* of small girls are adorned with prophylactic amulets, beads, buttons, mother of pearl, and jangly pieces of silver and base-metal jewelry, all designed to ward off the evil eye.

The women of the mountains of Jebel Haraz, lying to the southwest of Sana'a, wear smock-like dresses of burnished indigo from Tihama. The neckline down to below the waist is decorated with lines of chain-stitch embroidery, flanked by rows of base-metal sequins. Little pieces of mother of pearl are often attached close to the neckline and at the base of the central line of embroidery.

ABOVE
Man's tablet-woven *khanjar* belt, Sana'a.

BELOW
Woman's dress from northern Amran, embroidered on indigo-dyed fabric.

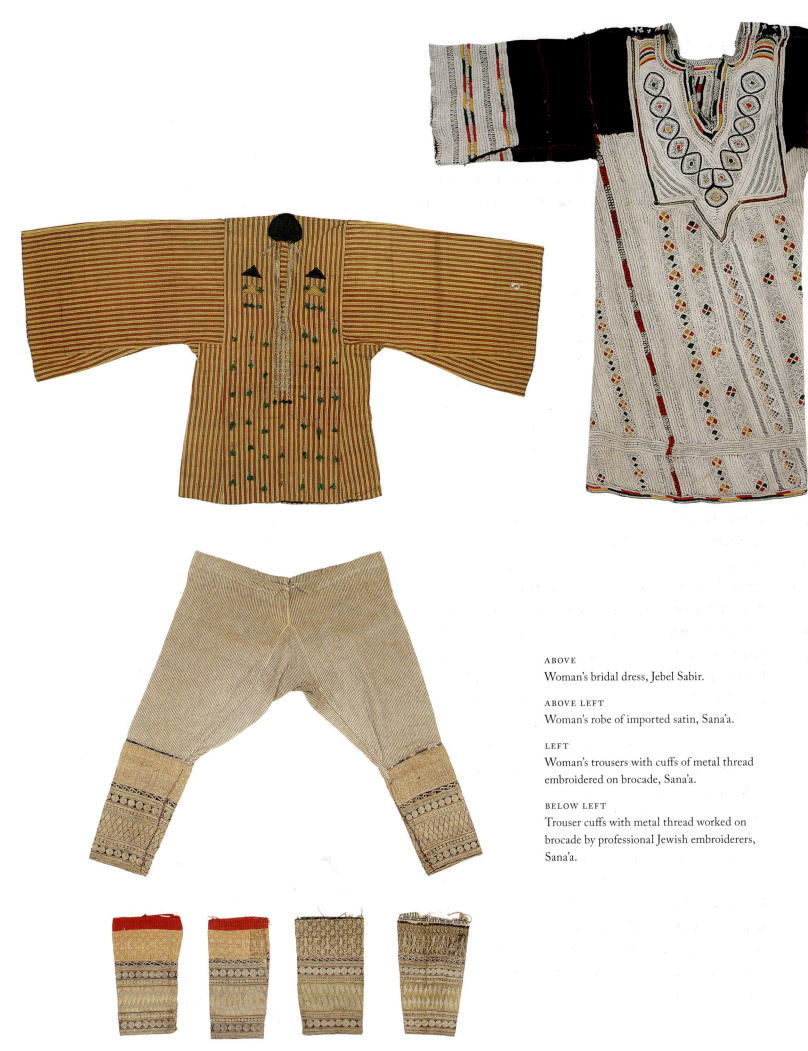

ABOVE
Woman's bridal dress, Jebel Sabir.

ABOVE LEFT
Woman's robe of imported satin, Sana'a.

LEFT
Woman's trousers with cuffs of metal thread embroidered on brocade, Sana'a.

BELOW LEFT
Trouser cuffs with metal thread worked on brocade by professional Jewish embroiderers, Sana'a.

ABOVE
Woman's dress, adorned with couched metallic braid, Bayt al-Faqih, Tihama.

Northeast of Sana'a, the women of the fortified villages of the plateau north of Amran are garbed in a similar manner. Their dresses are of the same kind of indigo-dyed cotton from Zabid, but they are more profusely embroidered with a multiplicity of protective patterns that possibly betray an influence from nearby Africa just across the Red Sea.

Some of the most interesting women's costume comes from the Tihama coastal region. Dresses with very wide sleeves for ventilation in the extremely humid climate of the Red Sea coast are to be found north of Hodeida. The sleeves and skirt are edged with material akin to striped Indian *mashru*, and the collar is edged with multiple rows of metallic strip made in a technique worked with pins and cushions like bobbin lace. This method is used from the Iranian side of the Gulf through Oman, where it is known as *talli*, and throughout southern Arabia. The rest of the dress, which is of black cotton, is embellished front and back with couched metallic braid, laid out in a regular fashion, though some parts of it form protective patterns. This dress is worn with a version of the high conical straw hat popular with rural women in many parts of Yemen.

From Bayt al-Faqih to the south of Hodeida comes a fitted version of the Tihama dress which bears a vague resemblance to Ottoman military uniforms of the nineteenth century. Fitted

ABOVE
Woman's dress from Jebel Haraz, made of burnished indigo cotton from Zabid.

BELOW
Girl's hood of burnished indigo-dyed fabric, Sana'a.

YEMEN 143

ABOVE, TOP RIGHT AND ABOVE RIGHT
Asba marriage caps, adorned with coins and other metallic ephemera, rural north Yemen.

RIGHT AND BELOW RIGHT
Women's kerchiefs from Taiz, of mill-printed cotton edged with *talli*-work metallic trim.

BELOW
Embroidered veil, embellished with mother of pearl, Sana'a district.

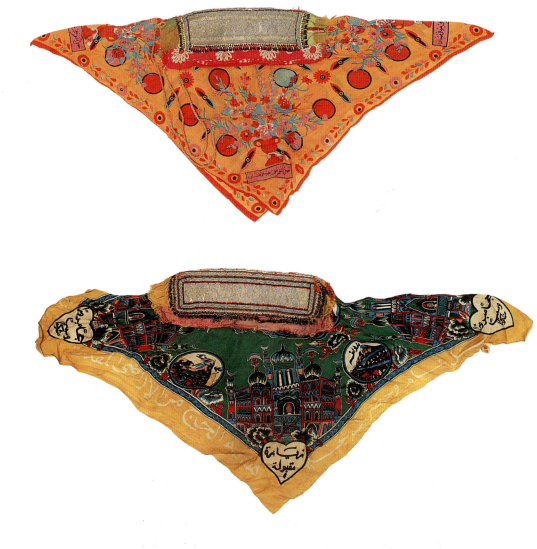

ABOVE
Sitara, Indian block-printed shawl.

LEFT
Indian tie-dyed and metal-brocade shawl for rural and urban use.

ABOVE
Woman's tie-dyed woollen *mamour* veil, with *rsaja* embroidered head panel, Sana'a.

BELOW
Bedouin dress, embellished with metal-thread embroidery and tinsel, Hadhramaut.

dresses with heavily embroidered fronts are worn by the women of Jebel Milhan and Jebel Sahir.

Taiz, the old city of the south, looks down from its mosques towards Aden and the southern coast. Both here and in Aden, the modern fashion for a woman's veil is to wrap a square black satin scarf closely around the head, leaving the face bare. The older style in Taiz was to fold a European headscarf of cheap printed material diagonally in half and sew on a strip of metallic lace for the forehead area. Older yet is a scarf of black voile folded in the same way but embroidered in floral patterns with flat metal thread.

Home to many Bedouin is Hadhramaut, stretching for miles along the Yemeni coast of southern Arabia. Formerly a patchwork of tiny statelets, it is famed for its traditional architecture consisting of blocks of houses grouped together and rising up many storeys. The Bedouin women wear a gaudy velvet dress embroidered in metal thread with geometric patterns embellished with tawdry finery, the most valued objects being plastic replicas of George V gold sovereigns.

THE PRESENT

Textile production in the nineteenth century and throughout most of the twentieth has been restricted to the dyeing and burnishing of indigo cotton cloth in such centres as Zabid, and the weaving in cotton of men's waist-wraps at such places as Bayt al-Faqih in Tihama. Embroidery continues to be practised as a domestic craft throughout the country to adorn items including wedding dresses and children's costume. Metallic lace trims are also still popular and continue to be made. The professional metal-thread embroidery that was the work of Jewish embroiderers ceased with their emigration to Israel in 1962. Overall, though there is less hand-weaving and dyeing than in the past, the demands for ceremonial costume from such a tradition-bound society continue to keep the Yemeni hand-crafted textile industry in a remarkably healthy state.

ABOVE LEFT
Woman of the Tihama wearing an imported printed cotton headscarf.

LEFT
Women in block-printed Indian veils, Al-Mahweet.

YEMEN **147**

Iran

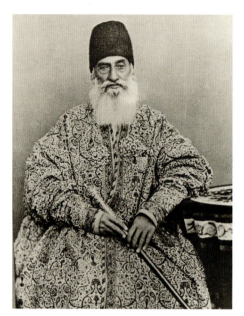

Iran, formerly known in the West as Persia, is a country – and was often an empire – that for considerable periods dominated the Middle East. The culture and arts of the region have a long and illustrious history, with Persian civilization dating back more than three thousand years, to before the times of King Darius the First and Alexander the Great.

Even in pre-Islamic times, textiles were important not only for utilitarian purposes but also as expressions of wealth and status. Wool has been a staple of Persian textiles for nearly two millennia. While the Iranian landscape is a seemingly inhospitable vista of mountain ranges and rocky deserts, this terrain in season provides excellent pasture for sheep and goats. It also sustains a nomadic lifestyle for large groups of pastoralists to this day. The migrations of the Qashqai and the Bakhtiari in the southern part of the country, and the Shahsavan and the Luri in the west, are spectacular events, with thousands of men, women, children and their domestic animals moving over hundreds of miles of rough ground to and from their winter and summer pastures.

In addition to wool, silk has long been a staple. The Persians were intermediaries in the silk trade between China and ancient Rome, and the knowledge of sericulture – long a state secret of the Chinese – had reached Iran by the third century AD. Persian silk manufacture became a great industry for both home and export use. The northern provinces of Iran – Azerbaijan, Tabaristan and Khorasan – were, in particular, renowned centres of sericulture. Indeed, Tabaristan was historically the greatest producer of silk yarn in the whole of the Muslim world.

The arrival of the draw-loom from Syria at about the time sericulture was introduced to Persia sparked a fashion for complex figured silk textiles. These fine fabrics were woven under the beneficent rule of the Sasanians, the last pre-Islamic dynasty in Iran, and they were of such value that some were traded as far afield as Western Europe to be incorporated into church vestments.

Muslim conquest led to the end of the Sasanian dynasty. The invading Arabs annexed existing state textile factories, but traditional designs continued to be produced, and these were at first little changed. It is recorded that in the eleventh century AD

PAGES 148–149
Rayon batik scarf from Osku for Turkmen women, Iran; *kalamkar* bath towel, Isfahan, Iran; Art Deco hook-work and appliqué cover, Rasht, Iran; *mafrash* silk cover, Karabakh, Azerbaijan.

OPPOSITE LEFT
A dervish at prayer in typical dress, *c.* 1930.

OPPOSITE RIGHT
A member of the Iranian royal household, wearing a brocade coat, *c.* 1910.

ABOVE
Russian roller print made for the Persian market.

the Shia Fatimid caliph Al-Munstansir owned prodigious quantities of textiles, including great tents worked with birds and elephants in the Persian manner.

The royal *tiraz al-khassa* workshop produced fabrics for the court alone, and quality was strictly supervised. The *tiraz al-amna* produced textiles for the wealthy. The *tiraz* system, along with many cities and craftsmen, was destroyed by the Mongol invasions of the thirteenth century, but it was revived in Iran in the late fifteenth/early sixteenth century under the Timurids and Safavids.

Under the Safavids, Shia Islam became the state religion of Persia. Shia Islam was tolerant of depictions of human and animal forms, and the figured textiles of the Safavids were extremely popular, whereas in the rest of the Islamic world non-figurative designs were now the norm. Under Shah Abbas (1587–1629), at his new capital of Isfahan, sericulture and silk weaving were greatly encouraged, and state workshops for both the court and the wealthy flourished. *Abrishum* (raw silk) was exported in bulk to Russia and Europe. Large communities of Jews and Armenians gathered at Isfahan and were intimately involved in the textile trade, the former specializing in dyeing and embroidery, the latter in export. During the Safavid era, fine patterned textiles were used for clothing but also for furnishings, animal trappings, tents and street bunting. Velvets became fashionable under Shah Abbas, too, often voided and incorporating gold brocade.

TECHNIQUES

Velvet Ikat Weaving

The process of hand-weaving velvet (*makhmal* in Farsi) from silk yarn is very complex. The fabric's distinctive pile is produced by means of supplementary warps, which are raised over grooved metal rods inserted into an open shed with the weft. When weaving has proceeded far enough for the raised warps to be secure, they are cut along the groove in the rod with a sharp knife to form dense tufts, and the rods are then removed. The manufacture of silk-velvet ikat is yet more time-consuming, as the supplementary warps have to have a pattern tie-dyed into them before the complicated process of weaving can begin. The only place where velvet ikat is even rarer and more prized than Iran is Central Asia.

The desert city of Yazd in Iran was a renowned centre for the making of velvet ikat and, up to the early twentieth century, so was the ancient bazaar town of Kashan. Examples of these

THE PERSIAN WORLD

textiles date back at least as far as the seventeenth century. One mainstay of Kashan weaving was the *pardah* (curtain). These were woven in pairs, typically 3–4 feet wide (1–1.2 m) and 6–7 feet deep (1.8–2 m). They generally had a floral border running along both sides, and the central field was most often a pleasing scene of one or two cypress trees set between peacocks. Other popular patterns included repeats of tigers' heads, and sometimes the human figures so beloved of the Persian Shia world. At the bottom of the curtain, the weaver would inscribe in Farsi the date on which he commenced weaving and the date on which he finished. On average, a *pardah* took three months to make.

Further mainstays of the local velvet ikat tradition were panels of roughly 18 by 36 inches (45 x 90 cm), with small floral or geometric repeats. These were used to form the central fields of baby hammocks made of leather with an appliquéd leather border. Colours used for both the hammock panels and the *pardah* curtains were combinations of red, black and magenta, sometimes with lime green details.

LEFT
Velvet ikat curtain, with typical patterns of cypress trees and peacocks, Kashan. The curtain is inscribed at the bottom with the time of its making.

ABOVE
Velvet ikat curtain, Yazd, first half of the nineteenth century.

IRAN 153

Brocade

Kashan and Isfahan were also famous for their fine silk brocades, examples of which have been found dating back to at least the seventeenth century. These brocades were patterned with repeats of the *boteh*, or 'Paisley' cone, and were known as *termeh*. In more recent years, shawls and furnishings woven in wool on jacquard looms with the same patterns have been the speciality of towns including Yazd and Isfahan.

Warp-Ikat

Yazd was also famous for a variety of silk and mixed silk and cotton textiles (plaid-patterned material for tablecloths and wrapping cloths were a speciality). Today it is the last remaining centre in Iran for the weaving of warp ikat in silk or rayon. Warp-ikat yardage is woven on wide pit-looms, with the warp threads taken over a high beam and weighted with bags of sand or soil, in the same manner as Afghan or Central Asian looms. The warp ikat is made using an ancient resist-dyeing technique in widespread use across Asia, whereby the patterning of the textile is obtained by tying fibre resists tightly around the warp threads that have been stretched out on a frame. The tied hanks are then immersed in a dye bath. In Yazd, the silk or rayon yarn is tied to order and dyed by professional dyers and then passed to the weaver. Among the products woven are curtain lengths with the typical Iranian pattern of cypress trees and peacocks.

ABOVE, ABOVE RIGHT AND RIGHT
Eighteenth-century silk brocades, Isfahan.

154   THE PERSIAN WORLD

ABOVE
Woman's bag lined with Russian trade cloth, Yazd.

RIGHT
Early twentieth-century silk brocade, Isfahan.

BELOW
Nineteenth-century woman's jacket of Isfahani silk brocade.

IRAN 155

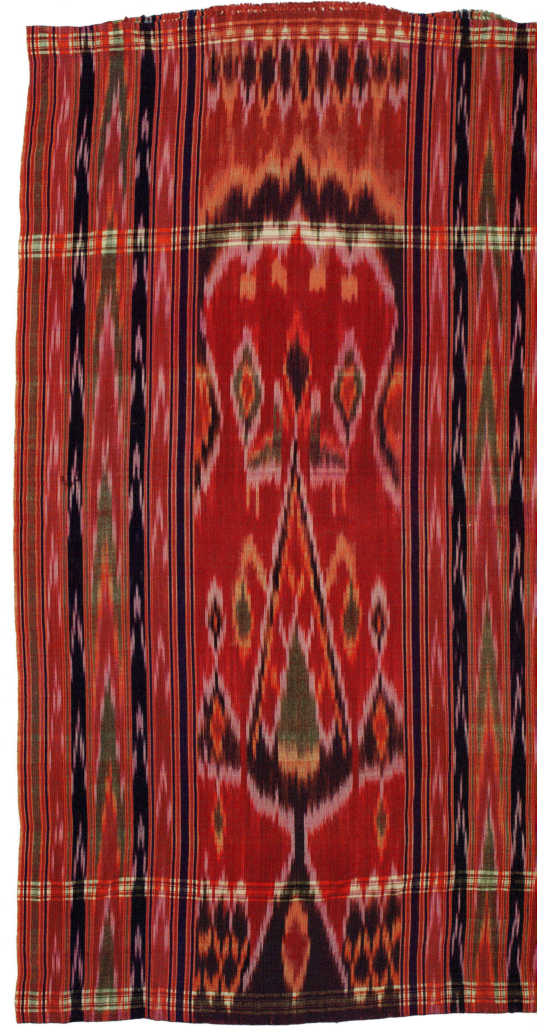

ABOVE
An elderly ikat weaver at work in Yazd.

RIGHT
Warp-ikat silk curtain, Yazd.

BELOW
Detail of warp-ikat silk curtain, Yazd.

OPPOSITE LEFT
Camel-hair weaver trimming cloth on the loom, Muhammadieh, Na'in district.

OPPOSITE RIGHT
Angami, Kerman-weave shawl used as a cummerbund in Syria.

Camel-Hair Weaving

Camel hair is the preferred material for a wealthy Arab man's traditional outer garment, the *aba* or *bisht*, tailored from two narrow strips of fabric: one forms the neck and shoulders, the other is sewn to it to make up the skirt of what is an open robe. Iran is a major and much valued source of this prized cloth. Bushehr, Ahvaz and Na'in are the major centres of camel-hair weaving in Iran. All these places are extremely hot during the summer, and Na'in suffers from bitter winters. In order to escape the summer heat and winter cold, the weavers of Na'in work underground in a weaving shed excavated from limestone to a depth of about 10 feet (3 m), then roofed over. Visitors walk down some steps, eyes adjusting to the semi-darkness after the bright desert sunlight, to see the aged weavers working at their pit-looms either side of a walkway. They weave yardage about 30 inches wide (75 cm), of varying grades, and they use camel hair from Baluchistan (the finest grade is woven from hair plucked from the camels' humps). The Na'in weavers sell their wares by the roll for a fairly good price to wholesalers from Qom and Isfahan, who sell it on to Iraq, Syria, Kuwait, Saudi Arabia and the Gulf states. Each weaver takes about ten days to weave a 20-foot (6 m) roll. In that time, he can weave more of the coarser cloth but less of the finer grade, though he is compensated in the latter case by a premium on the price he receives. At periodic intervals during the weaving process, the cloth on the loom is combed with a home-made metal device rather akin to a nutmeg grater, shaved with an instrument like a large cut-throat razor, and ironed.

Kerman Tapestry Weaving

Iran has always been a major market for the fabulous *jamawar* (tapestry-woven shawls) of Kashmir. Walking through Iran's picturesque bazaars, it is not uncommon to come across ragged fragments of eighteenth- and nineteenth-century Kashmiri 'moon' shawls. The collapse of the industry, caused by the loss of its most important market after the French were defeated in the Franco-Prussian war of 1870, had dire consequences for the weavers of the Kashmir valley. Poverty and starvation became a harsh reality that drove them out. Some found work at the looms of the north Indian plains, in such towns as Lahore, but there were so many destitute weavers that it was impossible to find meaningful employment for them all. This grim situation was partly alleviated in the 1890s by the actions of the Qajar Shah of Persia, Naser al-Din, who sponsored the revival of a weaving industry in the southeastern town of Kerman. Kashmiri weavers and ancillary workers were brought to the town. Using local and imported wool, they wove shawls in the Kashmiri tapestry technique both for home consumption and for export to such traditional *jamawar* markets as Syria and Russian Azerbaijan. Patterns were those favoured by a Persian clientele and eschewed the bold motifs of the Kashmiri shawls that had been destined for the French and English markets. In the early years of Kerman *jamawar* weaving, when the weavers were native-born Kashmiris, standards of production were high, and it is difficult for the uneducated eye to distinguish Kashmir from Kerman: the patterns and the tightness of the weave are almost identical. As the twentieth century progressed, however, standards slipped and the work became

ABOVE
Detail of an *angami*, a Kerman-weave shawl used as a cummerbund in Syria.

ABOVE RIGHT
Late nineteenth-century woman's Kerman-weave jacket.

RIGHT
Quilted mat faced with a fragment of an eighteenth-century Kashmiri 'moon' shawl.

much coarser, so that by the 1940s very little fine work was being attempted. No *jamawar* are now woven in Kerman.

Tablet Weaving

The earliest known tablet-woven textiles in the world were found in a grave dating to 375 BC at El Cigarellejo in Spain, but this ancient technique is still practised in Iran by such nomadic groups as the Bakhtiari. They use it to make narrow bands, belts and straps. (The technique is fully described in the Syria section of this book; see p. 103.) While most tablet weaving can be distinguished by its distinctive, warp-twined appearance, the actual fabric should not be twisted. It is essential to maintain tension to prevent this, which means that the weaving-in-progress is not transportable. The most sophisticated exponents of this technique are therefore sedentary rather than nomadic.

ABOVE LEFT
Woollen tapestry-woven shawl, Kerman.

LEFT
Panel of Isfahani silk and metal-thread brocade.

ABOVE
Bakhtiari tablet-woven animal strap.

Kerman *Pateh* Embroidery

Probably around the same time as the introduction of *jamawar* weaving to Kerman, embroidery in the Kashmiri style became a feature of the textile production of the town. *Pateh* motifs are typically Kashmiri, and are generally worked with a needle on twill-woven red woollen cloth similar to Kashmir *raffal*. *Boteh* and floral representations of gardens predominate. Alternatives to the red cloth are orange and white. Embroidery on white is the most prestigious and expensive, as the embroiderer has to fill in all of the design with tight stitchery so the white ground does not show through. Woollen thread in eight different colours is used. Square covers, rectangular cushion covers and curtains made in sets of four are the items produced. As with Kerman weaving, the standards of embroidery quickly deteriorated. Modern-day examples, rather crudely worked on imported woollen fabric, are available today at a price in the bazaars of Kerman.

Rasht Work

Rasht is a port town on the Caspian. Nestling beneath green, rain-fed hills, it was long a centre of Russian influence. Its embroiderers specialized in making furnishings – curtains, cushion covers, tablecloths and all manner of decorative cloths – from mill-made broadcloth, baize or flannel. This kind of material was used because the edges do not fray when cut and hence do not need to be turned under, saving a great deal of labour. Onto a typically red ground are appliquéd floral motifs cut out of the same material but in contrasting colours. The whole is then edged and embellished with tambour-worked chain stitch. Counterchange appliqué was also a speciality of Rasht. In this technique, two differently coloured sheets of felt or baize are laid on top of one another. Identical motifs are cut out of both by simply cutting through the two layers at once. The motifs from one felt are sewn into the voids in the other, and vice versa, to form two identically patterned textiles. This seems to be an older and more time-consuming technique, only found on very antique examples, and the method appears to have long fallen into disuse. Rasht work had a strong export market up into the neighbouring Russian territories, and many examples found their way to Europe.

ABOVE
Pateh curtain embroidered with designs of a cypress tree, peacocks and other birds, Kerman.

BELOW
Pateh embroidered panel, Kerman.

ABOVE
Art Deco hook-work and appliqué cover, Rasht.

BELOW
Late nineteenth-century hook-work cover, Rasht.

Isfahan Embroidery

Isfahan, Shah Abbas's beautiful capital, is a centre for many crafts, including enamel work, but is most noted for its textile work – its *termeh* brocade weaving, and especially its embroidery. Embroidery with a needle is known as *suzan-dozi*; with a hook, as *golab-dozi*. Metal-thread work is a particular speciality. Hanging bags made up of small squares of fabric embroidered in real silver thread with floral motifs are highly prized. Rare and also highly valued is the silk hook-work on silk *pardah*, embroidered with martial and picnic scenes from the medieval Persian lexicon. Both these styles seem to have died out in the second half of the nineteenth century. Most famous is *nakshe* ('embroidered' in Farsi), a term particularly applied to nineteenth-century women's trousering of a rich floral pattern. Commonly known in Iran simply as 'Isfahani', this expensive embroidery combines robustness and a delightful delicacy in a unique manner. The designs are always of diagonal parallel bands filled with close floral ornamentation. It is likely that the embroidered version was derived from a woven original. *Nakshe* was used for various garments other than trousers, and because it was famed for its toughness it was also employed for covering boxes, purses and cartridge pouches.

BELOW
Nineteenth-century hook-work and appliqué cover, Rasht.

IRAN **161**

ABOVE
Nineteenth-century patchwork, Rasht.

LEFT
Nineteenth-century professionally embroidered *nakshe* panel, Isfahan.

OPPOSITE TOP LEFT, TOP RIGHT AND CENTRE LEFT
Khouri khanum ('Sun Maiden') sequin embroideries, Isfahan district.

OPPOSITE CENTRE RIGHT
Metal-strip embroidered cuff from western Iran.

OPPOSITE BELOW LEFT
Metal-thread embroidery on velvet with cypress motif, central Iran.

OPPOSITE BELOW RIGHT
Metal-thread purl embroidery on Kerman-weave pipe bag.

162   THE PERSIAN WORLD

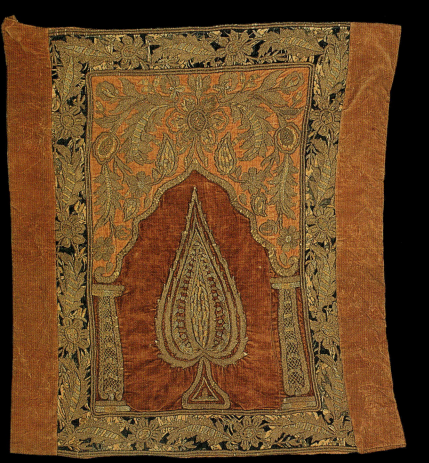

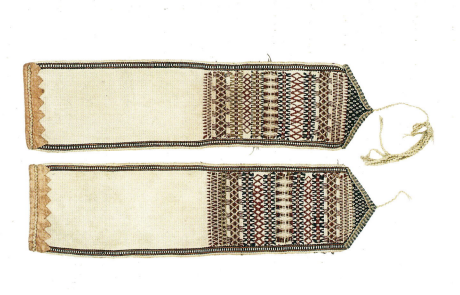

Block Printing and Painting

Isfahan is a centre for block printing (formerly there were others, including Yazd). There are no records of when this technique was taken up in Iran, but it can be surmised that it was popularized by the influx of craftsmen from India during the reign of Shah Abbas in the seventeenth century (a process that reversed the flow of the previous century, which had seen Safavid craftsmen taken to Mughal India). Block prints were always cheap and ephemeral, and had little chance of being preserved over the centuries unless they were used as the lining for clothing or the backing for quilts. The situation is further complicated by the fact that Persia was a highly important export market for *kalamkari* work from the port of Masulipatnam in eastern India, and there were no doubt Indian craftsmen working in Persia at the same time. Indian *kalamkari* are a combination of block printing and painting. In fact, the word 'kalamkari' means 'pen work', named after the *kalam*, a pencil-shaped piece of wood bound with fibre near its tip. The bound fibre acts as a reservoir for dye or molten wax, which can be squeezed through gentle finger pressure down onto the tip

TOP LEFT
Embroidered Turkmen puttees, northeastern Iran.

ABOVE LEFT
Bakhtiari women's glass-bead-embroidered caps.

LEFT
Kaisal Bash dress, decorated in the *baft i nakhoni* ('finger-nail' weaving) technique, northeastern Iran.

ABOVE
Woman's metal-thread-embroidered trousers, Gulf coast.

OPPOSITE
Kalamkar bath towel, Isfahan.

164 THE PERSIAN WORLD

of the *kalam* and out onto the base cloth to colour it or to apply a wax resist on it. The textiles that resulted, with their chintz-like floral designs in indigo blue and a deep chay red, found a ready Persian market. As furnishings, decorative squares, curtains, bath towels or quilted bath mats, they were a staple of domestic life in the nineteenth century. To supplement these imports, a parallel industry producing *kalamkar* (the Farsi term) by the same techniques of printing and painting was very active in Persia, and it can sometimes be difficult to distinguish between the Indian product and the Iranian one. Persian *kalamkar* are mostly cruder and of slightly inferior colouring to the Indian originals, and some stylistic devices such as peacocks in the corners indicate imported origin. Primitive block prints in two or three colours were applied on hand-woven cotton at Nazafarabad. They were mainly used as linings. In 1923 Reza Shah, the founder of the Pahlavi dynasty, banned – among many other things – the import of foreign textiles. This gave a great stimulus to the indigenous *kalamkar* industry. Workers, particularly in Isfahan, began printing tablecloths, curtains and floor spreads with wooden blocks in chemical colours. There was also a fashion for large painted cloths with blocked borders, which were used in tea-houses as the backdrops for story-tellers relating tales from the *Shah-Nama*, the heroic exploits of the kings of Persia.

OPPOSITE
Kalamkar block-printed and painted curtain, Isfahan.

ABOVE LEFT
Painted *Shah-Nama* cloth showing a hunting scene.

LEFT
Mid-nineteenth-century *kalamkar* curtain, made in India for the Persian market.

IRAN

Batik on Silk

Iran is a producer of silk headscarves and shawls that are patterned in the batik process, with a wax resist being applied using wooden blocks. Osku, near Tabriz, and Kerman are centres of the craft. The batik makers of Osku claim descent from Azerbaijani refugees who fled Russian takeover in the early nineteenth century. The main market for Osku scarves are women of the Qashqai and Shahsavan nomads and the Turkmen. Each has particular colour preferences. The Shahsavan, for instance, favour white, golden yellow, red and black, while the Turkmen prefer black, violet, yellow and white. Before the Second World War, silk was used as the base cloth, but afterwards cheaper rayon was substituted (silk was reintroduced in the 1960s and '70s). The printed motifs are diamond shapes and smaller geometric elements, together with *boteh*, fish, flowers, birds and leaves in any combination that takes the printer's fancy. The blocks are simply carved out of cheap wood. Motifs that are to be light-coloured are printed on in wax or painted on by hand. The scarf is then dipped in a violet dye bath. The waxed-over portions resist the dye. The designs to be violet-coloured are then waxed over and the scarf is dyed black. After drying, the fabric is de-waxed, then the portions to be violet and white are waxed over, and the scarf is dipped in a yellow dye bath. The scarf is de-waxed by being washed in kerosene, then is aired until the kerosene odour has disappeared. Washing and passing through a hot roller complete the process.

OPPOSITE LEFT
Kalamkar cloth of yardage imported from India.

OPPOSITE ABOVE RIGHT
Kalamkar cloth, Yazd.

OPPOSITE BELOW RIGHT
Mid-twentieth-century *kalamkar* cloth, Isfahan.

ABOVE LEFT
Rayon batik scarf from Osku for Turkmen women.

LEFT
Kalamkar prayer cloth, Isfahan.

IRAN

OPPOSITE ABOVE
Nineteenth-century pin-stripe-weave cotton man's coat, Isfahan.

OPPOSITE BELOW
Chuga, Bakhtiari man's woollen jerkin.

LEFT
Namad, Turkmen felt mat, northeastern Iran.

BELOW
Plaid silk/cotton weave, Yazd.

ABOVE
Early twentieth-century revival of silk lampas, Tehran.

LEFT
Nineteenth-century Russian roller print with 'cypress' pattern for the Persian market.

BELOW
Kalamkar eating cloth, Isfahan.

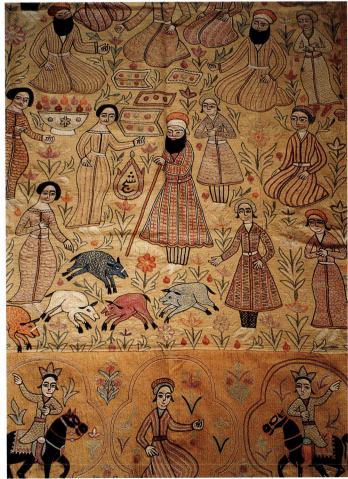

THE PRESENT

The practitioners of most present-day Iranian textile crafts are few and far between and advanced in years. This is true of the camel-hair weavers who labour in the underground workshop at Na'in and the warp-ikat weavers of Yazd, who toil in the backs of the cloth shops catering to the tourist trade. There are several crafts – including warp-ikat weaving – that are in great danger of dying out through a dearth of skilled artisans. Already, the only reminders of the once-magnificent weaving tradition in Kashan are the demonstration looms operated at the local crafts school.

ABOVE
Dervish of Isfahan in his ceremonial costume.

ABOVE RIGHT
Silk hook-work embroidery depicting a hunt and picnic, Isfahan.

RIGHT
Detail of an imported Indian block print from Ahmedabad.

The Caucasus

The high Caucasus mountains dominate the isthmus of land that lies between the Black Sea and the Caspian Sea. Of fabled beauty, they cut off the fiercely independent, war-like peoples of the mountains from the fertile lowlands of Christian Georgia and the oil-rich desert that covers much of Muslim Azerbaijan. Though Georgia became part of Russia in 1800, and Russia wrested northern Azerbaijan from Persia in 1828, the Muslim highlanders were to retain their independence for another few decades. From the eyries of Daghestan, the heroic resistance leader Imam Shamyl mobilized the Chechens, his own people the Avars and many other local, ancient Muslim tribes, and fought the might of the Imperial Russian army for thirty years before being forced to surrender in 1859. The Cherkess (Circassians) on the opposite Black Sea coastal region to the west were finally defeated in 1864, whereupon they emigrated *en masse* to the Ottoman lands, settling in the Balkans, Anatolia and Syria. The Chechens of the northeastern Caucasus are resisting the Russians to this very day.

The Caucasus has maintained its own textile traditions, and interesting styles of embroidery are to be found all over the region. Azerbaijan is justly famous for its pile rugs and for its flatweaves, embroideries and printed textiles, which displayed a cultural affinity with neighbouring Iran. Women of the villages of Daghestan weave large, thick, woollen floor coverings in the ancient *soumak* weft-wrapping technique. Daghestan is also noted for its Kaitag silk embroidery, with a rich variety of designs interpreted in a highly individualistic style, of which some are derived from traditional Ottoman silks and velvets.

REGIONS

Azerbaijan

Despite two hundred years of Russian domination, Azerbaijan is very much part of the Persian world. It has the same traditions of silk weaving, metal-thread embroidery and block-printed wax-resist batik on silk. Sheki, in the hills near the Russian and Georgian borders, was a famous centre for silk weaving and, lying on the caravan routes, was even more prominent as a market and distribution centre for imported silks. Women's costume in the area consisted of a pair of divided baggy pants called *casqir* worn beneath a skirt, and a blouse worn underneath a short-sleeved *lavada* (bolero) of Kashmiri or Kerman shawl material, edged with silver braid. The outfit was topped off with a batik-printed silk headscarf (since the 1840s, of Russian mill fabric). Men wore long shirts over baggy trousers gathered at the ankle, with the typical Caucasian coat known as a *cuxa* or 'Cherkess', with *bandiroles* – loops to carry cartridges sewn above each breast.

The main glory of Azerbaijani textiles is the metal-thread embroidery that decorates articles for ritual and domestic use. Lovingly worked in metal-thread embroidery in the Persian style, and often lined with Persian silk brocade, are *möhür qabi*, little satin or velvet purses used for holding the circular- or half-moon-shaped prayer stones of moulded clay (*möhür*) that a Shia Muslim uses to protect his forehead from bruising while at prayer. Most of these prayer-stone covers were worked in or around the city of Baku, as were *daraq qabi* (comb covers) and little purses for keeping pocket watches. The comb covers were

often decorated with motifs of a pair of courting birds or sun-birds. This work was also a speciality in the Karabakh region.

Embroidery with a tambour hook, in a style reminiscent of Rasht work (see p. 160), was practised in Sheki. Medium-sized rectangular covers on mill-made felted woollen cloth are most typical. This work is known as *tekeduz*. In the Sheki region, textile workers make long pieces of pennanted bunting called *gaerdaek* to decorate shelves, and smaller ones called *taxla paerdaesi* for windows.

The ancient mulberry-wooded, silkworm-rearing and silk-weaving centres of Azerbaijan are Nakchivan, Shamakhi, Ganja, Shusa and Sheki. Hand-woven silk (*manjilig*) was made in Sheki up to the 1930s; after that, factory-woven silk (*davel*) took over in larger volume. Silk cloths of local and imported origin in a plaid pattern were used as *boxca* (an Ottoman word, indicating wrapping cloths), though *kalamkar* cloth imported from Isfahan was an acceptable substitute (see p. 167).

Silk weaving in warp-faced stripes was a speciality of Azerbaijan. In Sheki, artisans wove miniature bags in the shape of saddlebags, often edged in Persian silk brocade, for boys to carry their books to the local *madrasah* (Koranic school). Striped covers for *mafrash* (clothing bags), strapped either side of a donkey, to be transported on the transhumant herders' seasonal migration, are woven in silk in Karabakh, in the mountains and lowlands around Shusa, and in the Gazakh region.

The batik technique was also practised in Azerbaijan. Silk squares were blocked out in wax with wooden stamps to make women's headscarves. The most famous of these were large, square, silk wedding wraps called *julmandah*, decorated with complex floral and figurative motifs and the usual *boteh*. These were made at Sheki and in the province of Shirvan, near Iran. The style is very similar to those from Osku in Iranian Azerbaijan (see p. 169). Formerly, natural dyestuffs included madder and indigo, and more rarely various mosses, ginger, saffron, sandalwood and the dog-rose. Plums and onion, walnut and pomegranate skins were also sometimes used. A batik silk kerchief might be tied onto a house under construction to ward off the evil eye, and might then be given to the master of the house when the building was completed. Kerchiefs were also used at marriage ceremonies. The bride wore hers as a veil, while the groom was presented with differently coloured ones by relatives; one might also be tied around the neck of a sacrificial goat. Silk kerchiefs are the traditional present in any form of celebration, but a black kerchief is used for mourning.

PAGE 174
Avar woman reeling in freshly dyed woollen yarn, Daghestan.

PAGE 175
Embroidered cover, Gobustan, Azerbaijan.

OPPOSITE
Mafrash silk cover, Karabakh, Azerbaijan.

ABOVE
Striped silk bag, Karabakh, Azerbaijan.

RIGHT
Sequinned alcove cover, Shirvan, Azerbaijan.

BELOW
Nineteenth-century Persian velvet-ikat curtain from Kashan or Yazd, made for the Azerbaijan market.

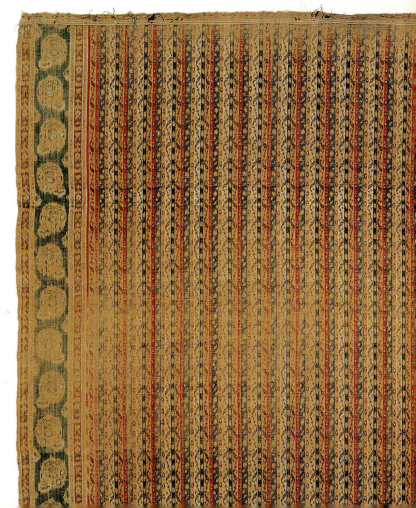

ABOVE
Metal-thread embroidery on velvet to be cut out to adorn slippers, Baku, Azerbaijan.

RIGHT
Zili-weave fragment, Gazakh or Shirvan, Azerbaijan.

BELOW LEFT
Woman's embroidered cap, Ganja, Azerbaijan.

BELOW CENTRE
Silver-embroidered mirror container, Baku, Azerbaijan.

BELOW RIGHT
Embroidered bag, Gobustan, Azerbaijan.

ABOVE
Silk *mafrash* cover, Karabakh, Azerbaijan.

BELOW LEFT AND RIGHT
Women's Kashmir-weave *lavada* boleros, Sheki, Azerbaijan.

Daghestan

Like much of the Caucasus, Daghestan is an area of extreme beauty – forests, hills and seemingly inaccessible peaks broken by dangerous torrents. It lies on the western shore of the Caspian Sea to the north of the modern state of Azerbaijan. The Daghestanis are a fierce, proud, independent people, who live in villages called *auls* deep in the hostile mountains, though many have now moved down to the capital and other towns in the littoral plains. Thirty-one different ethnic groups, each speaking different languages, may be found here, including the Avar, Dargin, Kumyk, Kaitag and Lezgin peoples.

The people are noted for their crafts, particularly metalwork, jewelry, woodcarving and textiles. Daghestani women weave carpets in blue and red on vertical looms in the *soumak* technique. Kumyk and Avar women weave large tapestry-woven double-warped carpets called *dum* and *davaghin*, which were frequently hung on the mountain-side colder wall of their terraced houses. The Kaitags and Dargins are also famed for their embroidery, stitching covers and hangings in fantastical designs. One of the origins of this work may lie in Ottoman embroideries, which would have been traded into the area and been known to the Daghestanis from the brief period of Ottoman dominance in the late 1500s. There are also influences from the prolific textile region to the south, Azerbaijan, and from the equally rich Central Asia. *Kaitag* are embroidered in silk on hand-woven cotton, or more rarely on silk, mainly employing types of couching stitch. Motifs are of simple flowers and birds, mythical beasts, horns, a central sun, all depicted in an often hooked form somehow reminiscent of the most primitive-seeming of ancient animist Central Asian stone carvings and later *suzani* embroideries.

Robert Chenciner, expert on Daghestani textiles, found from local people that *kaitag* are used ritually at birth, marriage and death. They also have everyday functions, such as their use as a shade for a baby's head when in the cradle. The face of the embroidery is always turned towards the baby, not the onlooker. Combined with blue beads and amulets, it helps to ward off the evil eye. *Kaitag* were also made by the bride to carry her dowry jewelry to her groom's house on the day of her marriage. In the region of Gapshima, *kaitag* were also displayed as cushion covers. They are also used at funerals. The face of the deceased is covered with an embroidery, again face down, in the same manner as a baby's face is shaded. The embroidery is never interred with the body, but is passed down within the family.

ABOVE
Avar metal-thread-embroidered window cover, Daghestan.

BELOW
Nineteenth-century *kaitag* embroidery, Daghestan.

OPPOSITE
Eighteenth-century rug-pattern silk embroidery, Azerbaijan.

THE PRESENT

Cheap and cheerful Russian printed textiles and factory-woven brocades replaced local hand-made work in the mid-nineteenth century. From the mid-1870s, synthetic dyes replaced natural dyes, especially locally cultivated madder, which was also more expensive. In the twentieth century the savage civil war was followed in the 1920s by Soviet repressions of *kulaks*, relatively prosperous self-employed country dwellers – there were no peasants in most of the Caucasus – and this literally killed off the hand-craft tradition. From the 1950s, after the transportations of the Great Patriotic War, there were leaden attempts by Soviet state artists to rediscover 'national' crafts. Today many looms are bare, and there is just one small natural dye-revival project in Daghestan, called Khan's Rugs.

Other crafts have not fared well either. Although silk is cultivated in Belokan and Lagodek by Avars living in north Azerbaijan, the cocoons are exported to Japan and Italy.

In Sheki, there is only one remaining silk batik printer still practising the trade, using long-handled blocks carved from the hardwood of pear and walnut trees. There is a small amount of reproduction embroidery produced in Daghestan, but most women only remember chain stitch. The wood-carving techniques have virtually no masters. The Amuzgi have been renowned since at least the twelfth century as armourers, and today there is one master of *bulat* (the strongest twisted, hammered, wrought steel) blade-making left in Daghestan. It is time for outside patronage and revival.

Uzbekistan

Uzbekistan lies at the heart of Central Asia. Populated by Uzbeks of Turkic origin – though with substantial Farsi-speaking minorities, especially in the towns – it is, along with a few textile centres in neighbouring Tajikistan, responsible for the production of some of the world's most visually dramatic textiles.

Nowadays we associate Central Asia with woven and embroidered silk products, but in fact – despite Khotan in nearby Chinese (East) Turkestan having a documented silk industry from the sixth century AD onwards – silk-rearing and weaving in Central Asia is a comparatively recent phenomenon as an important industry. Indeed, the territory covered by the modern republic of Uzbekistan was and is ideal cotton-growing country, to such an extent that in Soviet times cotton became a monoculture that eventually ruined the soil.

In Central Asia, silk-rearing and weaving first manifested itself in East Turkestan. It also became prevalent in West Turkestan, but slowly declined there due to endemic civil strife. It revived briefly under the Timurids in the fourteenth century, but it was not until the 1770s, when Shah Murad, Emir of Bokhara, established a silk-rearing industry in the Zarafashan valley to the north of the city, that the fabled sericulture of Central Asia really began to flourish. The wearing of highly decorative silk robes then became *de rigueur* for members of the court, their wives and the well-to-do in general.

The revival of sericulture meant that in the famous cities of Bokhara and Samarkand, Kokand and Shakhrisabz (and, after the Russian conquest of Central Asia in the mid-nineteenth century, the fast-growing towns of Tashkent and Pskent), thousands of workers were employed weaving silk fabrics and embroidering with silk thread. Highly dramatic warp-ikat robes were worn by the men, women and children of wealthy or prominent families, and the walls of their rooms were clad with the finest embroidered *suzani* hangings.

This world of textile opulence lasted until the full impact of the Soviet system devastated both the social hierarchy and the production system that served it with luxury goods. Weaving became co-operative and largely factory-based, and production became standardized. The complex five-dye *abra* fabrics of old were now produced in two or three chemically derived colours in simple designs, to be marketed as dress material under such trade names as Sputnik or Kremlin, and instead of the classic *suzani* created for the rich and powerful, embroidery was now restricted to the domestic sphere. However, with the fall of the Soviet Union and newly won independence, weaving and embroidery gradually at first, then lately with a rush, expanded enormously.

PAGES 182–183
Bolim posh, Urgut, Uzbekistan; warp-ikat *abr* silk *kurta*, Samarkand; white Tekke *chyrpy* for an old woman, Turkmenistan; painted 'hunting cloth', Herat, Afghanistan.

ABOVE
Nineteenth-century men wearing *abr* silk warp-ikat robes, Uzbekistan.

OPPOSITE
Suzani, with an embroidered pattern of floral repeats enclosed within multiple cockerels' heads, Urgut.

TECHNIQUES

Suzani Embroidery

The most classic of the textiles of the whole Central Asian region are the hangings embroidered with designs of flowers and meandering vines for the court and upper classes of Bokhara. The largest of these are known by the Persian word *suzani*. They – and smaller hangings – are traditionally worked on white cloth known as *karboz*, hand-woven out of cotton on narrow looms. To make up a wide piece of cloth, several – usually between three and six – long, narrow strips are sewn together. A specialist known as a *chizmachi* draws out the *suzani* pattern on the cloth. The strips that make up the hanging are then unpicked, and each strip is given to a different embroiderer. When they are finished, the strips are sewn back together to form the finished *suzani*. The fact that each hanging is embroidered by several different hands accounts for some of the pleasing irregularities and slight mismatches that counterpoise the perfection of the stitchery.

Much of what is known as Bokhara *suzani* work was not in fact embroidered in Bokhara itself but in nearby centres such as Chafrikan and Gizhduvan. In later years, mill cloth was often substituted for *karboz*. Silk was the primary embroidery thread, either locally produced or imported from India or China. However it was procured, it was dyed to the required colours by the predominantly Jewish dyers of Bokhara and other urban centres. The stitches used are *basma*, a laid and couched stitch, and *tambur*, chain stitch. There is another stitch, *kanda khayol*, which uses couching diagonal to the laid stitches.

In Shakhrisabz – the birthplace of Tamerlane, lying to the south of Samarkand – *suzani* and other hangings were

TOP LEFT
Embroidered *bolim posh*, held over the heads of a bride and groom, Urgut.

TOP RIGHT
Suzani, second half of the twentieth century, Urgut.

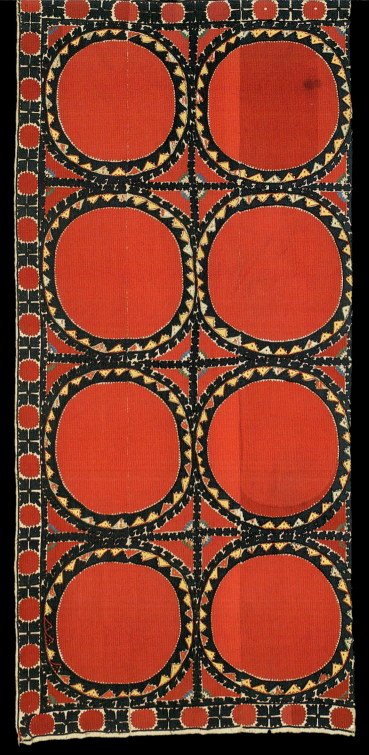

OPPOSITE CENTRE
Domestic *suzani* decorative panel.

OPPOSITE BELOW
Detail of cotton-on-silk embroidery on a *suzani* from Samarkand.

ABOVE LEFT
Oi palak, Tashkent.

ABOVE RIGHT
Suzani, Pskent.

LEFT
Oi palak, Tashkent.

OPPOSITE
Nineteenth-century *suzani* in the Ura Tube style.

LEFT AND BELOW
Professionally worked embroidered robe edgings from Shakhrisabz and other urban centres.

PAGE 190
Lakhai *ilgitsh*, southern Uzbekistan.

PAGE 191
Early nineteenth-century Lakhai *suzani*, southern Uzbekistan.

produced in a style very similar to that of Bokhara, but with bolder and more densely worked flowers and less wispy tendrils. Fine cross-stitch bags and *romal* (squares) are typical products of Shakhrisabz today. The *suzani* of the Ura-Tube region to the northeast of Samarkand also conform to the general Bokhara style, but the floral and vegetal motifs are more delicate in execution and regular in composition. Those of Nurata are of a similar delicacy to those of Ura-Tube, but with a more defined floral border and with tightly organized floral sprays set in an unadorned central field.

Distinct in style from the above are the very large (often 12 to 15 feet long; 3.5–4.5 m) *palak* hangings embroidered around Tashkent and Pskent. Typically, these hangings are densely embroidered in *basma* stitch in a mix of cotton or silk. One colour usually predominates, often red or purple. A common layout is the *ulduz*, or star design, with a central star surrounded by smaller ones set in triangles. The moon design, *oi palak*, has groups of three medallions set in two, three or four rows.

Some of the most prolific modern-day embroiderers come from the town of Urgut, near Samarkand. From around this area come *suzani* with very distinctive, complex, floral motifs in white or cream *basma* stitch, often on a yellow or green ground, repeated in a regular grid pattern all over the field (the same style seems to be practised in Samarkand itself). The commonest Urgut designs are of a central, reddish-coloured medallion framed within a spiralling, betendrilled, darker circle. Set in a square between smaller repeats of this pattern and embroidered on white cloth, these motifs have all the dramatic effect of a fireball set within a dark, whizzing Catherine wheel.

Another style practised in Urgut utilizes mainly chain stitch in black and is embellished with metal sequins set with glass beads. Children's hoods and the square *kolromal* that cover a bride's hands are made in this style. Modern-day centres for embroidery, in addition to those mentioned above, are Karshi, Surkhandarya and Kermine.

The fertile valley of Ferghana, meanwhile, produces embroidery with stylistic similarities to nearby Tajikistan. *Djoinamaz*, *ruidjo* and other textiles are worked on brown or magenta mill cloth. In Ferghana, a small portion of a *suzani* is always left unfinished, so as to let any threatening devils, or *shaitan*, trapped inside escape. Ferghana women wear a coat, the *ferangi*, with tied-back sleeves when they go to visit a bridegroom's house. Made of fine silk, these are embroidered and the pockets, cuffs and lapels edged with woven braid. The linings are of *abra* silk woven in nearby Margellan.

All manner of wedding hangings are made throughout Uzbekistan. When a farmer marries, the groom's family decorates one half of the wedding hall with embroidered textiles, the bride's family the other. If one family is wealthier than the other and possesses more and richer hangings, it will lend some to the other to hang on their side so as not to embarrass them. A wide variety of embroideries – now largely worked on mill-made cloth – are produced as part of the wedding trousseau. Large *suzani* and slightly smaller, square hangings, *barposh*, are hung on the wall facing the entrance of the house. *Bolim posh* embroideries, between 4 and 5 foot square (1.2–1.5 m^2), are held or draped over the heads of the bride and groom at the end of the wedding. Long, embroidered bands, *zardervori*, decorate the walls.

Probably the most characteristic articles of Uzbek embroidery are those 12 to 18 inch square (30–45 cm²) cloths known as *laliposh*, embroidered with floral designs. When the groom comes to visit the bride, she brings in a tray with six or eight nan breads (the number must always be even), sweets and halva, covered with the *laliposh*. Embroidered pillows, *takhiaposh*, are stacked on top of the bedding chest, which is itself covered with a *suzani* worked on *karboz* cloth and nowadays also with a glitzy metal-thread embroidery. A rich family will have up to four *takhiaposh* stacked up on the chest.

The most charming domestic article of Uzbek embroidery is the *sandilikposh*. In the cold Central Asian winters, a charcoal stove is placed in a pit specially prepared in the earthen floor of one of the interior rooms. The pit is covered with a table and then with a number of quilts. The ladies of the household can slip their legs underneath the quilts to be warmed, and tea is served on the square, embroidered *sandilikposh* that covers both table and quilts. These *sandilikposh* are decorated with embroidered teapot designs.

Patchwork pillows and square covers (*romal*, also known as *kuro-yastic*) are made all over Uzbekistan, the rest of Central Asia and into northern Afghanistan. Many made their way to the West in the 1960s, but were used as floor cushions and wore out.

Lakhai and Kungrat Embroidery

The Lakhai and Kungrat Uzbeks are to be found in the Surkhandarya region of Uzbekistan, in southern Tajikistan and across the Amu Darya (Oxus) river in northern Afghanistan in a region centred on the town of Kunduz. A branch of the Uzbeks, the Lakhai claim descent from Karamysh, the sole surviving brother of Genghis Khan. Lakhai was the name of Karamysh's youngest son, whose only legacy was that he should take whatever he needed from his brothers. The Lakhai long used this legend as an excuse for the most outrageous brigandry. They remained predatory nomads until crushed by the forces of the Emir of Bokhara in the later part of the nineteenth century, after which time most of them became sedentary agriculturists. In the 1920s some of the tribe rose under the leadership of Ibrahim Beg to fight the encroachments of the Bolshevik government, and they were one of the most important components of Enver Pasha's *basmachi* ('bandit') army. By 1930 they were defeated, and many were forced to take refuge in northern Afghanistan and eventually settled around Kunduz. The rest of the tribe remained to suffer forced collectivization in the Soviet Union just across the Amu Darya river.

Lakhai women have, however, retained their ability to create extraordinarily vivid and uninhibited textiles. On both sides of the river they embroider hats, purses, bag-faces and the V-shaped hangings, *segusha* (used to decorate piles of quilts), also found among other Uzbek groups. The most beautiful textiles are worked in silk on imported baize in the form of square- or shield-shaped bag-faces. Known as *ilgitsh*, they are too fragile to ever actually have been used as bags. They are embroidered using mainly chain stitch with bold, often asymmetrically composed motifs of flowers and such talismanic creatures as scorpions and spiders. A Lakhai bride would hope to have three or four of these *ilgitsh* ready for her dowry before she finishes the period of seclusion that precedes marriage. The *ilgitsh* were then hung in pairs on the walls opposite the pile of bedding that occupies the place of honour at the rear of the yurt or dwelling. The base of this bedding pile was formed by a large embroidered textile in the shape of an open-topped box, a *mafrash*.

A related group of Uzbeks, the Kungrat (traditionally sheep herders, where the Lakhai were formerly horse breeders), embroidered broadly similar articles, often on a black rather than a red ground, with more regular, geometric and symmetrically composed motifs.

Many of the once-nomadic Uzbek groups embroider triangular or V-shaped *segusha*. The often blank top ends of the *segusha* are tucked between the layers of bedding positioned at the rear of the dwelling. Frequently displayed in sets of two or three, the older examples are of hooked geometric forms

RIGHT
Man's robe, embroidered in silver and gold thread, Bokhara, nineteenth century.

BELOW
Woman's headband embroidered in metal thread, Bokhara.

worked in silk cross stitch in predominantly yellow, black, green, red and magenta. The newer ones are embroidered in simpler floral motifs with a much smaller range of colours. Embroidered in cross stitch in the older style are also purses, small tasselled hangings to adorn the bedding pile, and the puttee-like strips known as *piey pech* that are tied around the bride's hands at a wedding.

Cap Needlework
In the present day, embroidered skullcaps are the most obvious everyday display of needlework. The most popular design for men is known as *chusti*, after the village of Chust in Ferghana. These caps are of white or black silk, or synthetic material, and are in the shape of a low four-sided pyramid set on a band. They are designed to be folded up flat and put into a pocket, and then to be taken out and put on again for formal occasions, especially visits to the mosque. On each of the four sides of the pyramid are embroidered motifs of the almond, *badom*, or chilli pepper pod, *kalampur*. Instead of being directly embroidered, the designs are most often cut out of cardboard, bound with thread and then stitched onto the cap. The chilli pepper motif is reputed to derive from an old Tajik design that is in reality a cockerel's wing. In pre-Islamic times, all of the cockerel – head, wings and feet – would have been shown in profile. Women wear a cap of *iroki*-style metal-thread embroidery of the same basic shape.

Metal-Thread Embroidery
Bokhara was the unrivalled centre for metal-thread embroidery in Central Asia, with many workshops catering for the needs of the Emir. Gold-work embroidery was practised in the region long before the advent of silk. Archaeological remains of women's garments from the first century AD in the Tashkent area already show traces of gold-thread embroidery.

Metal-thread embroidery in Central Asia is known as *zardozi*. The metal thread, *kalebatun*, would originally have been made locally, but in the years before the Bolshevik Revolution it was most often imported from India, Europe or Iran. In the main, the wearing of metal-thread embroidery was restricted to men, there being a superstition that if a woman touched a man's metal thread it would turn black. Despite these beliefs, part of a well-off Bokhara woman's wedding costume was a *zardozi* headband called a *peshonaband*.

Metal-thread embroiderers were organized into craft guilds whose membership was restricted to men, though within the family many wives and daughters were also skilled at the work. Male relatives of established guild members were taken on for long apprenticeships. Each guild occupied its own *guzar*, or quarter of the town, and had its own constitution. The metal thread, worked on a frame, was couched down with a thread known as *pechak*, which was the same colour as the background cloth. There are two broad classifications of work: *zaminduzi*, in which the background cloth is completely covered

in embroidery, and *gulduzi*, which has floral patterns with a lot of the ground visible. The cloth to be embroidered was usually velvet, chamois leather or wool. The velvet was either locally produced or imported from Turkey, Syria, India, Iran or Europe.

In the late nineteenth and early twentieth centuries, embroiderers attached to the Ark, the palace fortress of the Emirs, made robes for royalty, court officers and their wives. For the Emir's generals, they made Russian-style military overcoats. After the last Emir was deposed by the Communists in 1920, the artisans lost their great patrons and, although they were organized into co-operatives after 1930, the quality of their work steeply declined.

Block Printing

The block printers, or *chitgar*, of Central Asia are now known more for their historic production role than for the present quality or quantity of the fabrics they produce. Up until the 1930s, block printing was a thriving craft in Bokhara, Ferghana, Tashkent and Samarkand, as well as Khojent in Tajikistan. Vapkent, near Tashkent, was a particularly important printing centre. The products were wraps, sheeting, yardage, floor- and prayer cloths. Because these were everyday items – made of printed, hand-woven *karboz* or mill cloth – they were neither of great value nor very durable, and consequently few older examples have survived in their entirety. Glimpses of past glories are found in the lining of *chapan* coats and the backing of old embroideries and quilts. Patterns tended to be floral and geometric, and the blocks used were of carved wood. All makers produced prints with larger or smaller floral designs used respectively to cover the top and bottom of quilts. Favoured motifs were seeds, amulets, the almond with its protective symbolism, and running water which was used for borders. In the 1930s Stalin forbade working from home. The printers then worked in co-operatives, until in the 1950s competition from factory-made prints drove them out of business.

The preparation of dyes is long and complex. Although chemical alizarine is now used for red, black is derived from a long-soaked and boiled mixture of iron filings, vegetable oil, wheat flour, gum and lentils. The mordant for black is tannin derived from the pistachio tree. Yellow, now chemical in origin, was formerly obtained from apricot sap mixed with an aqueous solution called *ochicktash*, mixed with pounded flowers. The *chitgar* first blocks out the black outline and then fills in the yellow before steeping in alizarine. The finished cloth is dried in the sun and ironed. Prior to 1957, the block-printed cloth was always callendered with stones on both sides to give it an attractive sheen.

ABOVE
Simple block print on cotton *karboz*, Ferghana Valley.

Abra Silk Weaving

The pride of all Central Asian fabrics is silk *abra* (from a Persian word, meaning 'cloud-like'). This sumptuous warp-ikat textile is unrivalled as the world's most stunning visual display of the dramatic possibilities of resist technique. It was Shah Murad who provided the raw material in the 1770s, when he re-established the silk industry in the Zarafashan valley north of Bokhara with workers brought from Merv.

All Central Asian *abra* are warp-faced warp ikats. The warps are always of silk; the weft, depending on the place of origin, either silk or cotton. The most exciting *abra* were made in Bokhara or Ferghana, traditionally with silk warp and weft. The colours of the Bokhara ikats were predominantly bright yellows and reds, like the wild tulip that is native to these parts and a recurring motif in local crafts. Before 1930, production in Bokhara and other centres was always aimed at the rich and powerful. Men would wear colourful *abra* coats one over the other; women an *abra* smock (*kurta*) under an *abra* coat. These magnificent clothes were worn to impress, and perhaps to intimidate. Until the end of the nineteenth century, silk was reserved for the aristocracy; commoners could only wear cotton. Sugra Kasimova, a grand old lady of present-day Bokhara, describes how in her youth *abra khalat* (coats) were worn by the well-to-do for weddings, festivals and as formal visiting attire, and her father, one of the last Emir's generals, had twelve *abra* weavers working in the family courtyard.

In addition to the tulip, the *ola gul*, motifs popular in Bokhara were the ram's horn, *kutch cara gul*, and the combination that is probably most archetypical of Bokhara, a bright sun and scroll known respectively as *daira gul*, the tambourine, and *shona gul*, the flower. The *abra* of Samarkand was much simpler but equally as distinctive, relying on solid blocks of colour for effect.

OPPOSITE
Block-printed mattress cover of cotton *karboz*, probably from Vapkent.

TOP LEFT
Warp-ikat *abr* silk *kurta*, Samarkand.

ABOVE LEFT
Warp-ikat silk *kurta*, Samarkand.

LEFT
Karakalpak woman's *abra* veil.

UZBEKISTAN **195**

Production of *abra* was brought to an almost complete halt by the socialization policies of the 1920s. Between 1927 and 1929 all the craft workshops in Bokhara were closed down. The artisans, including weavers and dyers, were arrested. Many escaped and fled to Turkmenistan, Afghanistan or Iran. After this period, production was re-organized on factory lines, and the wearing of *abra* dresses and pyjamas was encouraged for the newly emancipated common woman. Bokhara weaving, probably for political reasons, was left to languish and production concentrated in Khojent in Tajikistan, the premier centre, and in Ferghana. In all these centres, weaving is still carried out on semi-mechanized looms, with up to eight treadles per loom.

Dyeing of the warp threads can often take place at some distance from the location where the weaving is done. For instance, the warp threads now woven at Bokhara are dyed at Shakhrisabz. In Margellan, where dyeing and weaving operations are in fact integrated on the same large site, thirty-seven different stages from raw silk to finished product are detailed. The warp silk yarns are bound to a pattern drawn onto them by the *averband*, or master dyer. The first dyeing is yellow, then the process moves from the lighter colours to the darkest. Popular in the Bokhara area were *abra* silks woven with a pink silk weft that gave a rosy hue to the entire fabric. The silk weavers also produced a shiny cloth in satin weave known as *atlas*.

In many workshops, *abra* silk was woven in tabby (plain weave) with a white cotton weft, making a fabric widely known as *adras*. If the weft is hidden in a dense warp-faced weave, the ikat-resist-dyed pattern stands out clearly. If, on the other hand, the warp is not so closely threaded, the thicker cotton weft shows as a horizontal rib.

ABOVE LEFT
Five-colour *abra chapan*, probably from Ferghana.

ABOVE RIGHT
Abra chapan panel, Samarkand.

BELOW
Child's *abra chapan*, Bokhara or Ferghana.

OPPOSITE ABOVE
Green *abra chapan*, Samarkand.

OPPOSITE BELOW
Abra chapan, Samarkand.

PAGE 198 ABOVE
Abra, showing a sun and ram's horn design, Bokhara.

PAGE 198 BELOW
Nineteenth-century *abra* cover, probably from Bokhara.

PAGE 199 ABOVE
Nineteenth-century *abra* cover, probably from Bokhara.

PAGE 199 BELOW
Nineteenth-century *abra* panel, Samarkand or Ferghana.

196 CENTRAL ASIA

Baghmal Weaving

Early in the nineteenth century, at the height of production of luxurious fabrics, there appeared silk velvet ikat, *baghmal* – the most costly and exclusive weave of all. For its manufacture, a complex threading of a double warp was necessary. A foundation warp of plain orange or pink silk threads was threaded alternately with an ikat-dyed warp several times the length of the plain warp and set on a separate beam. As the weaving with the cotton weft progressed, the ikat-dyed warp was raised separately over grooved wires inserted on alternate picks. After a section was woven, a sharp blade was run down the grooves, leaving the velvet pile with its clear ikat pattern held by the alternate pick of cotton weft. This costly fabric was used for wealthy women's coats and for children's hats. Very recently there has been a revival of velvet ikat for export, mainly through Istanbul.

Natural Dyeing

With the revival of an export market for Uzbek textiles, there has been a revival in natural dyeing. Reds and pinks are obtained from oak gall and madder roots; brown from walnut husks from Samarkand. Dried pomegranate rinds give gold. Indian natural indigo gives blue. Onion skins mixed with fresh mulberry, quince and vine leaves give a vibrant buttercup yellow.

TOP
Contemporary *baghmal* yardage from Bokhara.

ABOVE RIGHT
Woman's *baghmal* cap, Bokhara.

RIGHT
Karakalpak *aq jegde* from Samarkand, worn over the head in a similar way to the Uzbek *paranja* or Turkmen *chyrpy*.

ABOVE
Kiymeshek veil, made of red *ushiga* decorated in chain stitch with various horn motifs: typical Karakalpak designs include cattle horns and talismanic beasts, but can also represent such humble domestic implements as carpenters' planes.

BELOW
Karakalpak *shapan* lined with printed cloth, Khorezm.

PEOPLES

The Karakalpaks

The Karakalpaks – literally, the 'black hats' – live mainly in the delta of the Amu Darya river as it enters the Aral Sea, though Karakalpak villages are scattered all over the region and can be found as far away as the Ferghana valley. Of mixed but predominantly Turkic descent, the group probably formed in the northern Aral region during the sixteenth century, but for the past several hundred years have been settled in Khorezm, the former khanate traditionally ruled from the ancient city of Khiva. They are settled in houses and are farmers and herders, but they formerly lived in yurts.

The Karakalpak weaving style has many unique features, though in recent centuries it has been influenced by the Turkmen, their sometimes predatory neighbours. It is the embroidery of the women that is justly famous. They embroider dresses, coats, oversleeves and headcovers – items of clothing that are reserved for special occasions such as marriage. They concentrate their embroidery on female attire, though sometimes the seams or edges of men's costume may have a little needlework.

The most famous garment is the *kiymeshek*, a hooded veil that covers the hair, shoulders, chest and upper back but leaves the face uncovered. Twentieth-century *kiymeshek* were embroidered on the front in open chain stitch on imported red or black broadcloth known as *ushiga*; the rest of the veil was made up of ikat-patterned silk, which experts on the Karakalpak David and Sue Richardson attribute to Jewish weavers from Khiva. The use of fulled wool *ushiga* may originate from imported British broadcloth, although this was superseded by Russian-made cloth from the late nineteenth century onwards. What little costume survives from before that date was embellished with counted-thread embroidery in cross stitch in raspberry-coloured silk on hand-woven *karboz*, called *bo'z* by the Karakalpaks. There was a period in the late nineteenth century – before the universal adoption of broadcloth for the front and edges of the veil – when cross stitch was worked on rectangular pieces of *shatirash* (red and black chequered hand-woven cotton cloth), which were then applied to the veil.

One of the rarest Karakalpak costumes is the richly embroidered indigo cotton *ko'k ko'ylek* wedding dress, which went out of fashion in the late nineteenth century. Its rarity is partly because such dresses were cut up following the death of the owner and shared among her family. In some cases, pieces were smoked over a fire by local shamans for magical purposes.

THE PRESENT

Since the dissolution of the Soviet Union, independent Uzbekistan has once again become a vast textile workshop, producing above all embroideries, warp-ikat silks and even velvet ikat. Often encouraged and funded by Turkish merchants, much of the Uzbek supply is made available to the world through that great entrepot, the Istanbul bazaar. The customer must beware, however, as many new products are marketed as antiques, and the best modern *abra* and *suzani* can be almost indistinguishable from the antique original; even so-called experts have been caught out – in itself a tribute to the enduring textile skills of Uzbekistan.

Local markets are also thriving. In the marketplace at Ferghana, women sell quilted *chapan* coats and hats, which they stack up in great piles upon their heads. Not all individual textile crafts are faring so well. In Margellan, one old man, Achmadaliyev Salijon, still practises block printing from home, but – working part-time, as and when the few orders for weddings and festivals come in – he has no one else trained to take over from him when old age forces retirement. He works at a low table using *khalib* blocks. He and another printer in Ura-Tube use old blocks. He states that there is one man who makes new blocks in Kokand, but they are crude and not deep enough. He knows of one printer still working in Tashkent and another in Kashgar. It is to be hoped that future generations pick up the skills of these artisans, and that the magnificent textile heritage of Uzbekistan can flourish in all its guises.

ABOVE
Uzbek woman wearing a *paranja* shawl, commonly used as a headcovering by all manner of contemporary Uzbek women.

BELOW LEFT
Bokhara woman in a wedding outfit of silk velvet ikat, worn with a metal-thread-embroidered *peshonaband* headband.

BELOW
Woman unreeling silk cocoons, Margellan.

Turkmenistan

The Turkmen are a people of mixed Turkic and Iranian descent, who live between the Aral Sea and the Iranian province of Khorasan. Excellent riders of both horse and camel, they have long mastered the navigation of the harsh deserts that make this one of the most arid regions on earth. Though traditionally nomadic, they did at times occupy urban centres such as Merv, one of the world's richest cities before it was destroyed by the Mongols in the thirteenth century, and the fortress of Geok Tepe before it was conquered by the Russian army in 1881. Greatly feared by their neighbours, the Turkmen themselves once made their living by raiding, pillaging and slaving. Now mainly settled, they live in Turkmenistan, centred on the capital Ashkhabad and the ancient Merv, and in Uzbekistan, northeast Iran and northwest Afghanistan. They are generally farmers where there is enough water, and pastoral nomads where there is not.

Turkmen are traditionally divided up into twenty-four tribes, known as *halq*, of which the most prominent are the Tekke, Yomut, Saryk, Kizil Ayak, Chub Bash, Esari, Chodor, Arabachi and – reputedly the oldest – Salor. All the groups embroider envelope-shaped bags, the smaller ones for storing little valuable articles and the larger for soft items such as bedding. Turkmen women are great weavers, embroiderers and felt makers, creating splendid rugs, kelims, and yurt and animal trappings, and traditionally making all their own clothes and embellishing them with fine embroidery. The women are very emancipated and go around unveiled except for their custom of covering their mouth with a scarf.

COSTUMES

Women's Dress

Turkmen women wear a shift-like dress known as a *köynek* over a pair of baggy drawstring trousers (*balaq*) made of cheap, disposable material. They also wear a kerchief, undercoat, hat and an overcoat worn over the head like a shawl. The cuffs, yoke and hem of the dress and the cuffs of the trousers are embroidered with closely worked floral and geometric motifs. For those groups that wear it, the band of the bun-shaped hat is stitched with the same motifs as the dress and trousers, as are the cuffs, vents and lapels of the undercoat, though in the case of the Tekke a row of running stags is often added to the cuffs. Trouser cuffs are often of silk, as they are the only part of the garment that can be seen beneath the *köynek*. Care, attention and expense is lavished on these. When the rest of the trousers are worn out, a new pair can be sewn onto the beautiful cuffs, which are most often a dowry item. To help preserve them, a braid made of camel hair is attached to the bottom edge of the cuff to prevent the embroidered part from being worn away. Traditionally, a coat made of silk or velvet and decorated with silver jewelry or old coins was worn over the shift and trousers. The Yomut and the Tekke each had at least one version of this coat. For special occasions, the Tekke (though not since the nineteenth century the Yomut) wear a heavily embroidered *chyrpy*, a coat draped over the head and shoulders like a cloak. The sleeves of this garment are usually vestigial – tapering flaps, often tipped with silver and imported trade cloth, and linked together halfway by a small strip of embroidered or woven cloth known as a *gerbi*.

Children's Dress

As is the case with rural peoples from time immemorial, the Turkmen lavish attention on their children. For nomadic pastoralists, children are wealth and will in time provide ready helping hands to care for flocks and herds and fulfil all the tasks necessary for an itinerant way of life. Beautiful little fringed bibs are made by both Tekke and Yomut women for their infants. Fringed with tassels, these are usually embroidered, and sometimes incorporate valuable material such as *abra* ikat, or even a worn piece of the most prestigious fabric of all, velvet ikat. As the Turkmen are highly superstitious, children's smocks and shirts are often adorned with snakes made out of human hair to ward off the evil eye. Unmarried girls wear a heavily embroidered skullcap known as a *börük*, or among the Tekke a *taxya*, which they use from early girlhood until the time they are married. The whole of the ground is embroidered.

Men's Dress

Men nowadays wear a Western-style cotton shirt and trousers, but often topped with a traditional long silk coat, or *qirmizi*, embroidered restrainedly at collar, cuffs and side slits. Boys wear a similar cap to that of the girls, as do the men, though the men's tend to be unembroidered. The bushy black or white lambswool hat known as the *telpek* is still conventionally worn by men. Neither men nor women take off their hats in company, as this is considered impolite.

TECHNIQUES

Weaving

Turkmenistan has more than adequate supplies of raw cotton, and sericulture is also strong. Turkmen women are great weavers of cloth as well as rugs. Working on a multi-heddle pit-loom, they weave plain, striped or plaid fabric in silk or cotton to a maximum width of 12 to 14 inches (30–35 cm). Various shades of red, the favourite Turkmen colour, predominate, and yellow is also popular. Woven strips can in addition be black, white, green or blue. All silk material is known as *cepbetew göwderi* or *malay*. Silk/cotton mixes are called *qalbiri* or *sowsam*. Often a contrastingly coloured stripe is woven along the selvedge of the cloth, which is then incorporated into the colour scheme of any cloth or clothing made up from the material. Lengths of this home-woven fabric are made up into scarves, veils and other items of clothing for the family. Triangular sections are introduced to widen garments where necessary.

PAGE 203
Turkmen women at a Soviet literacy class in the 1930s.

TOP
Tekke child's smock.

ABOVE
Tekke child's *baghmal* bib.

BELOW
Tekke child's *abra kurta* with amulet and snake motifs.

OPPOSITE
Tekke boy's smock.

LEFT
Chodor *kurta*.

BELOW
Rare Tekke *chyrpy*, embroidered on a green ground.

BELOW
Chodor *kurta*.

BELOW RIGHT
Tekke *chyrpy* showing the block-printed lining.

206 CENTRAL ASIA

ABOVE
Chodor caps.

RIGHT
Esari felted bag.

Embroidery

Although Turkmen are divided up by tribe and it is easy to distinguish between examples of embroidery from the different groups, there is a general commonality of embroidery style. Turkmen women embroider in open chain stitch and a variant on buttonhole stitch. Women of the Yomut and the Tekke are by far the most productive embroiderers among the Turkmen tribes.

Patchwork

Turkmen women are famous patchworkers, making cushions to recline against out of red and black mill cloth decorated with inserts of more valuable and prestigious hand-made fabrics such as *abra* silks. There are not many beautiful old examples left, as they were bought up from both Turkmenistan and Afghanistan in the 1960s and taken to the West, where they were used as covers for cushions and bolsters until they wore out.

Felting

Turkmen women are great felt makers. The covers of their yurts are of felt, and felt is also used to fill up any cracks in the yurt to keep the cold winter winds out. The raw material, sheep's wool, is readily available. The finest grade is kept for weaving, and only the second grade used for felting. One of the Turkmen's most decorative felts is used as a horse cloth and decorated with black and red coloured spirals against a plain ground. To make felt, the wool is laid on a reed mat. It is teased up using switches, then dampened and rolled up in the mat, with constant pressure being applied. Eventually, a naturally coloured felt results. If coloured details are required, dyed wool is put into the raw wool as and when the pattern requires.

PEOPLES

The Chodor

The Chodor live in the northeast of Turkmenistan and are also found on the neighbouring Mangyshlak peninsula, to the north in Kazakhstan, jutting out into the Caspian Sea. They are prolific embroiderers, and most of their embroidery is worked on a red ground. In the past this would have been Russian broadcloth; in more recent times it is whatever red mill cloth is available in the local bazaar.

The Esari

The Esari are especially noted for their embroidered covers for women's ponytails.

The Tekke

The Tekke are prolific embroiderers, making beautiful *chyrpy* in dark colours, yellow and white. Younger women wear them with a blue or black ground; older important women wear them with a yellow ground; and the most important women of all wear them with a white ground. Very occasionally the Tekke have been known to embroider also on a green or red ground.

The most profusely embroidered *chyrpy* are covered with motifs of tulips and other floral designs (Central Asia is the home of the tulip). More common are *chyrpy* embroidered with motifs of rams' horns and geometric devices all along the edges of the coat, above the vents and on the arms. The finest work – which is often taken from an old, worn-out *chyrpy* – is reserved for the lapels. This is often bought in from a professional embroideress. When the *chyrpy* wears out, this piece is taken off and transferred to a freshly embroidered garment. The sleeves,

TURKMENISTAN 207

TOP LEFT
Tekke summer *chyrpy*.

TOP RIGHT
Yomut child's smock.

ABOVE
Tekke embroidered camel trapping.

RIGHT
Tekke *chyrpy*, embroidered on an unusual red ground.

ABOVE
White Tekke *chyrpy* for an old woman.

ABOVE RIGHT
Soviet-era Tekke neckties.

RIGHT
Yellow Tekke *chyrpy* for a middle-aged woman.

TOP
Kurta with block-printed lining, possibly from Merv.

RIGHT
Arabachi *kurta*.

BELOW LEFT
Yomut woman's silk shawl.

BELOW RIGHT
Yomut plaid silk shawl.

210 CENTRAL ASIA

LEFT
Embroidered Yomut purses.

ABOVE
Embroidered Yomut children's caps.

which are often vestigial, are always tied back. Older *chyrpy* are lined with beautiful block-printed cloth.

Tekke *chyrpy* are often dated in either Arabic or Cyrillic numerals just below the armpit, above the vent. The quality of embroidery worked today is still very high. Twentieth-century curiosities are the elasticated ties embroidered with Communist symbols or Russian landmarks. Recently, there have come onto the international textile market light summer *chyrpy* of green or white silk with applied strips of usually red silk in bird's head or ram's horn motifs.

The Tekke are also famous for their animal trappings. Pentagonal fringed panels in felt, broadcloth or woven pile, known as *asmalyk*, are hung either side of the lead camel in a wedding procession. Horse cloths for the fabled Akal Tekke horses are also labours of love. These are made up of a central strip that runs down the back of the horse, fringed with lozenges of cloth. The flap that falls over the horse's forehead is heavily embroidered.

The Arabachi

The Arabachi are notable for wearing *chyrpy* embroidered with bold cerise flowers set against an indigo blue cotton ground.

The Yomut

The Yomut are probably more numerous than the Tekke, but are not such prolific embroiderers. Yomut territory stretches up the east coast of the Caspian Sea as far as the gulf of Qara Bogaz and then eastwards across the desert as far as the ancient city of Khiva. Yomut can also be found in northeast Iran, between the Atrek and Gorgan rivers. Yomut women sometimes favour a technique of appliquéing or merely tacking down little protective triangles in differently coloured materials on children's clothing and hats.

THE PRESENT

Turkmenistan has gone through remarkable changes since the break-up of the Soviet Union. From being a Soviet backwater it has become an independent nation assiduously courted by powerful foreign countries due to its vast mineral wealth, particularly its deposits of natural gas. Ashkhabad, the capital, has changed out of all recognition in the last twenty years. This newfound wealth has had profound effects on the production of hand-made textiles. Up to the early 1990s the standard of domestic weaving and embroidery was very high indeed, but with prosperity standards are beginning to slip and the temptation to buy in ready-made textiles rather than producing and decorating them locally has been hard to resist. There is some investment coming into the country. Turkish entrepreneurs are trying to revive the textile crafts with a view to marketing them through the Istanbul bazaar. It is to be hoped that these entrepreneurs have the same remarkable reviving effect as they have had in Uzbekistan.

Tajikistan

Tajikistan is a land of Persian speakers, with Afghanistan to the south, Uzbekistan to the west, Kyrgyzstan to the north and China to the east. The embroidery of the plains people is related to that of neighbouring Uzbekistan and has particular similarities to that found in Ferghana Valley, birthplace of Babur, the first Mughal emperor of India. The embroidery of the mountain people relates to the embroidery styles of Afghanistan.

Arabs introduced Islam to the area as early as the seventh century AD. They were supplanted by the Samanid Persians, and Samarkand and Bokhara (now in Uzbekistan) became centres of Persian culture. The area later became part of the Emirate of Bokhara, then in the nineteenth century the Russian empire began to spread into Central Asia. In the 1920s local *basmachi* ('bandit') insurgents fiercely fought the Bolsheviks in an attempt to establish independence, but were ultimately defeated. A long period of Soviet oppression and secularization followed. In 1991, after the collapse of the Soviet Union, Tajikistan declared independence but this was marred by the breakout of a violent civil war.

TECHNIQUES
Embroidery

In a Tajik house, every part of the wall is covered with embroidered articles. There are embroidered pouches for combs; covers for mirrors, *oinakhalta*; covers for tea-leaves, *chaikhalta*; and all manner of *suzani* hangings. Niches in the walls are covered with special embroideries. Embroidered bands known as *zardervori* are hung along the upper part of three walls – the two longitudinal walls and one end wall. At a Tajik wedding, skullcaps and dresses belonging to the bride decorate the bridal house, and square embroidered *romal* cloths are prominently displayed.

Djoinamaz, or prayer cloths, are also embroidered. Nowadays, the embroidery is worked on mill cloth, with red often being the background. A *mihrab* in singles or multiples is embroidered onto the cloth, the open ends of the prayer niche often curling up to suggest a spiral. Pre-Islamic elements, such as pomegranates symbolizing happiness and fertility, or worms and centipedes symbolizing the fulfilment of wishes, are frequently embroidered on either side of the *mihrab*. More up-to-date articles such as teapots and samovars symbolizing hospitality are often depicted on secular items of embroidery.

One of the most beautiful embroideries is the *ruidjo*. The plain, unadorned, central field is framed with floral motifs along three sides. The bottom edge is left unembroidered and – most importantly and highly symbolically – is always unhemmed. The *ruidjo* is used as the bedsheet for a bride's wedding night and is displayed afterwards as proof of her virginity. When treasured old sheets are used for successive weddings, the soiled parts are cut off, so the *ruidjo* tends to become shorter and shorter with the passage of time. These needleworked items form part of the general Central Asian tradition and can be found all over the area, particularly in Ferghana and the Persian-influenced urban centres.

The mountain Tajiks also wear gorgeous embroidered clothes. Men's shirts and women's *kurta* (loose shifts) are embroidered at the cuffs, collar and vertical neck-slit. Embroidered belts for men and women, respectively the

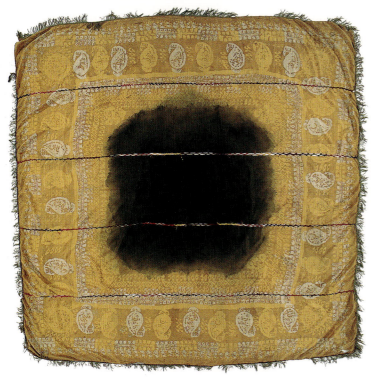

PAGE 212
Tajik blacksmiths at work, wearing skullcaps typical of the region.

PAGE 213, CLOCKWISE FROM TOP LEFT
Wax-batik silk scarf; wax-batik silk scarf; wax-batik silk scarf; tie-dyed cotton shawl; tie-dyed cotton shawl; wax-batik silk scarf. Khojent is a centre for wax batik, South Tajikistan for tie and dye.

RIGHT
Ruband wedding veil, Tajikistan.

FAR RIGHT
Tajik *suzani*.

kamarband and *takband*, are also worn. The most notable item is the bride's *ruband*, or wedding veil, which covers her whole face and chest, and is embroidered in floss silk in deep reds, usually on a white ground, with motifs of peacocks and flowers in a style and use of stitchery reminiscent of both Tajik Afghanistan and Hazara district in Pakistan (the peacocks represent the bride and groom). Karathegin and Darvaz are two important centres of embroidery in the mountain Tajik style.

Large hangings of a layout similar to the *palak suzani* of Tashkent and Pskent are embroidered around Khojent, but with a more floral treatment and with more of the ground left showing. Colours are magenta and black worked in floss silk on undyed *karboz*.

Tie-Dye
Tajikistan is famous for its tie-dyeing, both on cotton and silk. Large shawls are made with a centrally placed circle of polychrome dots and rather crude tied decoration at the corners. The shawls are worn tied around the woman's head, with the bulk of the garment hanging down her back. Cotton shawls are usually predominantly of a yellow pattern against a brown ground. Silk shawls favour pink or purple as a ground.

Batik
Tajikistan is a major producer of the silk squares so beloved of Central Asian women. Used as headscarves, these have a batik pattern. Motifs are mainly floral, though on occasion there are novelties such as Soviet cars. The resist is applied with wooden blocks – a technique used on silk all over Central Asia and also the Middle East. The craft may have been introduced from neighbouring Iran, where Osku and Kerman are traditional centres.

Ikat
Tajikistan is also a great centre for *abra* dyeing. Many of the ikat *chapan* coats that come onto the Western market and are assumed to have come from Uzbekistan are in fact from Tajikistan. All Central Asian *abra* are warp-faced warp ikats. The warps are always of silk; the weft, depending on the place, either of silk or cotton. The most exciting *abra* was made in Bokhara or Ferghana in Uzbekistan, but much of the more common work was made at Penjikent, Khojent and other centres in Tajikistan.

THE PRESENT
Garments, carpets, rugs, embroidered items and other textile goods form a substantial part of the national economy of Tajikistan, one of the poorest countries in Central Asia, particularly following the civil war of 1992 to 1997. Local materials – cotton, silk, wool and leather – are used locally, and cotton is in addition a major export. Many textile-manufacturing plants in the region have been modernized using money from foreign investors, especially Americans, South Koreans and Italians. It is to be hoped that these will continue to produce the spun and woven products for which the country has long been known, and it is to be hoped that the lowlands of Tajikistan will continue to be planted with cotton and mulberry trees for some time to come.

Kyrgyzstan

The Kyrgyz, like the neighbouring Kazakhs, are of mixed but predominantly East Asian stock. Traditionally horsemen and herders of the steppe and hills, until recent times they lived in yurts. The pastoral nomads take their flocks to pasture in the high mountains in the summer and to the lowland valleys during the winter. Their livestock consists of Bactrian camels, horses, yaks, cows and sheep. Kyrgyz are to be found not only in modern Kyrgyzstan, whose borders were drawn up by the Soviets in the 1930s, but also in Afghanistan, Tajikistan, Ferghana Valley in Uzbekistan, as far north as Tuva in Siberia and east into Chinese Xinjiang. The Kyrgyz textiles most unaffected by the outside world were those of the Wakhan panhandle in Afghanistan. The Afghan Kyrgyz, driven from their homeland into Pakistan by the Russian invasion of 1979, have now been resettled in Turkey, and their magnificent embroidered felt textiles are a thing of the past.

The Kyrgyz are relatively late converts to Islam; though it was introduced as early as the eighth century AD, intense exposure did not occur until the seventeenth century. Islamic influence is today comparatively strong among the southern Kyrgyz. Local men wear skullcaps, observing the Muslim custom that the head is the part of the body closest to God and must stay protected and covered. The Kyrgyz man's cap, or *kalpak*, is the only item made of felt that is still worn today.

COSTUMES

Men's and Women's Dress

Historically, Kyrgyz clothing was made of leather, fur and wool. Cotton and silk textiles were considered luxuries and bought in from outsiders. Leather-on-leather appliqué was once practised among the northern Kyrgyz. *Yalandravon*, a brightly coloured, ikat-dyed, striped cotton produced in Khojent (Tajikistan), was particularly popular used as either a headscarf or a girdle. At least until the end of the nineteenth century, women would weave narrow widths of cloth in wool on a ground-loom using a single heddle with the warp suspended from a tripod. This fabric – of a maximum 14 inches (35 cm) wide – was used to make up men's and women's clothing. A marked difference in styles can be noted, especially for women, between the north and south of the country. Styles from the north tend to be more austere and to be influenced by the Kazakhs and inhabitants of southern Siberia. In the south, the more highly decorative fashions of the neighbouring Uzbeks and Tajiks are reflected. In the north, the bride dons a white veil when riding from her parents' house to the home of her prospective in-laws. In the south, the bride wears an embroidered silk veil covering her whole face throughout the wedding ceremony. Women of both north and south wear a tunic dress over baggy drawstring trousers. They also wear an embroidered apron, or *beldermichi*, often of black velvet edged with fur. This apron, though part of the dowry, is a mark of motherhood.

ABOVE
Tush kyiz, embroidered arch decorating the far interior wall of a yurt.

TECHNIQUES

Embroidery

Kyrgyz women make large 'pi'-shaped hangings of Chinese-influenced designs in silk chain stitch on an imported black velvet ground. These are used in the yurt, or *ger*, to cover or frame piles of bedding when they are not in use. Square hangings with sparsely embroidered, vegetal-like motifs scattered across a black or red ground are hung up in the yurt. Nick Fielding, an expert on the Kyrgyz, states that some of these motifs are known as 'horseshoes'. The Kyrgyz name for the square hangings is *ayak kap*, which prosaically translates as 'tool box'. The hangings correspond to the Uzbek *oinakhalta*. Like the Uzbeks, the Kyrgyz embroider envelope-shaped bags that are also used as hangings. Of additional note is the *ashkana chij*, a screen woven from sedge and dyed wool wrapped into a decorative pattern and used to fence off the kitchen area within the yurt.

Many Kyrgyz textiles are made of felt, and much embroidery is carried out on the felt, often using asymmetric designs in wool. The northern Kyrgyz especially also embroider on buckskin, and pride of place goes to the men's buckskin trousers known as *samya sam*.

The masterpiece of southern Kyrgyz embroidery is the *chach kep*, the embroidered cap that has earflaps and a long, relatively narrow tailpiece that covers a married woman's twin braids. The top of the cap is not sewn up; it is simply a cylinder of cotton drawn together at the top and tied up with white cotton thread. The earflaps are embroidered in silk in diamond shapes, and the tailpiece is also closely embroidered. Raspberry and black are the dominant colours. The *chach kep* is further decorated with mother-of-pearl ornaments, pearls, coral and a variety of circular pendants. The whole is covered with an enormous white cotton turban called an *ileki*. The northern *chach kep* is of the same shape, but much more sparsely embroidered, with floral motifs in silk that are vaguely reminiscent of some *suzani* from the mountain Tajiks. Russian anthropologist Klavdiya Antipina states that the embroidery on southern *chach kep* was often so fine that it could take up to one and a half months to complete.

TOP
Man's felt hat.

CENTRE
Embroidery on leather.

RIGHT
Embroidered leather pot-holder.

THE PRESENT

Kyrgyz women still produce a wide range of textiles, mostly out of felted sheep's wool, though traditional patterns are nowadays being adapted to suit tourist and export markets. Hand-made felted and stitched floor coverings, known as *shyrdak*, are still made for yurts and dwellings. *Tush kyiz* – large, colourful, ornately embroidered wall hangings, traditionally made to commemorate marriage – are a longstanding tradition, but are seldom, if at all, produced now. The colours and designs, which include flowers, plants, stylized horns, animals and emblems of Kyrgyzstan, symbolize local customs and rural life.

LEFT
Chach kep, women's embroidered caps.

BELOW
Embroidered bedding cloth.

Afghanistan

The mountains that dominate the landlocked country of Afghanistan are known as the Hindu Kush, which literally means 'Hindu killer', since it was here that the Hindu slaves brought back by the raids of Mahmud of Ghazni and his ilk in the early centuries of the second millennium were worked to death in the fabled lapis lazuli mines of Badakhshan. A harsh land of mountain and desert, prone to periodic outbreaks of violence, Afghanistan has bred tough peoples of great independence of mind, who have rarely if ever submitted to a foreign conqueror for any appreciable length of time.

The majority of the population, and the traditionally dominant race, are the Pushtun (sometimes spelled and pronounced 'Pukhtun'). They live in the south and the east of the country, and can also be found in the tribal areas and North West Frontier Province of Pakistan. To the west and in the mountains of the northeast are people who speak Dari, a dialect of Farsi, and are generally known as Tajiks. To the north of the Hindu Kush lie the plains leading down to the Amu Darya river, which are inhabited by Uzbeks and Turkmen, true Central Asian peoples, some of whom are relatively recent incomers, refugees from the Bolshevik Revolution from 1917 onwards. All of these are followers of the Sunni branch of Islam, except for some of the Tajiks of Badakhshan who are Ismailis (followers of the Aga Khan). In the central mountains, the Hazarajat, live the Hazara, Mongoloid people reputed to be the descendants of Genghis Khan's hordes. They are Shia, and traditionally at the bottom of the social pile. For all that, Hazara women are the most skilled embroiderers in Afghanistan, which for a nation famed for its embroidery is quite an accolade.

TECHNIQUES

Domestic Embroidery

The Afghans are, for the most part, nomads and peasants. The greater part of the land is arid mountain and desert, with the latter, in times of rain, forming the nomads' traditional grazing grounds. What arable land there is, is not very fertile. So for nomad and peasantwoman alike, although they work very hard, there are long periods when they have time on their hands. This fact, combined with – for cultural and religious reasons – the strict division between the sexes, and the varying degrees of seclusion to which women are subjected, means that a great deal of a female's time is taken up with sewing. Women are largely illiterate and have no schooling, except perhaps the tuition they receive in embroidery as young girls. Each district or tribe has its own embroidery style, which is passed down largely unchanged from mother to daughter.

Most Afghans are poor and do not have large houses, if they have houses at all. Consequently, most embroidered items are on a small scale. It is rare to find embroidered hangings with the stature of Central Asian *suzani*. An Afghan woman

ABOVE
Pit-loom weaver of Herat.

OPPOSITE
Turkmen or Uzbek patchwork from northern Aghanistan.

will embroider dress-fronts, cuffs, hems and pockets. Purses are embroidered and given by the would-be bride to her betrothed and his friends as proof of her skill. Belts, rifle-straps and covers, as well as horse- and camel trappings, are also embroidered gifts from the bride to the groom. Cushions are made, and in the Uzbek north betasselled hangings known as *popet* and befringed *saigosha* (V-shaped hangings) are embroidered in silk cross stitch in geometric or floral designs to decorate piles of quilts when these are not in use.

Professional and Semi-Professional Embroidery
The southern city of Kandahar has always been famed for its embroidery. Kandahar is nothing if not hot, and Kandahari clothing is therefore designed for coolness. The men wear baggy *salwar* (trousers), a light cotton shirt with a slit opening to one side of the chest, and an enormous turban. Panels are either embroidered by the women of the family or, more often, are bought-in professional work from the bazaar. The embroidery is fine counted threadwork in satin stitch. The thread in the past would have been silk, but is now almost always synthetic. The whole of the chest panel, which reaches down to waist level, is covered with angular floral motifs that leave very little of the ground showing. The embroidery thread is usually light-coloured against a light-coloured ground, which gives a very subtle effect. Nowadays, some of this work is done on the very sophisticated sewing machines that have recently become available.

Braiding and Other Accoutrements
Kabul was famous for its velvet garments decorated with couched metallic braid. Hazara tailors made waistcoats with large interior pockets for both male and female nomads, most of whose garments otherwise lacked pockets. Ornate wedding dresses and jackets were made in a similar style for both settled and nomad brides and bridegrooms. Both types of garment, but especially the dresses, have a very martial effect, which is not surprising, as the makers were military tailors who worked outside the artillery barracks. The dresses are always known as 'Topkhana dresses', Topkhana being the Persian term for 'fort, or place of the artillery'.

Weaving
Afghanistan, in general, was famed for its weaving and dyeing. Kabul was a noted centre for indigo dyeing, and a kind of thin purple silk fabric much used as dress material was woven both here and at Herat (the southern Punjabi city of Multan also exported this silk to Afghanistan). Herat still resounds to the clack of the pit-loom, a sound long absent from Kabul. Headscarves for men are the main products of Herat's pit-looms today, a speciality being light silk shawls with each face of contrasting colours. In Jellalabad were woven the dramatic striped silk and cotton shawls of the Hazar-Booz nomads, who in days of yore used to bring down woven rugs from north Afghanistan to the plains of British India, where they would buy guns which they would smuggle up through the Khyber

Pass under the noses of the frontier guards of the Raj. Turkmen women from around Balkh, meanwhile, are famous for weaving narrow lengths of silk in the characteristic Turkmen red with yellow borders. These are used for dressmaking and for scarves.

Ikat, Tie-Dye and Batik

North Afghanistan, with its predominantly Uzbek and Turkmen population, has many of the crafts of Central Asia. *Abra* (ikat) is made in Akcha, near the Amu Darya river, as are tie-dyed silk scarves. *Abra* was previously woven in silk, but for many years production has been in rayon using chemical dyes. The tie and dye is roughly done in vivid chemical colours, but to great visual effect. One of the specialities of Akcha is the block printing in black of thinly outlined patterns over the tie-dye. Tie-dye work was also done at nearby Andkhui.

OPPOSITE
Woven Hazar-Booz eating cloth.

ABOVE LEFT
Uzbek yurt hanging of tasselled netting suspended from a warp-faced panel.

ABOVE CENTRE
Baluch netted bag, southern Afghanistan.

ABOVE RIGHT
Silk double-weave shawl, Herat.

RIGHT
Tie-dyed silk shawl, made in Andkhui or Akcha.

AFGHANISTAN **221**

'Hunting Cloths'

One of the most fascinating groups of textiles made in Afghanistan are the *chireh*, or 'hunting cloths', of Herat. The basic design is drawn out in ballpoint by the last surviving practitioner and his family, who live near Gohar Shad's mosque in Herat. The motifs are shaded in using a tight wad of old rag dipped in black, yellow, red and green inks. Mainly they depict leopards wrestling with snakes, quails, rabbits and male lions, though unshaven men with long knives and shotguns shooting small birds are sometimes featured. According to French scholar Pierre Centlivres, who in the 1960s did research into hunting costume in northern Afghanistan, there was a tradition of hunters dressing up in painted costume that imitated the animal they were stalking. Perhaps the 'hunting cloths' of Herat lie within the same tradition.

OPPOSITE
Painted 'hunting cloth' from Herat, with typical design of a leopard and snake with fighting quails.

RIGHT AND BELOW
Printed and painted 'hunting cloths' from Herat, featuring hunters and scenes from the hunt.

222 CENTRAL ASIA

Afghanistan 223

ABOVE LEFT, ABOVE RIGHT
AND BELOW LEFT
Hazara embroidered teapot covers.

LEFT AND BELOW RIGHT
Hazara prayer cloths.

224 CENTRAL ASIA

ABOVE
Velvet 'Topkhana' wedding dress, embellished with couched metallic braid, Kabul.

BELOW
Hazara prayer cloth.

PEOPLES

The Hazara

The Hazara embroider in a variety of styles, depending on which part of the Hazarajat they inhabit. In some places they embroider in surface satin stitch in a manner reminiscent of Sindh. In other places they embroider teapot covers depicting a full tea service – teapot, cups, saucers and all (this is an anomaly, since they themselves drink tea from bowls and have only ever seen pictures of cups and saucers). The Hazara around the city of Ghazni embroider in two styles: they make purses with closely stitched, multicoloured, diamond patterns in which they keep the holy soil brought back by pilgrims from the sacred Shia shrine of Karbala in Iraq, and they also embroider in brightly coloured satin stitch depictions of the same shrine onto square white cotton kerchiefs to be used as prayer cloths for men. In a variant of the latter style, Hazara women embroider face-veils for their wedding, which are rectangular pieces of white cotton fabric attached by being tied on with a headband.

The Pushtun

Some of the most prolific embroiderers are the Pushtun nomads of the south. The Katawaz group embroider in chain stitch in orange, green or purple silk. As well as dress facings, they embroider rectangular tray and teapot covers, fringed with blue beads to ward off the evil eye. The Katawaz are wealthy not only from their abundant flocks but also from the fact that many of their men go to Delhi and other cities in India to practise the profession of extortionate money-lending. Their wealth is reflected in the abundance of their embroidery. The Haruti, another Pushtun nomad group, embroider in the same style, but with markedly finer stitches. Women of both groups adorn their dresses with beadwork made up of Bohemian beads.

One of Afghanistan's most memorable embroidery styles is from the environs of Mukur, a small town between Ghazni and Kandahar. Panels for the sleeves and front of the young Mukur bridegroom's wedding smock are embroidered in green, fawn or wine-coloured silk on a white cotton ground. Worked in open chain stitch, the dramatic, swirling, impressionistic patterns incorporate suitably disguised pre-Islamic symbols denoting fertility. A myriad of cockerels' heads are supposed to be indicative of the many sons to come. Likewise indicative of fertility are the women's marriage shawls of the Pushtun nomads from the Kayser area northeast of Herat. A line of

226 CENTRAL ASIA

OPPOSITE TOP LEFT
Dress cuff, eastern Afghanistan.

OPPOSITE TOP RIGHT
Pushtun smock panel, Mukur.

OPPOSITE CENTRE LEFT
Pushtun bridegrooms' purses, southern Afghanistan.

OPPOSITE BELOW LEFT
Pushtun woman's embroidered legging.

OPPOSITE BELOW RIGHT
Pushtun Koochi hook-embroidered silk shawl, possibly worked in Multan.

RIGHT AND BELOW RIGHT
Haruti nomad teapot covers, southern Afghanistan.

ABOVE
Pushtun sleeve, Mukur.

BELOW
Pushtun gun-cover, southern Afghanistan.

BELOW RIGHT
Bridegroom's smock panels, Mukur.

AFGHANISTAN 227

ABOVE
Pushtun *rumal*, eastern Afghanistan.

LEFT
Pushtun bridegroom's smock panels, Mukur

red diamonds in appliqué or embroidery runs vertically down the back of the shawl, often bordered by applied male fertility symbols in cast metal.

The harsh mountains bordering Pakistan shelter many other groups with a strong embroidery tradition. Some, like the Mangali, are Pushtun; others are not. The Mangalis of Terri Mangal are semi-nomadic herders who traditionally wandered freely across a frontier they did not recognize. Mangali women wear loose-fitting smocks in black cotton embroidered in very tight stitchery in raspberry-coloured silk around the cuffs and hems and more heavily around the neckline and pockets. The embroidery, though floral in design, looks as though it has been influenced by British military embroidery, once prevalent along the frontier. Underneath their dresses, the women wear very narrow leggings with extremely hard-wearing embroidered cuffs. The leggings are designed to concertina down in folds over the women's calves. Mangali bridegrooms, meanwhile, wear a tight-fitting coat adorned with the same kind of embroidery around the vents of the jacket, with the addition of metallic braid and mirrors positioned around the rest of the garment.

The Pashai

The Pashai are a semi-nomadic shepherd group found north of Jellalabad up into Nuristan. The men wear white cotton *kurta* (loose shirts), beautifully quilted in fine black stitchery. The women wear a similarly shaped garment, but with less quilting and with embroidery along the neckline, cuffs and shoulders, and lines of vertical stitchery at the back. Pashai women's *kurta* can be of indigo blue cotton or can show a rough block print on a blue ground, most likely signifying Indian origin. The most recent *kurta* are nearly all on white or black material. The harshly coloured yellow thread for the embroidery on recent *kurta* is synthetic. Pashai women wear a variant of the Mangali women's leggings, but without the tightly embroidered cuffs.

TOP
Nomad woman's shawl, Kayser district, northeastern Afghanistan.

ABOVE
Pashai man's smock, Nuristan.

RIGHT
Pashai woman's dress, Nuristan.

The Lakhai

The women of the Lakhai tribe of northern Afghanistan – a branch of Uzbeks – create extremely vivid embroidered textiles. They are particularly renowned for their *ilgitsh* (square or shield-shaped bags worked in silk on imported baize), hats, purses and V-shaped hangings known as *segusha* (see the Uzbekistan section of this book; p. 190). Variants of these textiles are also made by other Afghan Uzbeks.

The Tajiks

Both Uzbek and Tajik women (the Persian-speaking mountain-dwellers) embroider curtains and prayer cloths with floral motifs, using couching stitches in a manner reminiscent of the *suzani* work of Central Asia. Often the styles used by the Tajiks within Afghanistan are indistinguishable from those of their cousins across the Amu Darya river in Tajikistan.

ABOVE LEFT
Lakhai square.

ABOVE RIGHT
Uzbek quilt pile decoration.

ABOVE
Hazar-Booz silk embroidered border.

RIGHT
Tajik embroidered prayer cloth.

230 CENTRAL ASIA

ABOVE LEFT
Waistcoat, possibly from Nuristan.

ABOVE RIGHT
Koochi embroidered sleeve panels.

LEFT
Koochi beaded dress, southern Afghanistan.

BELOW LEFT
Katawaz nomad dress of Indian brocade.

THE PRESENT

Sadly, Afghanistan is still war-torn, particularly in the south – far from ideal conditions for making the hand-worked textiles for which the country is famous. The nomads are now mainly settled in mud villages and no longer wander with their flocks; no more can the nomadic Pushtun groups known as Koochis (or Powindah) be seen wending their way between southern Afghanistan and Pakistan, the women driving their donkeys with a swirl of brightly coloured skirt amid the dust. Now there are landmines everywhere, and the women who were formerly nomads but are now settled no longer need to reinforce their dresses with tightly embroidered panels. In parts of the country, fortunately, it remains impossible to separate an Afghan woman from her needle, and hand-weaving has revived. As long as there are weddings and births to be celebrated, the tradition of domestic embroidery will flourish and beautiful embroidered items will still be made.

AFGHANISTAN

The Mughal World

India

The modern state of India contains one of the largest Muslim populations in the world – well over one hundred million spread over the whole country. They are descended from invaders, their spouses and converts, beginning with the first Islamic incursion in the eleventh century by the Afghans Mahmud of Ghazni and Muhammad of Ghor. Turkic and Afghan rulers followed these two conquerors over the next three centuries – a period that culminated in the glorious Mughal empire founded in 1526 by the Timurid Babur and lasting till the deposition of the last Mughal, Bahadhur Zafar Shah II, in 1858. The word 'Mughal' derives from 'Mongol', recalling the original Timurid homeland in the Central Asian steppes. It was these early, Persianized Mughals who brought their customs to India and formed the basis for the Indo-Persian culture that dominated during the golden age of empire.

Islam has had a profound effect on all aspects of Indian culture. While Muslims were never able to convert the vast Hindu majority, Islamic codes of dress and modesty were adopted in many of the courts, and particularly in the cities under direct Muslim rule. Imported skills were added to the existing indigenous mastery of the arts of weaving fine cotton fabric and colour-fast dyeing. Many textile arts became the prerogative of Muslim workers, due either to the immigration of artisans from the Arab, Persian and Turkish worlds or to the conversion of low-caste Hindu workers who wished to improve their social status and identify with their Muslim patrons. To this day, professional textile practitioners – be they, weavers, block-printers or tie-dyers – are very likely to be Muslims. Major weaving centres of long standing are to be found all over India – in Gujarat and across the Gangetic plain from Delhi to Bengal; across central India, particularly the Deccan plateau; and in the Dravidian south.

TECHNIQUES
Brocade Weaving

Ahmedabad in the Gulf of Cambay, and the port of Surat to the south, were famous as silk and metal-thread brocade-weaving towns. Ahmedabad was the principal city for *kinkhab* brocade weaving until a great fire broke out there at the beginning of the fifteenth century. *Kinkhab* brocade often featured rows of evenly spaced metal-thread motifs of flowers, or even human figures, against a plain single-coloured silk ground. The courtly Mughal ideal of beauty that was followed was typified by rows of floral elements, in which each individual element could stand alone, and sometimes did. The writer and scholar Robert Skelton has attributed this taste to the European botanical

PAGES 232–233
Jamawar tapestry-weave 'moon' shawl, Kashmir, India; Molesalaam appliqué, Kathiawar, India; *amli* needlework shawl, Kashmir, India, 1860s; Baluchi embroidered *pashk* dress, Pakistan.

ABOVE
Mutva woman displaying a patchwork quilt, Banni Kutch.

OPPOSITE
Embroidered woollen tablecloth, Kashmir.

LEFT
Brocade shawl, Benares.

ABOVE
Kinkhab brocade cover, Ahmedabad.

BELOW
Brocade 'calligraphy' shawl, Benares.

drawings that were in vogue in seventeenth-century India (this style was to influence the silk textiles of Safavid Persia: in previous centuries the influence had been the other way round, with the Persians affecting the styles of Indian textiles). The acme of brocade weaving under the Mughals was the *patka* (sash) worn by noblemen and noblewomen. The sash was bound two or three times around the waist, then usually tied at the front so that the brocaded ends hung down in such a way that their floral motifs were clearly visible. This type of weaving survives in the brocaded saris of Paithan in central India. By the end of the eighteenth century, the main centre of brocade weaving had become Benares, under British auspices. In the nineteenth century, a style evolved that showed intricate floral and vegetal patterns, influenced by European tastes. That style persists to this day.

Mashru Weaving

Mashru – a warp-faced silk and cotton fabric, usually striped but sometimes with arrow-head ikat details – was woven in many places in India. Gujarat was a major centre, though it is

236 THE MUGHAL WORLD

ABOVE
Jamawar tapestry-weave 'moon' shawl, Kashmir.

BELOW
Detail of *jamawar* tapestry-weave shawl, Kashmir.

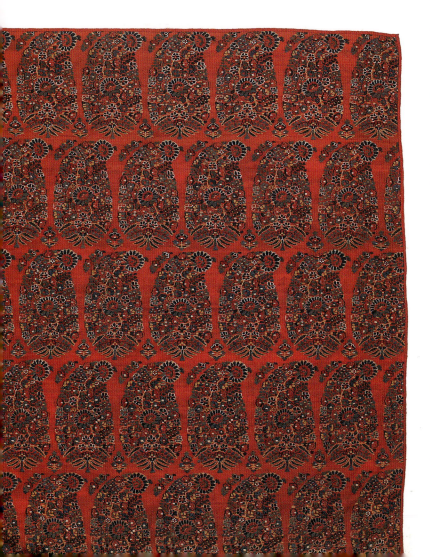

thought that the Gujarati style was much influenced through trade by the *mashru* of Turkey and Syria: they are certainly very similar. The fabric was also woven in the south at such centres as Hyderabad and Thanjavur, and is still woven today near Mandvi in Kutch. *Mashru* means 'permitted' in Arabic. According to one of the hadiths, an orthodox Muslim male is not permitted to wear silk next to the skin. *Mashru*, however, has a cotton weft, so if the fabric is worn with the silk-warped face out, the cotton lies next to the skin and the fabric is permissible.

Muslin Weaving

Muslin was one of the first materials that made India famous in the West. It was woven in Dacca and its environs in East Bengal from the long-staple cotton found in a specific area by the banks of the River Meghna (this territory is in present-day Bangladesh, so the development of the industry is covered in the Bangladesh section; see p. 260). Muslin was known by a variety of names, the most common being 'mal-mal'. The very finest were known by such sobriquets as 'woven air', 'crystal spring' and 'morning dew'. This kind of fabric was the premier export to Europe until over-production, a change in fashion and the development of machine-woven textiles in Europe ruined the Bengali weavers and threw Bengal into what was to be centuries of poverty. Other muslin-weaving centres were Lucknow and Benares in modern Uttar Pradesh. They, like Bengal, were famous for their figured muslins.

Kashmir Shawl Weaving

The beautiful Vale of Kashmir is justly famed for its textiles, above all for the Kashmiri shawl. Going back to the fifteenth century, skilled weavers were reputed to have been brought from Turkestan to the valley, where the relative geographical isolation ensured that the concentration of skilled workers could be built up and maintained. The valley's location at the crossroads of some of Asia's great trade routes also gave it access to markets for its textile products.

The classic Kashmir shawl – known as a *jamawar* – was woven out of pashmina wool derived from the fleece of *Capra hircus*, a Central Asian mountain goat. This wool was always imported from Tibet or Xinjiang and was never produced in Kashmir itself. There were two grades of pashmina, the finest coming from goats in the wild. The pattern on the shawls was formed from the weft threads alone, woven in the twill-tapestry technique. Making a shawl in this manner was a long,

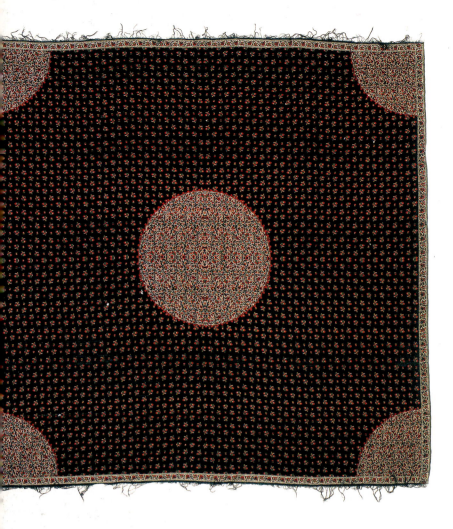

LEFT
Jamawar tapestry-weave 'moon' shawl, Kashmir.

ABOVE
Man's *jamawar* tapestry-weave robe, or *angarkha*, Kashmir.

OPPOSITE
Details of *jamawar* tapestry-weave shawls, Kashmir.

slow process. From the beginning of the nineteenth century, as designs became more complex, production was split between two or more looms. The woven pieces were then finely sewn together, the joins being virtually invisible.

Exports of Kashmirs created a fashion market in Europe. In the late eighteenth century, attempts were made in England and then in Scotland to imitate the shawls, and by 1808 weaving had begun in Paisley. Production also soon started in Nîmes, Lyons and Alsace in France. The wearing of both genuine and imitation Kashmir shawls quickly became highly fashionable. From 1818, the jacquard loom greatly simplified the weaving of complicated designs in Britain and France, and this in turn influenced the design of shawls in Kashmir. European, particularly French, demand led to an expansion in production, but this expansion turned out to be a prelude to the collapse of the industry. Kashmir shawls could no longer compete in quality with the best Paisley and Lyons shawls, and were often outmoded and expensive by the time they arrived in the West. In any case, they had by now lost their sense of exclusivity. In the end, the Franco-Prussian war of 1870 saw the complete demise of French demand.

It is misleading, however, to think of Kashmir shawls only in the Indo/European context. Persia and the Ottoman empire were vast, rich markets, and even today it is not uncommon to come across fragments of eighteenth-century Kashmiri *jamawar* in the Iranian bazaars of Isfahan, Tehran and Yazd. Striped shawls were specially made for both empires and were often used rolled up as men's cummerbunds. In Damascus, Kashmiri shawls for this purpose were known as *angami*, meaning 'Persian' in Arabic, and reflecting the country through which they were imported (also encompassing the late nineteenth-century copies made in Kerman in southeast Iran). Other strong markets for Kashmiri shawls were to be found in Azerbaijan and southern Russia.

Kashmir still produces many beautiful textiles today, though most now have a uniformity of style that inevitably comes with catering to the mass market. The shawls are still made all over the valley, but are now patterned by embroidery rather than weaving, though weaving has been revived at Basohli in Jammu Province. Pashmina shawl manufacturers cut down on import costs by using the hair of goats reared in the high, arid Changthang region of Ladakh.

Embroidery

It was initially the Muslims who were famed for their needlework and tailoring, the Hindus traditionally favouring draped, uncut and untailored fabric (of course over the centuries, due to Muslim and later European influence, tailored clothes have become *de rigueur*, especially for men). One of the most notable forms of needlework was the *chikan-kari*, or *chikan*, work of Lucknow. This is a kind of whitework, thought to have originated in Bengal and to have been practised in Dacca and Calcutta. The *jamdani* weaving of Dacca must have been influential (see 'Bangladesh', p. 260); so too eighteenth-century European whitework. The pattern of predominantly floral designs is stitched using untwisted white cotton or silk (and now rayon) on the surface of the fabric. The textile historian Sheila Paine has observed that there are six basic stitches, which are used in combination with a series of stitches for embossing flowers and leaves. At the beginning of the twentieth century, the quality of *chikan* work suffered a catastrophic decline, due to the loss of court patronage. The industry then became orientated towards the mass market. Now all the base fabric is mill-made, and cotton/polyester mixes and thin silk are used in addition to cotton. While there are still embroiderers who work to commission, the vast majority of the work remains cheap and rough, and is used to decorate the *salwar kameez* and other garments that are exported abroad or sold inexpensively in bazaars all over India.

At the beginning of the nineteenth century, the *amli* (needlework) shawl was introduced into Kashmir (embroiderers here, like weavers, were always male). The *amli* was a very fair imitation of the *jamawar* loom-woven shawl, but could be made more cost-effectively. Maps of Srinagar were a favourite design, and shawls embroidered with human figures were also very popular. After the collapse of the Kashmir shawl industry, needleworkers turned to the embroidery of tablecloths, coverlets and other domestic items. While shawls are still embroidered with a needle, much of the sewing done in the Kashmir valley today is *ari* (hook) work.

Appliqué

Appliqué is generally a domestic craft in India, and is often associated with castes that have a military background, such as the Rajputs. The Molesalaam, a Muslim land-owning caste of Saurashtra, are famous for their appliquéd friezes and canopies with dramatically drawn figurative work.

OPPOSITE ABOVE
1860s *amli* needlework shawl, Kashmir.

OPPOSITE CENTRE
Embroidered woollen jacket, Kashmir.

OPPOSITE BELOW
Memon woman's embroidered *aba*, Kutch.

ABOVE LEFT
Memon woman's embroidered *aba*, Kutch.

ABOVE
Embroidered *aba*, Kutch.

LEFT
Shawl embroidered in wild silk for the Haj pilgrimage market, Calcutta.

INDIA

OPPOSITE
Detail of a Molesalaam appliqué, Kathiawar.

ABOVE AND BELOW
Metal-thread-embroidered velvet covers, northern India.

Metal-Thread Embroidery

Zardozi (from the Persian *zar*, meaning 'gold', and *dozi*, meaning 'embroidery') is reputed to have originated in Persia and been brought to India by the Mughals. Originally, these textiles of great cost – made with pure silver and gold threads, pearls and precious stones – were used for royal regalia, ceremonial costumes, palace furnishings and religious purposes. Muslim men still practise metal-thread embroidery all over India, but particularly in the northern cities of Delhi, Agra, Gwalior, Lucknow and Calcutta. Traditionally they produced garments, hangings (often in the Persian style), furnishings and animal trappings for the courts, whether the central Mughal courts at Delhi, Lahore and Agra or the regional courts. In the second half of the nineteenth century, they worked for the well-to-do, including the dominant English. In more recent times, they have often been reduced to producing the umbrellas and horse-trappings that are hired out for the urban wedding processions that take place at the end of winter. As they have always done, the *zari* workers tend to work on velvet of local or imported manufacture, though heavy silk and brocade are also used.

The material to be embroidered is stretched out on a *karchob* (frame). Two men usually work on the same piece at the same time. Metal-thread purls are made from tightly wound wires coiled into springs with smooth, rough or facetted surfaces. The purls are couched onto the fabric, or small sections are cut and applied like beads. *Zari* work is often combined with *ari* chain stitch, or *badla* work, in which flat metal thread is drawn through the fabric, knotted at the back and then smoothed off. Today there are thousands of workers involved in the industry, with a high turnover due to the strain on eyesight.

Nowadays Surat produces nearly all India's *zari* metal thread for brocading and embroidery, as well as the thin silver wire used for weaving. In Mughal times, Surat was the principal port for Haj pilgrims making their way to Mecca. These pilgrims provided the market for *zari*-work weaves and embroidery. The industry declined in the nineteenth century, due to competition from French machine-made metal thread. It revived in the 1920s, then lost some of its main markets in Pakistan in 1947, but today it has recovered through partial mechanization and through the introduction of artificial *zari* thread, consisting of copper wire silver-gilded by electrolysis, thus being much less prone to tarnishing.

Block Printing

Cotton is the fabric most associated with India, and brightly coloured, floral-patterned block prints are the most common of all Indian textiles. The age-old indigenous mastery of dyeing and mordanting is utilized to produce cheap but beautiful furnishings, bedding, cloths and shawls that are printed using wooden blocks carved out of close-grained hard wood such as shisham. The workers are mostly though not exclusively Muslim males, and their ancient craft is practised all over India though concentrated in the north, particularly in Gujarat and Rajasthan. Gujarat, except in times of severe drought, has always been a prosperous state, with an extensive coastline and historic trading links with the Middle East, Africa and Southeast Asia. Its economy has long been highly dependent on the manufacturing of cotton textiles. Gujarati block-printed cottons have been excavated from the middens of Fostat, Old Cairo, and dated to the fourteenth century. Until very recently, there was also a section of the old city of Ahmedabad dedicated to the production of block prints for overseas markets, including Ethiopia and the Yemen. Cloth from Palmyra has been excavated that has exactly the same patterns as are used today at Balotra and Jodhpur in Rajasthan. Not only was the cloth exported from India, but also the workers themselves. There were Indian block-printers in Isfahan from the Persian Shah Abbas's time, and they were also to be found in the trading towns of Sumatra in the nineteenth and early twentieth centuries, applying patterns to order to the blank fields of the wax-resist *sembagi* chintz cloths that had been imported from the Coromandel coast. Wooden blocks are used to apply dye directly, but also to apply mordants and resists, be they wax or mud.

ABOVE
Nineteenth-century block-printed shawl, Deccan.

OPPOSITE
Silk *bandhani* with *badla* (metallic-strip) work, Kutch.

LEFT
Block-printed Shia shrine cover, Ahmedabad.

ABOVE
Contemporary embroidered *kurta*, Srinagar, Kashmir.

Tie-Dye

The term *bandhani* refers both to the technique of tie and dye and to the finished cloth. Indeed, the English name for a spotted handkerchief, 'bandanna', derives directly from this word. Rajasthan and Gujarat are famed for their prolific production of *bandhani*. When simply tied, these textiles are inexpensive and constitute one of the cheapest ways for women of poorer communities to dress in a colourful fashion. When tied with many delicate knots, especially in silk or fine cotton, they become the preserve of the richer classes, as the price rises steeply. The finest work of all is reserved for the weddings of the daughters of the Muslim Khatri tie-dyeing families themselves. Red on a black ground are the favoured colours. Fine work is done in Gujarat. Kutch has many workshops, but the biggest are found in Saurashtra, especially at Jamnagar, where the water is reputed to bring out the deepest red. The craft is also widely practised in Rajasthan, especially at Bikaner and Sikar, though many of the colours there are spot-dyed rather than the result of submersion in a dye bath.

THE PRESENT

India is still the heartland of hand-made textiles, and its artisans' mastery of the arts of weaving, dyeing and all the associated skills has been retained. Notwithstanding the profound economic and concomitant social changes of recent decades, there is still a strong demand for traditionally made textiles in town and country alike. Inhabitants, particularly in the rural areas, still wish to distinguish themselves in matters of caste, sex and social standing, and the most important visual indicator is mode of dress. Traditionally made articles of clothing – turbans, shawls, trousers or waist-cloths, skirts or saris – carry a social and religious symbolism. They also often bear the surface decoration at which Indian textile workers excel, be it woven, embroidered, tie-dyed, printed or batiked. Even if the domestic market ever shows a tendency to wane, the export market can take up the slack. Textile workers – many of whom are Muslim – have a valued place in the craft hierarchy, and that gives them a certain economic security in often volatile times.

Pakistan

The state of Pakistan was founded in 1947. It was made up of the Muslim-majority provinces of British India – that is, Sindh, Baluchistan, North West Frontier, West Punjab and East Bengal. After the war of independence in 1971, East Bengal (by then known as East Pakistan) seceded to form the state of Bangladesh.

Pakistan produces some of the most beautiful textiles of the South Asian sub-continent. These are now known and valued as much beyond the nation's borders as within them. The country – socially more conservative and hierarchical than its large Indian neighbour, and less industrialized – still produces textiles specific to the celebration of what might be termed 'change of life' events. Betrothals, marriages, circumcisions, funerals, all require specific items of clothing and accompanying gift-giving, often of a textile nature.

The required clothing is the product of the local weaver, dyer or tailor. Any surface decoration is still usually domestic embroidery applied by a female member of the family, or it may be bought in from a professional male or female embroiderer.

REGIONS

Sindh

The southernmost province of Pakistan, Sindh is an area of ancient Islamic influence (the Arabs conquered it in AD 712), and it is one of the core areas of the sub-continent for the production of fine textiles. The heyday of some of these textiles is, unfortunately, gone. For instance, the double-weave *khes* blankets once woven at Nasarpur, near Hyderabad, and in northern Sindh, are largely things of the past; also no longer worked is the professional embroidery in floss silk on cotton shawls for the European market and on little silk jackets for children. On the other hand, Sindh's traditional caste hierarchy has proved remarkably impervious to social change. Brides-to-be still embroider all manner of costumes and household articles as part of their wedding trousseau, and there is still a strong market for professional embroidery, albeit mostly practised as a cottage industry rather than on a workshop basis.

Punjab

Cotton is an abundant crop in agriculturally rich Punjab and forms one of Pakistan's major export commodities. The mechanized mills at Faisalabad (formerly Llyallpur), 'the Manchester of Pakistan', provide the vast bulk of the material for the province's clothing, but there are also other weaving towns. Among the most important are Multan in the south and Chakwal in the north. Artisans in Multan wove the thin purple silk that was exported up to North West Frontier Province and Afghanistan for use as dress material. Unfortunately, the craft of hand-weaving appears to be on the wane in Punjab.

ABOVE
Sindhi chieftain (seated), wearing a block-printed *ajarakh* shawl.

North West Frontier and Northern Region

The Pushtun province of Pakistan lies north and west of the Indus from Punjab. The textiles of this region have strong links to those of neighbouring Afghanistan. Traditionally, itinerant groups would travel back and forth across a largely unmarked border. Weaving and embroidery have long predominated. Long woven shawls of indigo-dyed cotton with red, crimson or magenta silk borders and ends were woven in Swat, Hazara district around Abbottabad, and Mansera. Shawls in a similar style were also woven for the North West Frontier Province market in the Punjabi market town of Chakwal.

Baluchistan

This vast and sparsely populated province lies at the mouth of the Gulf and borders Afghanistan to the north, Iran to the west and Sindh to the east. Its arid mountain and desert terrain contains an indigenous Baluch or Brahui tribal population, with some itinerant and settled Pushtun groups in the north. Embroidery styles, whether Baluch, Brahui or Pushtun, depend very much upon the geographical position of the group within the province, and very often relate to styles prevalent in neighbouring Afghanistan, Seistan Province in Iran or Sindh. Baluch women wear a characteristic smock-like dress known as a *pashk*, usually tailored from the cheapest dress material available in the local bazaar.

TECHNIQUES

Weaving

Pakistan has many different weaving styles. In Sindh, *farasi* (fine, woollen, geometrically patterned floor coverings) and storage bags are woven by Meher and Baluch groups around Badin. Sindh was also once famous for the weaving of the chequered silk *lunghi* worn as turbans by Maldhari cattle-traders. Thatta was the centre of this industry, and neighbouring Kutch and Rajasthan in India were major markets. These *lunghi* are now only woven in rayon just across the provincial border at Multan in southern Punjab. *Soosi* is another famous Sindhi fabric, once of black striped silk usually on a green ground, now inevitably of rayon, and used to make baggy *salwar* (trousers) for women. Nasarpur is a traditional centre for this work.

The only silk weaving still done in Multan is the weaving of olive-green turbans for the Afghan community resident in Pakistan. These turbans, made of imported Chinese silk yarn,

OPPOSITE
Phulkhari wedding shawl, embroidered in floss silk on cotton, Mansera.

TOP
Baluchi mirrored animal trapping.

ABOVE
Mirrored purses, Sindh.

BELOW
Woven *soosi* silk trousers, Punjab.

TOP LEFT
Waziristan woven shawl, northern Pakistan.

TOP RIGHT
Metal-thread-embroidered *kurta*, Hyderabad, Sindh.

ABOVE
Baluchi embroidered purse.

RIGHT
Silk embroidered *kurta*, Dera Ismail Khan district.

RIGHT
Metal-thread-embroidered *kurta*, northern Punjab.

are known as *mashaddi*, after the Iranian pilgrimage town of Mashad. Chequered double-weave *khes* blankets, almost always in two colours in the Sindhi manner, were also traditional Multani products. Formerly woven by hand, they are now made with a jacquard device on power-looms.

Lahore was once famous for its weaving of shawls in the Kashmiri style. It was also a major silk-weaving centre, though the industry was never large enough to support the cultivation and spinning of silk. Most of the yarn was imported from Central Asia around Bokhara and from northeastern Persia or Bengal. Striped silk fabric akin to Sindhi *soosi*, often in vivid colours, was used as the base material for women's *salwar*. The stripes could be in contrasting colours – yellow with red, or green with pink – or they could be of silver bound thread against a single colour.

At Chakwal in north Punjab, weavers work in silk and cotton, producing shawls and yardage for use in both Punjab and North West Frontier Province. Here were woven the white, or white with a thin lined red check, *lunghi* that in Punjab were worn as men's waist-cloths. The ends were of a wine-coloured silk and were designed to hang down decoratively to the front or the side of the garment. The same *lunghi* were exported to North West Frontier Province, where they could be worn as turbans.

Rectangular shawls were woven in Waziristan on the Afghan border, with striped red, black and yellow silk ends, an indigo-dyed cotton body, and one embroidered edge designed to be turned over to show off as a cowl. These shawls are unrivalled examples of the weaver's art. Women's shawls from other parts of North West Frontier Province are of black cotton with red or red-purple silk woven ends. Occasionally differently coloured lateral stripes, sometimes in an arrow-head formation, are introduced to the borders to give a contrast. Swat Valley and the area around Abbottabad and Mansera in Hazara district were noted centres for this kind of work. Long, narrower *lunghi* in the same style were used by men as turbans and sashes. Little of this kind of weaving is done nowadays, perhaps because of the unavailability of the right kind of silk, or indigo to dye the cotton – or, one suspects, because of the destruction and upheaval that accompanied Partition.

Patti cloth is woven by men from the fine undyed (or dyed brown with walnut husks) wool of local sheep on pit-looms in such centres as Chitral or the nearby village of Mogh, and used for the characteristic *pakol* caps, with their rolled-up brims. There are local variations in the way the brims can be stitched, but the cap is the most distinctive article of male attire and can be found on both sides of the Afghan–Pakistan frontier in the hilly regions bordering the Hindu Kush. The best place to buy a *pakol* is in the meandering little alleys of the famous *topi* (hat) bazaar in the old city of Peshawar. The finest and most expensive are made of the highest-quality *patti* cloth, the cheapest from cut-up discarded coats from Western countries.

Domestic Embroidery

Domestic embroidery for weddings and associated dowries in Sindh is still of a very high standard. All the dowry items are embroidered in floss silk or cotton, almost always embellished with *shisha* mirrorwork and couched threads, often of metal. Patterns are floral or geometric, but rarely figurative, as Sindh is an area of ancient Islamic influence. Most embroidery is worked by women either for themselves or their family, but it is not uncommon for lower-caste women to embroider dowry items for those of a richer caste. The most characteristic of all Sindhi embroideries are the *abocchnai* (wedding shawls) of the Dars and Pali land-owning communities, painstakingly embroidered by Meghwal women who belong to a low leather-working caste.

Pushtun groups in Dera Ismail Khan close to the Afghan border embroider shift-like dresses of cheap silk, envelope-shaped purses and cotton coverlets with areas of vivid, brightly coloured embroidery embellished with mirrors. There is also a healthy tradition of embroidery in the Hazara district in North West Frontier Province to the north of Pakistani Punjab. The style is known as *phulkari* (flower) work, and when no part of the ground cloth is left unembroidered it is known as *bagh* (garden). *Phulkari* are worked in the counted-thread method and always consist of embroidery on cotton cloth known as *khaddar*, hand-woven on pit-looms in relatively narrow strips. Typically, three strips are sewn selvedge to selvedge to make up a shawl. Before 1947, the Sikhs and Hindus of Hazara embroidered *phulkari* in a gorgeous deep gold colour on an apricot ground. However, the Muslims of Hazara have always preferred an indigo or white ground. Worked from the back, motifs are generally floral and geometric. *Takhia* (bolster covers), wedding shawls, *rumal* (square covers), dresses and *lunghi* sashes for a bridegroom are embroidered by the bride for the wedding. Occasionally on the wedding shawls, an area of white-on-white embroidery is worked. Embroidered *rumal* with intricate geometric designs are typical of Swat Valley. In Mansera, white wedding shawls often feature pre-Islamic, anthropomorphic, satyr-like designs on the borders.

The Shinn are semi-nomadic shepherds who live high up at the head of the valleys leading off from the Indus river and the Karakoram highway that runs alongside it. They are not Pushtun but are part of a group of peoples whom nineteenth-century ethnographers named the 'Dards'. Shinn women wear *jumlo*, black dresses with full skirts of multiple godets, with breast and cuffs finely embroidered in silk. The dresses are embellished with lead weights, key chains, zips, bath chains, padlocks and brass buttons. Sections of fine embroidery are rescued from old, worn-out dresses and incorporated into a newer garment. The dresses are worn over black jodhpur-like trousers, with embroidered cuffs usually adorned by a disc made up of lead weights or zips. The woman then covers herself

ABOVE
Baluchi embroidered *pashk*.

BELOW
Silk embroidered coverlet, Dera Ismail Khan district.

252 THE MUGHAL WORLD

with a *chuprai* (shawl), embroidered in red and yellow starburst designs edged with zips. Young Shinn boys wear caps and waistcoats embroidered and adorned in a like manner. Most beautiful of all, however, are the hoods in which mothers carry their babies. Another curiosity are the embroidered gun-butt covers that the young bride embroiders for her husband's Lee-Enfield rifle, for this is a region of constant blood feuds where no man goes out unarmed.

As is the case in Baluchistan, in those parts of North West Frontier Province that lie close to the Afghan border, the textiles and costume of the inhabitants are sometimes difficult to distinguish from those of their Afghan neighbours. Around Kohat, near the frontier with Afghanistan, Khatak women wore smock-like dresses of indigo-dyed cotton, embroidered on the breast with floral motifs and with the edges printed with *roghan* work (printing with a castor or sunflower oil-based gum to which pigment has been added). These dresses were worn with incredibly wide black and red striped cotton *salwar*.

The Ismaili peoples (followers of the Aga Khan) embroider caps, cuffs and dress edgings in stylized floral patterns using cross and tent stitch. Chitral, Gilgit and Hunza are the main centres of this style. In Chitral, *choga* (gowns) of *patti* cloth are often embellished with floral embroidery in a single muted colour on the sleeves and/or chest. Hoods of the same material, embroidered in coloured wool, are used for the babies.

Baluchi women wear their *pashk* over baggy *salwar* and under a large, all-enveloping shawl. The breast section of the dress is finely embroidered, as are the cuffs. An embroidered kangaroo-style pocket is added at waist-level, and sometimes two slits are incorporated on the sleeves near the breast to facilitate breastfeeding with modesty. Each of the different Baluchi groups has a slightly different style and, depending on their geographical position within the province, they relate to their neighbours just across the national or provincial borders. Most of the best 'Baluchi' embroidery used for the *pashk* is, in fact, the product of professional embroidery workshops in Jacobabad in northern Sindh.

LEFT
Embroidered wedding shawl, Hazara district, northern Pakistan.

PAKISTAN

ABOVE
Embroidered dress, Hazara district, northern Pakistan.

OPPOSITE ABOVE LEFT AND RIGHT
Shinn boys' embroidered waistcoats, Kohistan.

OPPOSITE BELOW
Embroidered dress, Kohat, North West Frontier.

PAKISTAN 255

Professional Embroidery

Zardozi metal-thread embroidery in the Muslim north Indian style (see p. 243) is a speciality of Karachi and other major urban centres. In former times, Memon (Muslim merchant-caste) women wore tie-dyed garments from Kutch, embroidered in a special gold-thread technique known as *marori*. In Lahore, professional male embroiderers worked in silk on wool or cotton, and in Mughal times made delicate floor-coverings, known as 'summer carpets', of cotton embroidered with silk in red and green. Sadly, these are all of the past, though male embroiderers specializing in beetle's wing embroidery are still to be found in the back streets of the old city of Multan, one of the very few places in the sub-continent left producing this once-famous Indian craft. The design is first pounced out onto the fabric, which is then stretched out on the frame. The mostly young workers (those still with good eyesight) sew in workshops open to the street to let in the maximum amount of light.

ABOVE
Shinn baby-carrying hood, Kohistan.

RIGHT
Embroidered wedding shawl, Hazara district, northern Pakistan.

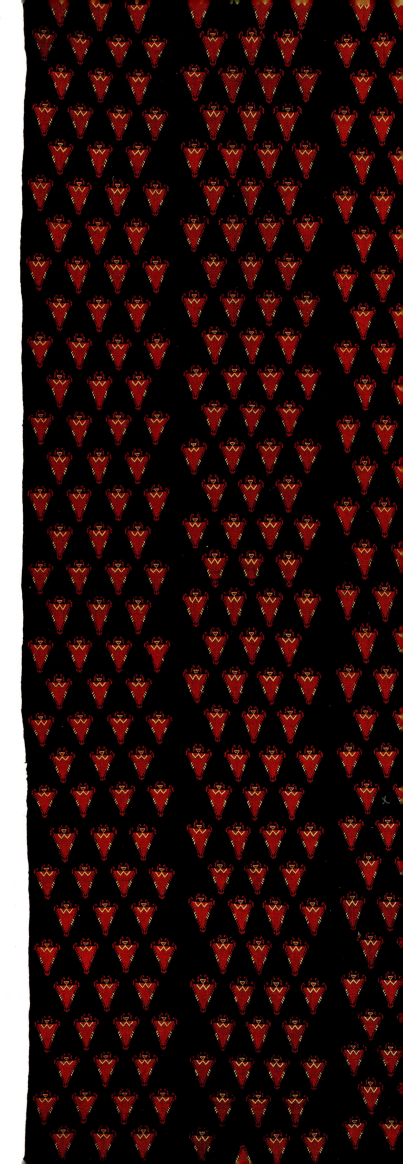

RIGHT
Nineteenth-century Memon embroidered cover, Sindh.

BELOW
Appliqué and patchwork quilt, Sindh.

Quilting

Sindh has a desert climate and cold nights, especially in winter, so quilts are needed as warm bedding. There are two styles of Sindhi quilt. One is a stitched quilt made of rags or discarded clothing. It would appear to be a style of quilting of indigenous origin. It has some similarities with the *kantha* tradition of Bengal and Bihar. Fascinating examples of this work are the quilts known as *kambiri*, worked in a repeated stepped diamond pattern by the Meghwal for the Dars and Pali land-owning castes. Quilted bags for the storage of clothing and other soft items are made in the same style. The other, more common Sindhi style is pieced cotton quilts, often decorated with squares of appliqué or reverse appliqué. These are most probably the influence of British, or more likely American, female missionaries in the latter part of the nineteenth century, though the Sindhi quilter today is highly unlikely to be aware of these origins.

Family groups of women work on an individual quilt, which is usually intended as a wedding gift, though any surplus quilts may be sold into the general market chain, which has its terminus at Karachi. Settled groups of farmers, herders, landowners and merchants require quilts as bedding; they are also used as spreads to cover beaten mud floors for social occasions. By far the highest-quality quilts, with very finely worked appliquéd patterns, are those made by the Meher, rich Muslim pastoralists of northern Sindh and the southernmost regions of Pakistani Punjab, bordering the Cholistan desert. The finest quilts used by the rich land-owners are often the work of much poorer women.

Tie-Dyeing and Block-Printing

The Sindhi style of *bandhani* tie and dye was relatively coarse, with patterns of white or yellow dots set against a red-brown madder-dyed background. Tando Muhammad Khan was one centre for this work. *Bandhani* fabric was made into the *ghaghra* (skirts) and *odhni* (shawls) of various Sindhi castes. The craft has been revived in Karachi, but by recent Muslim Khatri immigrants from neighbouring Kutch.

The pride of Sindhi block printing is the blue and red (traditionally, indigo and natural alizarine) *ajarakh* cotton print of geometric designs, used by Muslim men of Sindh. This fabric is better known to the West as a product of Kutch and western Rajasthan, but Maliana, Tando Muhammad Khan and other small towns were the traditional centres of the work. Though still used and stamped out by hand for Muslim men's *lunghi*, *ajarakh* degenerated into simple black and red prints made using chemical dyes. In recent years, a major revival project has been underway, making use of natural dyes with a view to marketing the fabric as a prestige product for the Western market.

In the old city of Peshawar, simple floral designs, predominantly in red, are block-printed on cotton fabric. The main products are kerchiefs to be worn by men while visiting the mosque and long *dastarkhana* eating cloths to be spread out over matting before any kind of feast.

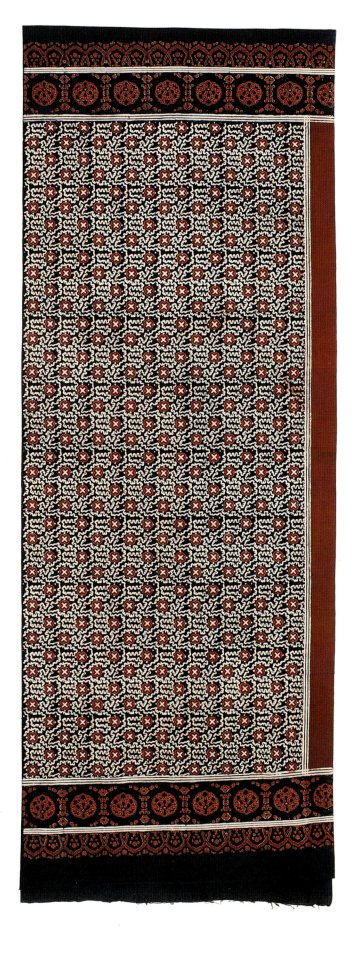

ABOVE
Block-printed *ajarakh lunghi*, Sindh.

LEFT
Sprang pyjama ties, Punjab.

THE PRESENT

The chaos after Partition uprooted textile worker and patron alike, and destroyed India-wide markets. Nonetheless, it is remarkable how much of the industry survived. Both the hand-crafted sector and the industrial sector are major employers. Weaving and embroidery by hand continue to flourish, particularly in Sindh, Baluchistan and North West Frontier, where an innately conservative social structure still requires textiles of a traditional nature to be worn both for ceremonial and everyday use. These conditions are unlikely to change in the foreseeable future.

LEFT
Clothseller at Hawke's Bay market, Karachi.

BELOW
Memon tie-dyed and embroidered shawl, Sindh.

Bangladesh

In Mughal times, East Bengal, now modern-day Bangladesh, was home to the weaving of muslins that were already world-famous. Highly skilled Muslim weavers employed a long-stapled variety of cotton, *Gossypium herbaceum*, which was grown by the banks of the River Meghna to the southeast of Dacca. The raw cotton was tightly spun for the weavers by expert Hindu women in the favourable humid conditions that prevail in Bengal's rainy climate.

The British East India Company took over the rule of Bengal after Clive's victory over Siraj ud-Daula at the battle of Plassey in 1757. The commercially minded British stimulated the production of muslin to such an extent that export markets were overwhelmed by glut. Weaving standards fell, and soon demand ebbed away and weavers were thrown out of work and cast into penury. The muslin industry collapsed, never to recover its former glories. The days when Bengal muslin was so esteemed that it was deemed a fitting gift for the Prophet's tomb at Medina are long gone. What remains of this fine tradition is the weaving of *jamdani* saris.

TECHNIQUES

Jamdani Weaving

A typical *jamdani* sari is made of figured muslin, woven of grey cotton, with usually blue-black designs and sometimes bright-coloured cotton and/or gold-thread details, and *kalka* (*buta* or Paisley) cones in the four corners. The saris and yardage that are mainly woven in Tangail district to the north of present-day Dhaka (formerly Dacca) are now plain muslin, but figured *jamdani* saris are still woven in the city and its environs.

The very finest *jamdani* saris of present times, however, have only about two-thirds of the thread count of those woven a hundred years ago. A relatively recent innovation for both *jamdani* and plain muslin weaving has been the introduction of silk threads.

To make *jamdani* garments, the weaver weaves a length from which four six-yard (18 ft; 5.5 m) saris are cut. They are woven on very simple looms made of wood and bamboo. The *ustad* (master) and *shagrid* (apprentice) work in tandem, the master calling out instructions either from memory or from a paper cartoon so that the apprentice can incorporate patterns into the weave. *Jamdani* are known by their patterns, which fall into three basic groups: the first is the most complex, covering the whole of the ground and known as *jaal*; the second is a floral or geometric pattern laid out on the diagonal and known as *terchi*; the third is a relatively sparse pattern of floral and tendril motifs laid out across the whole ground and known as *buti*.

Kantha Quilting

The pride of Bengal is the *kantha* quilt. These decorative textiles have figurative or sometimes geometric motifs scattered across the face. By changing the colours of the quilting stitches, images of humans, animals, and domestic and agricultural

ABOVE
Weavers displaying a newly woven *jamdani* sari outside Dhaka.

OPPOSITE
Late nineteenth-century *jamdani* sari, patterned with indigo-dyed thread.

OPPOSITE
Contemporary cotton white-on-white patterned *jamdani* sari, woven in a village outside Dhaka.

ABOVE
Contemporary charity *kantha*-work coverlet, Jamalpur.

implements can be formed. Sometimes these are emphasized by outlining in chain or running stitch. Up to seven layers of old saris or *dhotis* – in Bengal, woven of thin, light, permeable muslin – are quilted together to make up cold-weather quilts, eating cloths, purses and wraps for mirrors or precious objects.

The textiles may originally have been inspired by the sixteenth-century Indo-Portuguese embroidered quilts of Satgaon. Each Bengali district developed its own particular style. Rajshahi *lohori* (wave) quilts are worked by Muslim women on used but quite heavy, locally woven, cotton fabric for thick winter quilts. The finest *kantha* come from what is now Bangladesh, east of the River Meghna. *Kantha* from West Bengal and Bihar tend to be cruder, with the exception of those from Calcutta, which often depict scenes from city life. Images from the circus are common, such as strongmen and acrobats; so too figures from Bengali mythology, particularly *churel* (evil ghosts), portrayed as flap-breasted, snaggle-toothed old crones. Figures from politics and literature are popular as well: William Shakespeare, Queen Victoria and Lenin have all made an appearance, not to mention Marilyn Monroe and sailors from Second World War US aircraft carriers in later examples.

The patterns on Bengali *kantha* are worked mostly in black, red and green, the predominant colours of the woven borders of Bengali saris. At one time, the quilts were reported to have been worked in coloured threads drawn from these sari borders, but most if not all the twentieth-century *kantha* are worked in store-bought thread. Muslim *kantha*, finely worked in shadow quilting, usually have a plain ground with black *kalka* cones in the corners.

BANGLADESH 263

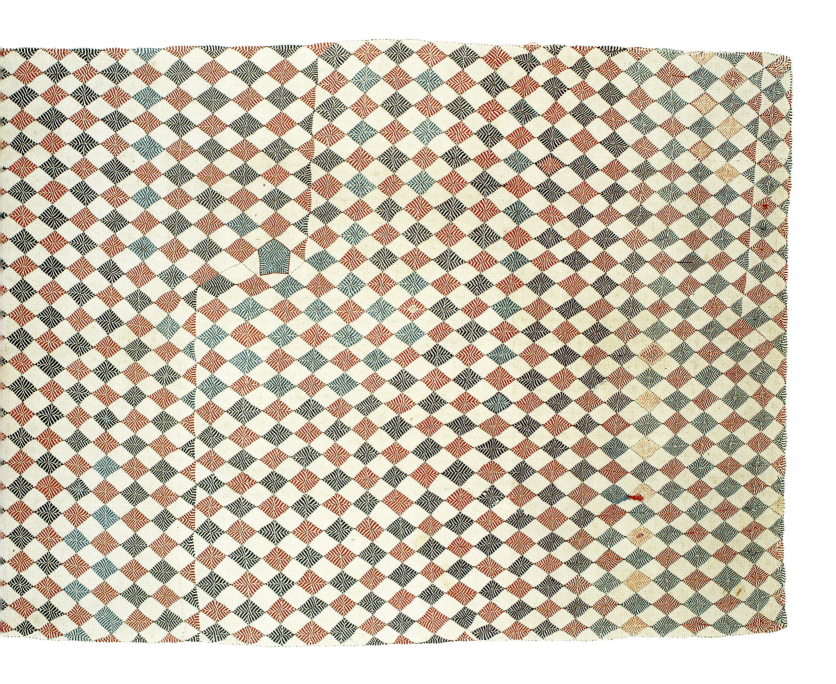

THE PRESENT

The advent of Partition in 1947 led to substantial movements of population into and out of East Bengal, though not on the extreme scale to be found further to the west. East Pakistan – and its successor state, Bangladesh – always retained a significant Hindu minority. There were changes in the composition of the textile workforce, but more important were the losses of Indian markets and rich Hindu patrons. Since the 1980s, there has been a distinct revival in the weaving of *jamdani* saris in and around the city of Dhaka, with considerable effort being expended to provide weavers with credit and marketing facilities. Today's *jamdani* industry can be considered to be in good health.

Rural women also still make simple, stitched *kantha* quilts for daily use, though the complex patterns of yesteryear are a thing of the past. What does flourish, however, is the commercial standardized *kantha* work marketed through charity outlets both within Bangladesh and abroad. Initiated by Canadian aid groups after the Bangladesh Liberation War of 1971, these outlets continue to provide paid employment for many rural women, especially those from Jamalpur district.

OPPOSITE
Diamond-patterned winter *kantha* quilt, Rajshahi.

ABOVE LEFT, ABOVE RIGHT AND LEFT
Kantha quilts, characteristically Muslim in their sparse decoration, limited to *kalka* cones in each corner.

Bangladesh 265

East and Southeast Asia

China

China has the largest population of any country in the world, and among the populace is a little-known but very substantial Muslim minority. Most of the millions of Chinese Muslims known as Hui are converted Han – the same racial grouping as the vast majority of the Chinese, and nowadays virtually indistinguishable from them apart from certain dietary habits and the fact that some of the women are now adopting the veil in order to re-emphasize their identity. Sadly, any specific textile or costume traditions have been lost in the process of the Communist Revolution and in the upheavals that followed during the Cultural Revolution.

Islam has been present in China for centuries. 'Search for knowledge, even unto China' is a saying attributed to the Prophet Mohammed, and indeed the Arabs were making long sea voyages from the Arabian Peninsula all the way to China as early as the seventh century. The country's oldest mosque – in the city of Canton (present-day Guangzhou), then the main centre of Chinese overseas trade – dates from that period, and is still used for worship today. Contact between the Muslim world and China grew during the Tang dynasty (AD 618–907), when many Arab traders arrived from the Abbasid lands. They became known as the 'black-robed Muslims'. 'Black-bearded and long-nosed', they formed a distinct and non-integrated community, and at first there was conflict. However, only four years after the Arabs had defeated the Chinese at the battle of Talas in AD 751 to gain control of Central Asia, Emperor Su Tsung appealed to the Abbasid Caliph to send him four thousand troops to help recapture his capital, Ch'ang-an, from rival Yan forces. Over time, Abbasid descendants and the descendants of other Muslim incomers integrated into Chinese society, a process much stimulated by the Mongol invasion that overthrew the Sung dynasty in 1260 to form the Yuan dynasty (Abbasid Baghdad had fallen to the Mongols in 1258).

Islam was but one of the religions that competed for the allegiance of the Mongol leaders, most notably Genghis Khan. But if the Mongols were at first thoroughly anti-Muslim (after all, it was Muslim cities such as Baghdad that they had been sacking), by the time Genghis's grandson, Kublai Khan, became emperor of China, many Mongol leaders had adopted the religion. There is evidence that, during the Yuan period,

PAGES 266–267
Batik sarong, North Coast Java; *cap* batik for Jambi market, Sumatra; Madras *sembagi* trade cloth for the Sumatran market, Indonesia; Maranao tapestry-woven *malong*, Philippines.

ABOVE
Uighur woman of Xinjiang, *c.* 1920.

OPPOSITE
Kyrgyz or Uighur woman's veil, Xinjiang.

types of textiles that had previously been rare imports started to be made in China, most probably due to the forced importation of skilled West Asian weavers into Chinese towns. Marco Polo, in his account of his travels through China at this time, describes the city of Ning-hsia in western China as inhabited by idolators, Muslims and Christians, and as being a centre for the weaving of a fabric understood to be made from camel hair. Here, he wrote, 'are made many cloths which are called camlets, the most beautiful that are to be found in the world and the best; and again of white wool, for they have white camels: they make of it white camlet very beautiful and good, and they make very great quantity of it and thence many of the said camlets are sent for sale to other parts, or merchants carry them to sell through many places and especially to Cathay and to other places through the midst of the world'.

The Mongol rulers also adopted the West Asian – originally Persian, and later generally Muslim – custom of granting robes of honour to notable vassals and visiting dignitaries. This procedure stimulated the production of such hitherto exotic imports as 'cloth of gold' in the West Asian manner within the boundaries of the Chinese empire. Production of this type of fabric continued, often alongside the indigenous tradition of producing metal-thread brocade.

Large Muslim communities formed in Gansu and Yunnan, and in such cities as Xian, and Kublai Khan appointed many Muslims to high office in civil and military administration. Later, under the Ming (1368–1644), the giant eunuch admiral Cheng Ho was to lead an enormous fleet of junks into the Indian Ocean to explore, trade and levy tribute. He was a Muslim from Yunnan. Unfortunately, upon his return, Ming China turned in on itself and foreign trade was discouraged where it was not banned outright. The Muslim communities had by this time long intermarried, and were now considered on a par with the Han.

REGIONS

Gansu

The arid province of Gansu is home to a large number of Hui. Many families here were once engaged in the caravan trade across the Gobi desert and have long been Muslim converts. Gansu was always a major area for the breeding of Bactrian camels. With its abundant supply of raw material, it became a centre for the weaving of camel hair.

Yunnan

In the southwest of China, the Jin Haw Muslims ran the mule trains that carried goods – including various textile wares – back and forth between Yunnan and Burma and Indochina. They, like other Muslim groups in Yunnan, have some Central Asian blood in their veins. In the thirteenth century, Kublai Khan drafted soldiers from Turkestan to the newly conquered Yunnan in order to defend the southwestern marches of the Celestial Kingdom.

Xinjiang

Eastern Turkestan forms the westernmost province of China, also known as Xinjiang. Its native inhabitants, the Uighur, and other groups are largely of Turkic descent. These peoples live in the famous oases that border the Taklamakan desert (Kashgar, Yarkand, Khotan and Turfan) and in the large city of Ürümchi, where they are now vastly outnumbered by Han Chinese. The Uighur have a tradition of embroidery, but are most famous for the production of felt mats. Kyrgyz – yurt-dwelling nomads – to be found in the southwest of Xinjiang also embroider items of costume and make felt. The town of Tashkurgan that lies between Kashgar and the Kunjerab Pass across the Karakorams is home to a group of Tajiks whose women embroider caps in cross stitch and wear a coin decoration on the back of the head.

THE PRESENT

The Hui are now largely urbanized and, on the face of it, indistinguishable from the Han. The Uighurs and other Muslim groups of westernmost China are under tremendous pressure from wholesale Han immigration into Xinjiang. It is nevertheless to be hoped that they will continue to make their embroidered and felted textiles as part of their attempt to retain their cultural identity.

OPPOSITE ABOVE
Late thirteenth-century Mongol decorative element.

OPPOSITE BELOW
Uighur felt, Kashgar, Xinjiang.

TOP LEFT
Woven *assana* mat, East Turkestan or Gansu.

ABOVE LEFT
Uighur yarn sellers in Kashgar market, Xinjiang.

Malaysia

In both the Malay peninsula and the eastern Malaysian states of Borneo, weaving was and is a vital skill, seen as a prerequisite to marriage. A mother was expected to provide the fabrics necessary to clothe her family. Highly skilled weavers could also sell their produce on the open market. Such weavers could even be adopted as suppliers to the courts, where fine and often ostentatious textiles were required for purposes of display and prestige.

As with the rest of the East Indies (what today is known as the Indonesian archipelago), Malaya and in particular Malacca was a magnet, attracting a vast trade in imported textiles. Cotton goods came from India (in all probability along with the techniques for growing cotton); silk fabrics and thread came from China. These two countries were the dominant cultural influences, and remained so until the coming of the Europeans with the Portuguese conquest of Malacca in 1511, though there was always a steady influx of textiles from Thailand, Cambodia and Java. Techniques of weaving, painting on cloth and resist-dyeing are thought to have come from India, and embroidery and the use of gold thread largely from China. From at least the middle of the second millennium, the complex double-ikat silk patola was brought by Muslim traders from western India to Malacca and other ports of Southeast Asia. This was a highly prestigious product and was incorporated into the ceremonies and rituals of the Malay courts. Patola patterns were later to be much imitated in locally made textiles.

For millennia, Malay groups have settled on the coast of the enormous island of Borneo. Converting to Islam from the fourteenth century onwards, they formed communities from which were drawn the rulers of small coastal states that traded with both Chinese settlers and the aboriginal peoples of the interior. The northwestern side of Borneo consists of the modern state of Sarawak, while to the northeast lies the state of Sabah, both forming part of the Federation of Malaysia. The independent oil-rich Sultanate of Brunei is bounded on the land side by Sarawak.

TECHNIQUES
Batik

Batik, usually with floral patterns, is for everyday use, often in the form of a sarong, the tubular skirt of cotton, silk or nowadays synthetic material worn by both sexes. *Songket* (metal-thread brocade) and *limar* (weft ikat, usually in silk) are prestige textiles for formal and ceremonial use. Yellow, red, green, blue, black and white are the most commonly used colours in textiles worn by Malay people. These colours can have both a social and symbolic meaning. Red, for instance, symbolizes bravery and blood. Batik is a relatively late introduction into the Malaysian textile repertoire. The states of Terrengganu and Kelantan on the east coast of the peninsula have produced batik in the North Coast Javan style only since the early 1900s.

ABOVE
Shaman of Sarawak seated in front of batik drapes.

OPPOSITE
Songket brocade sarong, Kelantan, Northeast Peninsular Malaysia.

Ikat

Ikat – the technique of tie-dyeing a resist into the warp or weft (or both) – is a method of textile decoration widely practised in Southeast Asia, but particularly in the Indonesian archipelago. In the Malayan peninsula and southern Sumatra, a prestige cloth in weft ikat, usually of silk and known as *kain limar*, is very popular for important ceremonies such as circumcision. Terrengganu and Kelantan states are the centres for this craft in Malaysia.

Weaving

Ilanun women are the most prolific weavers of Sabah. They weave on a back-strap loom, in a style very similar to that of their cousins across the water in Mindanao in the Philippines. They and Bajau women specialize in weaving *kain dastar* (headcloths), both for themselves and for other groups. The town of Kota Belud is the main weaving centre. Patterning is in the supplementary-weft technique. Motifs of horses are a favourite for Bajau *kain dastar*. The Bajau were once exclusively fishermen, but have for many generations engaged in farming and cattle- and horse-breeding. Skilled horsemen themselves, they also decorate their steeds with appliquéd trappings at festival times.

Songket Brocade Weaving

Songket metal-thread brocade on a silk ground is the pride of Malaysian weaving. Up to the beginning of the twentieth century, weavers in the northeast states used to embellish their *kain limar* with *songket* metal-thread brocade details. The East Coast Peninsula states of Pahang, Terrengganu and Kelantan are centres of this work, as are Brunei and the Sarawak towns of Kuching and Mukah. *Songket* is usually woven in two-yard lengths and is worn at marriages and other ceremonies as waist-, head- or shoulder-wraps.

Gold-Thread Embroidery

The Malays of Sarawak and Brunei embroider in metal thread, in a manner akin to that of peninsular Malaysia and the Malay regions of Sumatra and other parts of Indonesia. They produce pennanted bunting for the decoration of the bridal beds of state, worked in embroidery or felted or in gilded paper appliqué.

Tekatan gold-thread embroidery flourished in nineteenth-century Malaya under the patronage of the courts, most notably those of Perak, Johore and Pahang. Young women attached to the courts made betel-nut box covers, conical-shaped food covers and tray covers. They also made items to be displayed at weddings – pillowcases, bolster ends, bedcovers, valances, curtains, fans, prayer mats, Koran covers and other ritual objects. The gold thread was worked on velvet backed with starched cotton. The embroiderer would sit on the floor and work at an embroidery frame. The velvet was usually attached to the frame by a network of threads stretched out from the four sides of the fabric.

The first essential was to cut out the embroidery motif from the many layers of soft paper that were glued together to make a soft and supple template (manila card can be used instead). To hold this in place, the embroiderer applies a technique similar to underside couching, in which the fine thread used to hold the thicker couched thread is pulled with each stitch. In this way, the couched gold thread is brought down to the underside of the fabric. From the front, none of the couching stitches is visible and the gold threads look as if they are sewn through the fabric. Sequins and beads are usually

OPPOSITE
Tanjak headcloths for Bajau men, woven at Kota Belud, Sabah.

RIGHT
Songket brocade sarong, Kelantan, Northeast Peninsular Malaysia.

used to cover areas where threads join or where there are empty spaces created by broken pieces of the template. Great care, however, is taken to ensure that the embroiderer does not sweat onto the work in hand. The velvet base fabric is imported from Europe, and the gold thread from Europe and India. Motifs are floral and vegetal. *Bunga cempaka* (*Michela champaca*) and other aromatic flowers are popular choices. The state of Perak continues to encourage *tekatan* work in more modern forms.

Another form of gold-thread embroidery uses a pure gold filament which is worked on silk, organza or voile to make traditional headcovers for women. These are called *selayah* in Sarawak, and are usually 40 by 20 inches in size (100 x 50 cm), enough to cover head and shoulders. Less ornate *selayah* have less gold work and instead are covered with pigeon-eye or clove motifs. *Selayah* are worn by Malay women in combination with *songket* costume.

THE PRESENT

As throughout Southeast Asia, textiles are used in Malaysia to mark rites of passage – betrothal, marriage, birth, circumcision and death. Valuable textiles were also – in line with general Muslim practice – ceremonially granted to notable guests and dependants. This is still the case at the courts of the many states that make up the Federation of Malaysia, but at a less exalted level this custom has rather fallen into disuse. Batik, however, has always been popular, particularly with women, and the more important and traditional the occasion the more likely it is that batik-decorated clothing will be worn. This holds true for both ikat and *songket* brocade, though at such events it will probably be the men who are wearing items of costume composed of these materials.

Indonesia

The Indonesian archipelago stretches from northern Sumatra in the west to West Papua in the east, and consists of more than 17,000 islands. About ninety per cent of the population live on the three major islands – Sumatra, Java and Bali. Regardless of whether they inhabit the main or the outlying islands, locals have long channelled their riches from agriculture or trade (particularly the spice trade) into the ostentatious display of both home-woven and imported cloth.

Since Indonesia lies at the crossroads between the great civilizations of China to the northeast and India, Arabia and Europe to the northwest, continual waves of foreign merchants and traders have passed through its straits, bringing with them cultural changes that have had a marked effect on the development of the region's textiles. The impact of this has been felt most deeply on the littorals of the main islands, where it is visible in the sophistication of the materials produced there, the foremost example being Sumatra, with its extensive range of textile techniques. It was through this longstanding contact with foreigners that methods for weaving *songket* brocade and weft ikat on discontinuously warped looms were introduced into the Indonesian heartland, as were the resist-dyeing processes of *pelangi* (tie and dye) and *tritik* (stitched resist).

In the first millennium AD, the most pervasive outside influence was India. By the second century, Indian traders had begun to do business with the coastal peoples of Java, and by the fifth century a Hindu kingdom had been established there. Hindu-Buddhists were to rule over much of the archipelago for the next thousand years, the ancient empires of Srivijaya in south Sumatra (around modern Palembang) and Majapahit in Java being notable examples. A great deal of tie-dye work and stitched resist is still carried out in Sumatra and Java, almost certainly a result of trade contacts with India. Sumatra is also one of the very few places outside the South Asian sub-continent with a tradition of mirrorwork embroidery.

Throughout the second millennium AD, Chinese traders settled on the coasts of the main islands, bringing with them trade porcelain and embroideries, a rich design source for the Indonesian textile repertoire. In the seventeenth century, the Chinese were also responsible for the introduction of sericulture. In addition, their trading communities were to have a substantial influence on the batik industry.

The arrival of Islam with Indian Muslim and Arab traders had certain profound effects on Indonesian textiles, notably in the recent past the production of batik prayer cloths made on the Javanese north coast for the Sumatran markets of Jambi, Palembang and Bengkulu. These cloths are embellished with quotations from the Koran in Arabic script. Islam also led to the heightening of decorative embellishment and the lessening

ABOVE LEFT
Clan chief from Aceh wearing warp-ikat silk trousers.

ABOVE RIGHT
Balinese couple wearing batik waistcloths from North and Central Java.

OPPOSITE
Batik sarong, North Coast Java for the Minangkabau market.

TOP
Gold and mirrorwork embroidered strip, Pasaman, Sumatra.

ABOVE
'Magical' goldwork panel, Aceh or West Sumatra.

LEFT
Minangkabau man's embroidered jacket.

of the figurative element in Central Javan batik. It was the Muslim merchants, moreover, who brought the all-pervasive check or plaid designs used for the sarongs in which the Malay seafarers were soon clad. These merchants also introduced to the islands the most influential textile of them all, the fabled double-ikat silk patola cloth of Gujarat and the surrounding areas of northwest India.

Sumatra is the island with the most profound Muslim influences. Being the closest of the archipelago's islands to India and Arabia, rich in resources and lying on the vital sea-borne trade route through the Strait of Malacca, it was converted early and most thoroughly to Islam (though there are still substantial non-Muslim groups in the historically hostile and inaccessible highlands).

Major Malay Muslim groups inhabit the north (Aceh and the coast around Medan), the eastern islands of Riau, the south centred on Jambi and Palembang, and the west coast from Lampung to Bengkulu, up to the rich lands of the Minangkabau. All these regions are to a greater or lesser extent Islamic, and have adopted a thoroughly Muslim mode of dress. They have also been highly influenced by textiles from the greater Muslim world. It is common to find embroidered waistcoats brought home from the pilgrimage to Mecca and Medina, and the *tarbush*-shaped hats made or sold at Jeddah were also common souvenirs of the Haj. This kind of influence was not new. Aceh was a centre of Ottoman trade, and indeed it was once the easternmost extent of Ottoman naval power. It was here that such Near Eastern influences as metal-thread embroidery and the weaving of cotton or silk warp-ikat waist-wraps arrived and spread to other groups on the island, both Muslim and non-Muslim. The technique of weft ikat in silk is often associated with proximity to the major sea trade routes of Asia, and very often the weavers themselves are Muslims. Sumatra produces notable examples of this technique. Before the Second World War, metal-thread brocade was woven at many places on the island. This was indubitably another Islamic influence. *Songket* weaving in Sumatra is now restricted to Pandai Sikat and Palembang.

278 EAST AND SOUTHEAST ASIA

OPPOSITE RIGHT
Nineteenth-century *tapis*, Lampung.
The inset 'mirrors' are of gilded lead.

ABOVE
Minangkabau embroidery of a tree and
birds flanked by a pair of sacred *bouraq*.

TECHNIQUES
Embroidery
Throughout the Muslim parts of Sumatra, there is a tradition of making hangings to decorate the bridal bed of state, upon which wedding gifts are displayed and in front of which the bride and groom sit. The bed itself, carved in the Chinese manner and assembled by Chinese carpenters, is hung with pennanted hangings in the style of Gujarati *toran* from India. These hangings are embellished with metal-thread embroidery and, in the case of those from Pasaman district near Medan and those of the Minangkabau people of West Sumatra, also with mirrorwork, the mirrors being made in the port of Bengkulu. The metal thread may be worked free-hand but is more usually worked on a frame in the Near Eastern manner, and sometimes over card templates in the way of some Ottoman embroidery. The designs are often worked on red broadcloth of European, most likely English, origin.

Appliqué
Appliqué and reverse appliqué of gilded paper are also worked on red broadcloth, often combined with mirrorwork. This is a speciality of the Malay peoples of Pasaman.

Ikat
The technique of ikat is found all over Indonesia. Warp ikat has been practised on the outer islands and by aboriginal peoples in the isolated interiors of the main islands since time immemorial. Weft ikat in silk is a textile long associated with Muslim weavers. A complex weft-ikat technique involving the use of many bobbins of pre-dyed patterned yarn is restricted to coastal regions of the main islands and is, with the exception of the Hindu weavers of Bali, the prerogative of Muslim weavers. In Sumatra, weft ikat based on Indian patola patterns is woven in Palembang and on Bangka Island to make a cloth often incorporating gold brocade called *kain limar*, which is worn at important ceremonies such as that of circumcision. The Minangkabau, who, like many of the peoples of Sumatra had a glorious textile

INDONESIA 279

TOP AND ABOVE
Embroidered bed pelmets, Pasaman, Sumatra.

BELOW
Clan leader's brocaded silk sash, Batu Sangkar, West Sumatra.

OPPOSITE
Examples of *kain limar*, silk weft ikat, Palembang.

tradition that mainly died out with the advent of the Second World War, wove weft-ikat sashes with zigzag patterns in red and dark blue, also incorporating *songket* brocade. The Acehnese are unique in the archipelago in weaving warp ikat in silk in patterns very similar to those of Syria. The Bataks are deemed to have copied these patterns in their cotton warp-ikat *ulos* (shawls) from Aceh. In Palembang and along the north Java coast there is substantial production of weft-ikat sarongs, both for home consumption and for export to East Africa and the Yemen (in fact, many of the proprietors of the weaving workshops on Java are from Yemen). This type of sarong – short and practical – is ideal for seafarers. The ocean-going Bugis and Makassarese of Sulawesi weave a similar kind of sarong, but in silk.

Pelangi and *Tritik*

Tie and dye and stitched resist are two techniques that it may be assumed arrived from India, though both methods of resist-dyeing are also well known in China. The patterning of *pelangi* and *tritik* textiles in Indonesia follows very closely that of similar textiles from India. Palembang is still a great producer of silk scarves and shawls in both techniques. Most plentiful are *selendang* shawls, which combine the two methods with a central field of tie-dyed flowers against a dark ground, set within stitched-resist borders of *boteh* (Paisley cones) against an often red ground. Most desirable to the Western collector are the *lawan selendang* of Palembang. These are in 'moody' colours, with a central rectangle or diamond set into another rectangle. Because of the technique of stitched resist, the colours fade into each other where they meet. Before the Second World War they were worked on a mushroom-shaped frame using cheap Shantung silk. They are still made today in small quantities on imported silk. The central Javanese sultanates of Jogjakarta and Solo also produce simple tie-dye on cotton and silk, as do Bali and Sulawesi. In central Java they also make women's breastcloths in *tritik*.

Songket Brocade Weaving

Songket metal-thread brocade is esteemed all over the Indonesian archipelago, especially by the people who think of themselves as Malay. Usually made by women, it can be woven on a frame or back-strap loom. Palembang in south Sumatra and the Minangkabau country in west Sumatra were important centres of this work. Pandai Sikat and Palembang still have *songket* weaving looms, though the glories of *songket* from such

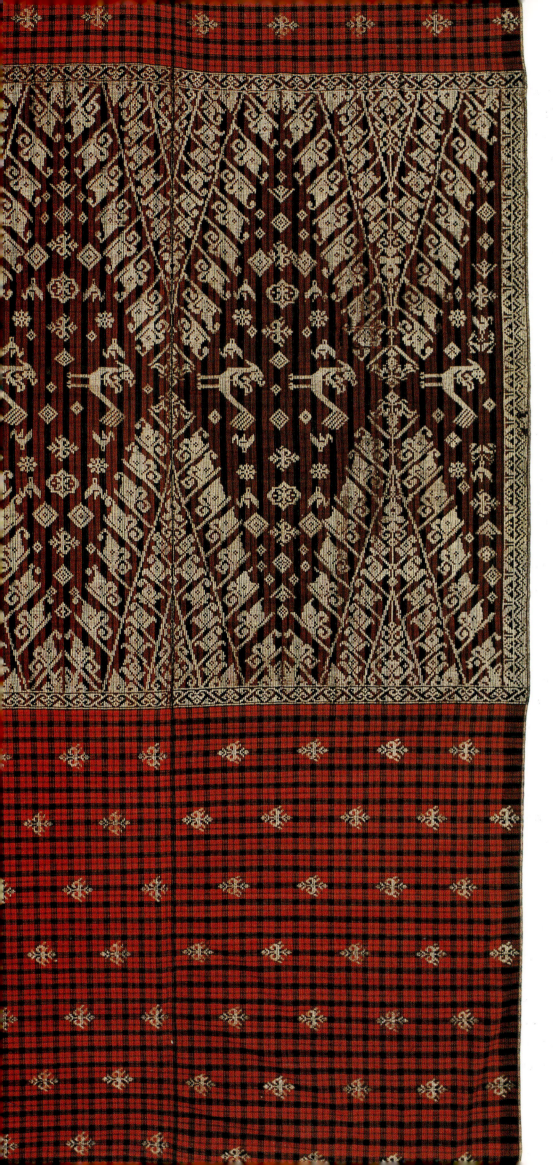

OPPOSITE ABOVE AND BELOW
Stitch-resist *lawan selendang*, Palembang.

LEFT
Cotton and metal-thread *weri* sarong from the Bimanese court, Sumbawa.

ABOVE
Tie-dyed, stitch-resist *selendang*, Palembang.

OPPOSITE AND ABOVE
Ritually important *weri* cotton and metal-thread brocade sarongs, woven on discontinuously warped body-tension looms, Bima, Sumbawa.

RIGHT
Cotton and silver brocade headcloth from the Bimanese court, Sumbawa.

INDONESIA

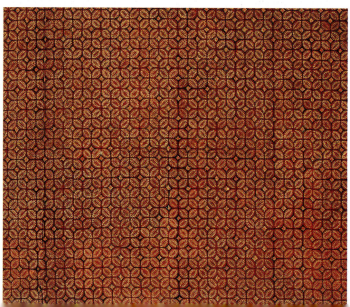

OPPOSITE ABOVE
Batik sarong, North Coast Java.

OPPOSITE BELOW LEFT
Cap batik waistcloth in the typical Central Javanese 'Broken Knife' pattern.

OPPOSITE BELOW RIGHT
Cap batik waistcloth, Gresik, North Java.

LEFT
Cap batik waistcloth, Gresik, North Java.

BELOW
Batik cloth for ritual use, South Sumatra.

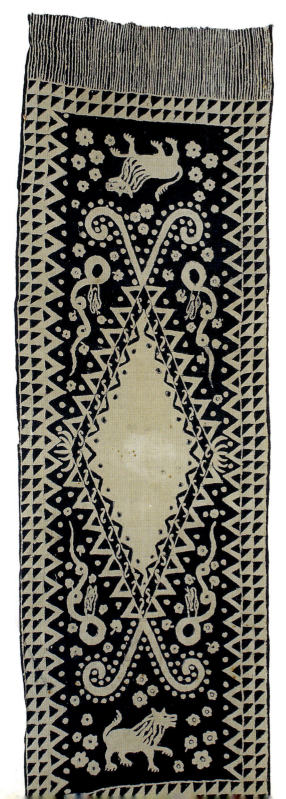

formerly famous Minangkabau centres as Batusangkar and Maralabuh are long gone. *Songket* is still woven by the Bugis and Makassarese on Sulawesi. On Sumbawa they use the technique to weave magnificent, often figurative, sarongs, as they do on a much more modest scale in Java and Bali.

Batik

Batik is the most renowned textile art of Indonesia. The technique – applying a wax resist before dyeing to form a pattern in negative – is known worldwide by its Malay name (meaning 'to draw with a broken dot or line'). Although the craft is practised in other parts of the world, it is on the island of Java that it has been brought to an acme of refinement. One has to go back to the seventeenth- and eighteenth-century painted chintzes of the Indian Coromandel coast to find anything that can rival Javanese batik for subtlety of colouring and mastery of dyeing processes. The *canting* – a little copper reservoir and spout attached to a wooden handle – is the instrument invented in Java to transmit delicate designs in molten wax onto finely woven cotton fabric. Making hand-drawn batik, which is known as *tulis* (literally, 'writing'), is a lengthy process whereby a waistcloth that needs to be waxed with identical patterns on both sides and dipped into multiple dye baths will take up to a month to complete. Throughout Java this is women's work. On the other hand, *cap* batik – a system pioneered in Java in the 1860s, in which a male worker prints out the batik designs in wax with the aid of a variety of copper stamps – is a much speedier process. As part of a factory-like production line, the worker can easily help to complete the waxing of up to twenty cloths a day.

The batik work of central Java is mainly produced around the courts of Jogjakarta and Solo, and is characterized by the use of soga brown and indigo blue dyes. It is among the diverse communities that settled on the north coast of Java that the predominant Muslim influence on Javanese batik can be seen. Unlike their neighbours the Chinese and Indo-Europeans, whose batik was highly figurative, the Arab batik-makers of Gresik and other towns of north Java such as Demak and Kudus – mainly of Yemeni origin, and originally attracted by the trade in sharks' fins from the Yemeni coast – had a preference for *jelemprang* patterns (derived from the eight-petalled lotus motif) and *ceplokan* patterns (featuring repeated geometric shapes), based on patola designs often worked in Islamic green.

The women of central Java and the north Java coast have a seemingly infinite repertoire of designs, and in the case of the batik-makers of north Java a very eclectic one. The latter always had a strong market in wealthy, resource-rich Sumatra. *Selendang* prayer shawls and *deta* headscarves were produced with batik designs in Arabic calligraphy and prominent Islamic symbols, mainly in and around the northwest Javan town of Cirebon. Two big export markets for this type of batik were Jambi and Bengkulu, both strongly Islamic and anti-colonial. The *deta* headscarves were folded, glued and pinned into neat turbans to be worn by men at weddings and other ceremonies. In recent years, *kalligrafi* batik has been imitated by screenprinting and sold into the same markets. Jambi was also the end market of blue and red *cap* (hand-printed) batik, with its strongly Indian-influenced repeated floral design. The deep, dried-blood-red colour of these batiks was from the dye vats of Lasem, a town in northeast Java that has always been famed for its reds. These particular batiks – both *selendang* and *deta* – were known as Jambi batiks, not because they were made there but because that is where they were sold. Sumatra, along with the other major islands, imported painted and printed textiles from both India's Coromandel coast and Gujarat. These textiles – particularly those with what might be called chintz designs – had a profound effect on the development of batik in Java.

THE PRESENT

Indonesia has the largest population of Muslims in the world. Since its independence in 1946, it has had a policy of using its rich resources, such as petroleum, to keep the cost of living low. This policy has enabled crafts to flourish and labour costs to be kept down. In a society that is very much governed by custom, there will always be a great demand for hand-made textiles to be worn at the many ceremonies associated with traditional Indonesian life. This fact alone helps to keep textile workers – be they batikers, weavers, tie-dyers or embroiderers – in steady employment, a fortunate situation that should continue for generations.

OPPOSITE
South Indian trade cloth for the Sumatran market.

ABOVE LEFT
Kalligrafi batik *deta* from Cirebon, North Java, but used by Minangkabau clan chiefs, West Sumatra.

ABOVE RIGHT
Kalligrafi batik *selendang* from Cirebon, North Java, but used by Minangkabau clan chiefs, West Sumatra.

The Philippines

The islands of the southern Philippines are close to the southeastern periphery of the world of Islam. Here Muslim peoples live side by side with animist and Christian groups. Though all are Malay-Polynesians, there have been historic tensions between the component groups.

The islanders were initially subject to influences from Buddhism and Hinduism when they began to trade with Indianized kingdoms in the Malay archipelago in pre-Islamic times. By AD 900 Chinese sea-traders had arrived in the area. In 1380 the Arab trader Karim ul-Makhdum established a sultanate on the island of Sulu, building a mosque and bringing Islam to the region. The religion was spread by Arab missionaries and seafarers, who often settled and intermarried, and brought elements of Arab culture with them that still today exist as an overlay to the indigenous culture.

The Philippines was colonized by Spain in the sixteenth century (indeed, the country is named for the Spanish king Philip II). Under the Treaty of Paris of 1898, it was ceded to the United States for the sum of 20 million dollars. On 4 July 1946 it was granted independence.

PEOPLES

The Maranao and Maguindanao

Mindanao, by far the largest island in the southern Philippines, is home to various Muslim groups, particularly in the west and along the string of islands that stretches from the city of Zamboanga towards Borneo. The most numerous of these groups are the Maranao, who live by Lake Lanao. They are closely related to the seafaring Ilanun, who are also to be found in coastal North Borneo and were historically the most feared pirates and raiders in the region.

Maranao men are great craftsmen, being famous for their inlaid metalwork. Maranao women are noted weavers. They wear an extremely wide silk sarong called a *malong landap*. This is worn with a long-sleeved blouse and a cloche-like headscarf. The sarong is inset with panels of tapestry weave in geometric or floral patterns against a purple ground. The rest of the garment is of gold or purple silk.

In the past, Maranao women made extremely fine abaca cloth woven from the bast fibres of the trunk of *Musa textilis*, a relative of the domestic banana tree. Large screens or curtains painted with designs derived from Indian or European trade cloths were made of this fabric and hung up to form the backdrop for important ceremonial occasions.

The neighbouring – and related – Maguindanao wear a similar *malong* to the Maranao, but in a more muted range of colours. Both groups also weave ikat textiles in silk as well as the favoured Muslim plaid, with purple as the dominant colour. The silk yarn has always been imported rather than home-reared, a consequence of the strong trading bent of these Muslim groups. Weaving in all of the groups is done by women.

The Tausug

The most sophisticated textiles of the area are found on the smaller islands, particularly Sulu, Basilan and Tawi-Tawi. The aggressive and much-feared sultanate of Sulu was, in the eighteenth century, the regional entrepot for the import of Chinese silk yarn. The island was mainly populated by the

OPPOSITE
A member of one of the warrior Moro tribes traditionally based in coastal Mindanao and the Sulu archipelago.

ABOVE
Maranao silk tapestry-woven *malong landap*.

OPPOSITE ABOVE
Maranao painted *abaca* cloth.

OPPOSITE BELOW
Maranao weft-ikat *malong*.

LEFT
Tapestry-woven *pis*, Sulu Island.

Tausug, who made their living from piracy, slaving and trading. By the mid-nineteenth century, it was awash with all manner of imported textiles – Madras handkerchiefs, Javanese batiks, gaudy European print kerchiefs, Chinese silks and satins, and chintzes either hand-made on the Coromandel coast or mill-made in Europe. Men's fashions were influenced by the Malay courtly style, but also by Arab and Chinese modes of dress.

Patterns from all this polyethnic array are to be found in Tausug textiles. Their most characteristic is the multi-purpose large square silk or more recently cotton kerchief, tapestry-woven, the geometric motifs being made up of tiny multicoloured squares. Used by men and known as a *pis siyabit*, it may be worn on the shoulder, wrapped around the hilt of a *kris* knife, or used as a headwrap. Women normally wore sarong and blouse, and, despite the prevalent use of imported cloth, were also accomplished weavers. The second masterpiece of the Tausug weavers' art is the *kambut* – a long narrow silk tapestry man's cummerbund. Tausug women also wove the tubular sarong so characteristic of this part of southeast Asia, again in silk tapestry. This was known as a *patadyong*.

The Yakan

The Yakan, who live on Basilan and at Zamboanga, weave the most sophisticated textiles in all of western Mindanao, specializing in complex supplementary-weft weaves. The Yakan equivalent of the Tausug *pis* is known as a *seputangan*, but among the Yakan it is an item of both female and male wear. The warp and weft are of cotton, and the supplementary-weft details are of differently coloured silks. Yakan men and women both wear a *badju* (shirt) with *sirwal* (trousers) that are wide on the drawstring waist and tight on the calves. Unlike their cousins the Tausug and the Samal, the Yakan earn their living from agriculture, rather than by fishing or trading by sea. No doubt it is for this reason that they are more conservative in their dress than either of the other two groups. They are certainly the better weavers. Their most sophisticated weave is *bunga sama*, which may be taken to mean 'flower work'. In this, the fabric is woven using up to seventy pattern sticks or heddles. *Sinuluan* is a colourful supplementary-warp patterned fabric, which is mainly used to provide material for male and female *sirwal*. *Inalaman* and *pinatupan* are, respectively, the more complex and the simpler variants of the supplementary-warp technique sarongs for Yakan women. The Yakan have a preference for patterning in a series of diamond shapes, which they incorporate into both their textiles and other types of craft.

The Samal

Another Muslim group, the Samal, are found all the way from Tawi-Tawi to the bay of Zamboanga. They always made use of imported cloth, and their best-known textiles are the bright multicoloured patchwork sails made for the *prahu* catamarans of Zamboanga Bay.

THE PRESENT

Weaving among the Maranao and related groups is still in a healthy state. The younger weavers still practise tapestry weave and ikat dyeing, though unfortunately not to the level of fineness that their mothers and grandmothers could aspire to. Abaca cloth is no longer made by these groups. Weaving in the chain of islands going from Zamboanga to Sulu is in decline, a process no doubt exacerbated by the chronic instability engendered by the periodic outbreaks of insurgency and piracy afflicting the area. In general, however, the Muslim peoples still require traditional items of costume for change-of-life events, and this requirement will keep the weavers and to some extent the dyers of Mindanao in gainful employment for the foreseeable future.

Sub-Saharan Africa

East Africa

East Africa is home to substantial populations of Muslims. Traditionally, it is believed that Islam first came to Africa when the Prophet Mohammed counselled a group of persecuted Muslims to flee to Abyssinia (present-day Ethiopia and Eritrea). Certainly, Islam had taken root on the east coast by the eighth century AD, spread by traders from the Arabian Peninsula and the Persian Gulf. Many of these merchants intermarried and settled in coastal East Africa (Zanzibar was a notable Muslim centre as early as the tenth century AD). These Muslims and converts formed the new Swahili community ('Swahili' is derived from the Arabic word 'Sawahil', meaning 'of the coast') – a merger of Arabic and East African cultures that unified previously disparate ethnicities and provided an enduring common identity. The majority of the textiles these Islamicized peoples used were imported, with any local production being woven on looms of a type familiar in Arabia and India. There are, however, particular textiles that are intimately connected with certain regions.

REGIONS

Ethiopia

The most beautiful examples of textiles from the Muslim peoples of East Africa are worn by the urban women of the ancient walled city of Harar in southeastern Ethiopia. Harar is a Muslim city with unique traditions. Among other crafts, it was renowned for its embroidery and the inclusion of imported, particularly Indian, fabrics into female costume. Marriage dresses are long, full smocks of indigo-dyed light cotton sewn up along a central longitudinal seam to form a V-shaped neckline. A piece of imported satin or damask of contrasting colour is sewn on to cover the shoulders, neck, breast and upper back. All the edges of this applied fabric and the neckline are outlined with delicate, restrained, floral embroidery in satin stitch. This forms identical patterns on the inside of the dress, and it is therefore possible to turn the garment inside out – a practice carried out at various stages during the marriage ceremony.

Underneath the dress, women wear jodhpur trousers of Kutchi *mashru* from India. The cuffs are embellished with a colourful, locally made braid. The outfit is completed with a tie-dyed rayon or silk shawl, also from India, confirming the strong trading links that extend from Harar across the Indian Ocean. Textile historians Barbie Campbell Cole and Peri M.

PAGES 294–295
Hausa blanket, Kano, Nigeria; Hausa trouser panel, Nigeria; Mende strip-woven cloth, Sierra Leone; Hausa wrap, Nigeria.

ABOVE LEFT
Swahili couple from the Comoros Islands.

ABOVE RIGHT
Eritrean Muslim woman, *c.* 1930.

ABOVE
Reversible wedding dress of indigo-dyed cotton, Harar, Ethiopia.

Klemm attribute the introduction of the wearing of this style of trouser to the need to protect the local girls' virtue from the licentious Egyptian soldiers occupying Harar between 1875 and 1885. Whatever the case, the Egyptian occupation produced profound changes in the type of clothing worn in the area. The fine cotton woven by local Galla (also known as Oromo) weavers was largely abandoned for luxury fabrics, such as silk and satin imported from India, China and Europe – a consequence of the opening up of new trade routes. The Galla still weave cotton for their own garments, which they smear with clarified butter to make them warmer and more waterproof.

Somalia

The Somalis – and related groups of the Ethiopian Ogaden, Republic of Djibouti and Somalia proper – traditionally wear cotton loincloths. They were once famous for their hand-weaving industry, and in the nineteenth century there was a strong export market for their cotton cloth, but nowadays they tend to wear imported fabrics. Like the north Sudanese, the Somalis weave on pit-treadle looms that are very similar to the pit-looms of Asia and the former cotton-weaving looms of the Swahili coast.

Kenya and Tanzania

The textiles most closely associated with Kenya – and East Africa in general – are *kanga*. These machine-printed cotton cloths are worn in pairs, known as *doti*. They were originally worn by Swahili women, but their use has now spread to women all over East Africa. The fashion for wearing them is said to have originated with imported European printed kerchiefs, which always came in rectangles consisting of six uncut kerchiefs, three along the top, three along the bottom. A woman in either Mombasa or Zanzibar is said to have cut a rectangle lengthways into two 3 x 1 kerchief lengths. She wore one length as a waistcloth and the other as a shawl. The style caught on, and Arab and Indian merchants began to imitate it, at first hand-printing with wooden blocks on imported cotton but rapidly turning to the mills of Europe, India and Japan to cater to the fast-rising demand. The first cloths, speckled on a dark ground, were called *kanga* (meaning 'guinea fowl'), as they resembled the birds' plumage. Over the years, the cloths have gone through many permutations. Those from the 1970s, made in Japan or China, were of relatively thick cloth, with bold, uncluttered designs; nowadays the cloths are printed in India

ABOVE
Woman's trousers from Harar, Ethiopia, made of imported Kutchi *mashru*.

BELOW
Wedding dress from Harar, Ethiopia, reversed, with a yoke panel of satin imported from Asia.

or locally, on much thinner cotton and with comparatively fussy designs. All *kanga* cloths, however, share one common element: they are always embellished with a proverb or message in Kiswahili. A spotted design might be emblazoned with 'Good luck brings wealth', a mango design with 'Love is like a cough – it never goes away', while a map of the world might suggest 'Even when we are separate, the memory will remain'. Every woman wearing a pair of *kanga* has a message to impart.

Zanzibar was for centuries an outpost of Omani power, and this fact is reflected in both the culture and dress of the Swahili people of the island. Zanzibari men wear a white cotton cap – embroidered in buttonhole stitch – similar to that worn in Oman. The designs on the cap are drawn out and holes pierced at appropriate places with the aid of a thorn. Embroiderers can be either male or female. Though the main centre of production is in the south of the island, the caps are marketed through the long winding bazaar in the capital, Stone Town.

THE PRESENT

Hand-made textiles are, and will remain, a rarity throughout the region. In Harar in Ethiopia, there is a limited amount of embroidery done for special-occasion clothing, such as wedding garments. The Somalis, meanwhile, are engaged in a seemingly neverending downward spiral of war and internecine violence – not conditions favourable for hand-weaving, which in any case has wasted away due to mill-made imports. In Kenya and Tanzania, much production of *kanga* cloth is now carried out in factories for local markets. East Africans will continue to dress in a most colourful manner, but the majority of their articles of dress will be machine-made or, as ever, imported.

RIGHT
Men's embroidered caps, Zanzibar.

BELOW
Machine-printed cotton *kanga*, Kenya.

West Africa

Islam came down across the Sahara desert from North Africa, and merchants would seem to have been the first proselytizers. Missionary activity has continued up to the present century and has resulted in substantial Muslim populations throughout West Africa, though in certain places Christian or animist groups predominate.

The coming of Islam to sub-Saharan Africa was, as in Southeast Asia, more the result of trade than of conquest. North African Muslim merchants wished to have dependable trading partners at the end of a long, arduous and dangerous journey. Trading trips could last two or three years, and there was little point embarking on them unless there was a reliable supply of wares to be obtained and honest buyers for the merchants' own goods. The North Africans needed trading partners with the same system of ethics as themselves, and to this end made converts to their own religion.

With the adoption of Islam came the acceptance of Muslim codes of modesty and dress. Heretofore climatic conditions meant that requirements for clothing were largely minimal, but after the coming of Islam a whole textile industry arose based on indigenous cotton and silk being imported across the Sahara, or later from European ships trading along the West African coast.

West Africa, however, produces textiles of its own, whose fame spreads far beyond their home region. Mostly woven in strips on a narrow horizontal loom, in a technique peculiar but not exclusive to West Africa, these textiles are often dyed in shades of indigo blue. Weavers (on both horizontal and vertical looms), dyers (primarily in indigo), tailors and embroiderers all contributed to the creation of the full, wide-sleeved robes known variously as *boubou*, *agbada* and *riga* in different regions of West Africa, but all of the same general style. Even non-Muslim men who aspired to the social standing of the wealthy, high-status Muslim merchants adopted this form of dress. Their wives also espoused Muslim codes of public modesty, and in turn needed voluminous robes and wraps. Thus began one of the world's most important – and still vibrant – textile traditions.

TECHNIQUES

Weaving

Weavers are to be found all over West Africa, from Senegal in the west to northern Cameroon and Chad in the east, and there are many men and women who are highly skilled at the craft. Men usually weave on the horizontal treadle-loom, women on the vertical loom, though as the years go by – especially among some peoples, such as the Yoruba in Nigeria – traditional sex

ABOVE
Muslim men of Central Nigeria, wearing embroidered *agbada* robes.

OPPOSITE
Mende *kpokpo* strip-woven cloth, with threads dyed indigo blue and kola-nut brown, Sierra Leone.

OPPOSITE
Wedding blanket, woven by the Fulani for the Tuareg.

ABOVE
Kassa blanket, Mali.

BELOW
Djerma man's strip-woven cotton cloth, Niger.

BELOW RIGHT
Tuareg mat, Mali.

demarcations are beginning to break down. Vertical looms have in many areas fallen into disuse completely. The horizontal looms weave thin strips that are then sewn together, selvedge to selvedge, to make up women's waistcloths and men's body-wraps. This method of making up cloth, though to be found in other parts of the world, is characteristic of West African weaving and is ancient (locally made strip-woven cloth dating back to the eleventh century has been found in the burial caves of the Tellem people in the Dogon area of Mali). The bulk of the woven strips are of plain white cotton and are often seen as rolled-up 'wheels' which have an established monetary value.

In the more sparsely populated areas of West Africa, a weaver will walk a considerable distance to his work and stay there until it is finished. Often he works just for his daily food, his patrons providing the yarn with which to weave. They will give him a present, such as a goat, on the satisfactory completion of the work, and then he will walk on to his next, often distant, commission. This system is only possible with the horizontal treadle strip-loom, with its small and easily portable heddles and moving parts. The weaver can build a frame for the loom out of locally available branches cut to shape at the new weaving site.

The Hausa weave the narrowest of strips (1 in.; 2.5 cm), and also the widest (18 in.; 45.5 cm). The former are used to make highly valued Tuareg veils, and the latter are so wide that they are often confused with the products of the women's upright loom. The narrowest strips are known as *turkudi*. Among the most important items produced on the Hausa loom are the patterned textiles that are used to make up the cotton blankets known as *luru*, sold in Kano market.

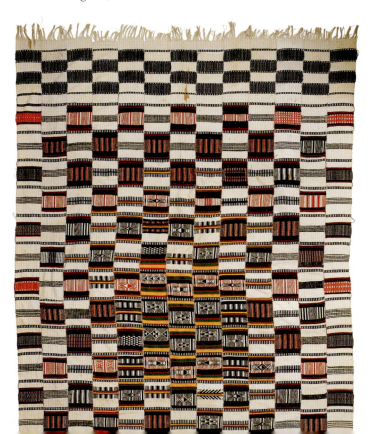

WEST AFRICA 303

TOP
Nupe robe, Nigeria.

ABOVE
Hausa *riga*, Nigeria.

OPPOSITE LEFT
Detail of embroidered Nupe robe, Nigeria.

OPPOSITE RIGHT
Embroidered robe, Bornu or Chad.

Embroidery

Embroidery is not nearly as widespread a craft as weaving. Where it takes place, it is the work of professional male embroiderers, and is considered very much a Muslim art form, particularly associated with the Hausa and Nupe people of Nigeria. The vast, deep-sleeved *boubou*, *agbada* or *riga* robe is worn by eminent West African men. Sometimes these are prominent non-Muslims, but the robe is a form of attire that is particularly associated with Islam. The embroideries are drawn out and often worked by impoverished Koranic scholars, who, as they are literate and adept at the art of Arabic calligraphy, are intrinsically competent designers. The fronts and backs of the robes are embroidered either by hand or machine. The collar and the breastpiece are typically adorned with the two- or eight-knife pattern; the breast pocket and back with a circle broken up into squares, a pattern recalling the cabbalistic pseudo-science of numerology. The material that makes up the robe can be mill- or hand-woven. The finest Lancashire cotton, European damask and strip-woven local cloth are all used, but the most prestigious and expensive cloth is the narrow-strip Hausa cloth, which is exported all over West Africa. Hausa hand- and machine-embroiderers are to be found in many countries in West Africa other than Nigeria.

Painting

Charm cloths and jackets inscribed with quotations from the Koran were traditionally used and worn for magical and protective purposes by Muslims, and occasionally non-Muslims, especially in times of war. Throughout the whole of the Muslim world, there is a strong belief in the protective power of the written word of the Koran. High-ranking Muslim warriors would wear a shirt inscribed with all, or part of, the Koran underneath their body armour. Examples have been found in Turkey, Iran and India, and also in North Africa, from whence it is thought the fashion for calligraphy cloths spread down, along the caravan trails, to West Africa. These textiles are most probably the work of Hausa craftsmen, in particular the Koranic scholars who traditionally supplemented their low income by drawing out embroidery patterns. Amulets – worn attached to the clothing of warriors or hunters – are also prevalent across West Africa. These are prepared by Islamic scholars or marabouts (holy men), who write out Koranic or magical inscriptions in locally made black ink, bless them with incantations, and bind them in leather or wild animal skin.

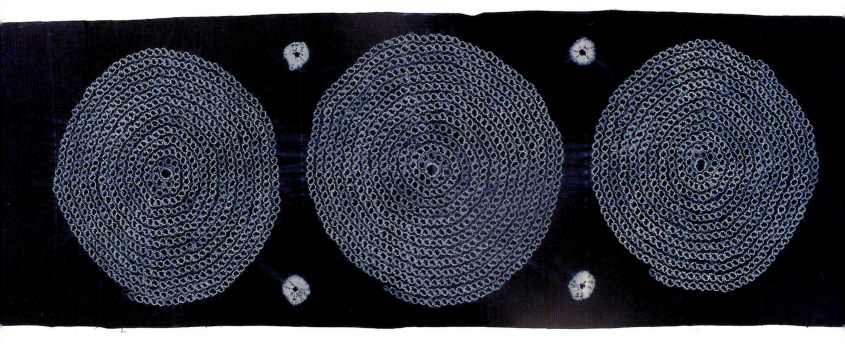

Indigo Dyeing

Indigo dyeing is one of the main means of colouring cloth in West Africa. *Lonchocarpus cyanescens* is the plant commonly used in the process, but synthetic indigo has largely replaced it. Various methods are employed to prepare natural indigo: either fresh leaves or balls of dried leaves kept back from the harvest or acquired through trade are steeped in a wood-ash lye, in vats or deep pits set into the ground and covered with lids. As far back as the fourteenth century, the Arab traveller Ibn Battutah visited Kano, the ancient trading city of northern Nigeria, and remarked upon the indigo dye-pits of Kofor Mata, which, nearly seven hundred years later, are still in use. Many types of cloth are dyed there, including plain new cloth, either hand- or machine-woven, and faded garments, be they old robes or worn-out blue jeans that need their colour refreshing. The bulk of the material dyed here, however, is new fabric to which a resist has been applied. In the secluded courtyards of old Kano city, near the pits, women work at tying in the resists to lengths of mill-woven cloth that, after dyeing, will be sold as women's body-wraps. The length of cloth is first folded into three and then tied so that, after dyeing, a repeat of a spiral design will be created. Concentric circles of ties radiate out from the middle until the tied but undyed cloth has a cone shape. Beans, grains of rice or chips of wood may be inserted into the ties to fill them out, or they may be merely sections of fabric tied with raphia or cotton. The resisted cloth is dyed by men in the pits by the usual indigo-dyeing method of regular dipping, followed by exposure to the air, so that the so-called 'indigo white' oxidizes and turns into 'indigo blue'. The resulting cloth, with its three motifs of concentric circles, is known by the name of 'Three Baskets'.

Leppi and *Ndop*

To the southeast of Nigeria lies the fertile and populous country of Cameroon. Although the population of the south of the country is largely Christian and animist, the north is Muslim and has many similarities with the neighbouring emirates of northern Nigeria. Places such as Maroua and Garoua were, like Kano, traditionally ruled by Fulani. For the most part, the weavers of Garoua and other centres in the north weave cotton (the north is excellent cotton-growing country). They use horizontal looms of the type found, with minor variations, right the way across West Africa. Tension on these types of loom is achieved by stretching the warp out a long way in front of the weaver and tying it to a stone or other heavy object, which is in turn mounted on a wooden sled. The weighted sled provides the necessary tension and is dragged towards the weaver as the weaving progresses. The horizontal loom lies within the men's domain, and the weaver produces narrow strips of unpatterned cloth from undyed cotton. These strips, widely known as *leppi*, are sold either in rolls or made up, by cutting and then sewing the strips together selvedge to selvedge, into cloths of standard dimensions. Among the main markets are the peoples of the grasslands of Cameroon, principally the Bamileke, Bamenda and Bamoun. Women of these groups stitch raphia resists into the cloths. They then send them back up north to be dyed in the dye-pits of Garoua (these pits provide indigo-dyed cloth for the whole country). When the cloths are returned, the women unpick the raphia stitches to form large hangings or skirts with geometric or occasionally figurative designs in white against an indigo blue ground. The Muslim sultanate of Foumban, capital of the Bamoun people,

produces probably the most interesting designs in this type of cloth. Its commonest name is *ndop*, but among the Bamoun it is known as *nteya*. The oldest type of *nteya* displays designs based on the spider's web, recalling a Bamoun creation myth. These textiles are used in the grasslands either as backdrops for the meeting of local Fon chiefs or, folded in two and edged with imported red broadcloth, as skirts for the professional male dancers who perform at 'cry-dies', mourning ceremonies held to commemorate an anniversary of death.

THE PRESENT

Cloth is practically an obsession in West Africa. In the seething public markets, magnificent-looking merchants, both male and female, preside over bolts of colourful mill-made cloth piled in mounds, but they also sell hand-woven cloth made locally from indigenously grown cotton, often dyed nearby in indigo. Cloth is not just an everyday necessity but a requirement for the many ceremonies that punctuate the year. Marriages, coming-of-age rites and funerals all require traditionally made, hand-woven cloth, and it is this that helps keep the practitioners in business. Unless and until the continent is brought fully into the globalized consumerist world economy, makers of traditional textiles will continue to prosper, and hand-woven and dyed textiles will remain the pride of West Africa.

OPPOSITE
'Three Baskets' indigo cloth, Kano, Nigeria.

ABOVE
Indigo dyer at Kofor Mata dye pits, Kano, Nigeria.

TOP RIGHT
Riding coat of strip-woven cloth, Benin.

ABOVE RIGHT
Fulani quilted helmet, Cameroon.

ABOVE
Painted charm coat, Ghana.

WEST AFRICA

Glossary

aba Tunic-shaped surcoat worn over trousers by Arab men

Abbasid dynasty 750–1258, based in Baghdad

abocchnai Embroidered wedding shawl, worn especially by the Dars and Pali land-owning castes of Sindh, Pakistan

abra Sumptuous warp-faced warp-ikat textile, traditionally with a silk warp and weft, woven and worn in Central Asia; speciality of Bokhara and Ferghana

appliqué Needlework technique whereby pieces of fabric are sewn onto a ground material to make a design or image

back-strap loom Weaving apparatus tensioned by the weaver leaning back against a strap or back-rest

baghmal Silk velvet ikat, Uzbekistan

bakhnug Woman's large rectangular shawl worn in Berber North Africa

bandhani Indian term for tie and dye

batik Resist-dyeing technique, whereby wax is applied to a fabric to retain undyed areas in a design

bisht Outer robe, often of camel hair, worn by Arab men

block printing Technique whereby wooden blocks are used to produce prints on a fabric

boteh Curvilinear shape, derived from Persia and perfected in the Mughal period in India; commonly associated with nineteenth-century European shawls, many of which were made in Paisley, imitating shawls from Kashmir; also referred to as *buta*, *kalka* and Paisley cones

buttonhole stitch Similar to blanket stitch, but with stitches closer together; any buttonholes required are cut after the stitching has been completed

callendering Giving a textile a glazed finish

cap batik Javanese method of using copper blocks to print wax onto cloth during the batik process

chach kep Woman's embroidered cap with earflaps and tailpiece, Kyrgyzstan

chay Plant of the madder family, whose root yields a red dye

chikan work Floral form of whitework, made using white cotton or silk (now mostly synthetic) thread on the surface of a fabric; speciality of Lucknow

chyrpy Embroidered coat worn by Turkmen women draped over the head and shoulders like a cloak, with vestigial sleeves

couching Technique whereby a thread is laid on fabric and attached by stitching with another thread

counter-shed The reverse of the natural shed

dishdashah Ubiquitous white cotton gown worn by men in the Arabian Peninsula

double-heddle loom In Africa, apparatus used for weaving strip-woven cloth; the heddles are joined to each other by a cord and operated by foot pedals (in depressing one pedal, the other is raised)

draw-loom Hand-loom capable of raising individual warps and therefore suitable for weaving complicated patterns

faggotting Decorative embroidery technique for stitching two pieces of fabric together

Fatimid dynasty 909–1171, based in Cairo

haik Length of cloth used as a body-wrap by Berber women

heddle Rod with loops, used on simple looms to lift a group of warp ends and thereby make a shed opening

hizam Girdle, often of silk lampas, woven and worn in North Africa

ikat Resist-dyeing process whereby designs are reserved in warp yarns (and sometimes weft yarns, or both) by tying off small bundles of threads with fibre resists to prevent the penetration of dye

jacquard loom Automated system of raising heddles in a specific order using punched cards

jamawar Tapestry-woven shawl; speciality of Kashmir

jamdani Fine cotton muslin textile woven in West Bengal and Bangladesh

kaitag Embroidery in silk on cotton, used ritually at birth, marriage and death, Daghestan

kalamkar Farsi term for Indian block-printed and painted *kalamkari* textile

kanga Rectangular printed cloths worn in East Africa in pairs, one around the waist, one around the shoulders

kantha Traditional quilted and embroidered cloth made with recycled fabric; speciality of Bengal

karboz White cotton cloth hand-woven on narrow looms, Uzbekistan

khaddar Hand-spun, hand-woven cotton cloth, Indian sub-continent

kinkhab Fine Indian brocade with rows of metal-thread motifs on a plain silk ground

kiymeshesk Distinctive Karakalpak hooded veil, Uzbekistan

kurta Woman's loose shift, Indian sub-continent and Central Asia

lampas Complex weaving technique, probably of Byzantine origin, with two sets of warps and two sets of wefts in weft-faced satin weave

limar Weft-ikat prestige textile, usually of silk, Malaysia and Indonesia

Mamluk slave dynasty 1250–1517, based in Egypt and Syria

mashru Satin-weave warp-faced textile with warp of silk (now mostly synthetic) and weft of cotton

mihrab Arched niche; in a mosque, it marks the direction of Mecca

Mughal empire 1526–1858, based in India

muslin Fine soft cotton textile, particularly woven in the region of present-day Bangladesh and northern India

Ottoman empire 1299–1922, with capitals at Bursa and, after 1453, Istanbul

oya Turkish needle-woven braid used as a border

patka Waist-sash with floral brocaded ends, worn by Mughal nobles

patola Double-ikat prestige textile woven in Gujarat and also exported to Southeast Asia

pelangi Indonesian term for tie and dye

pick A single pass of the weft thread from one selvedge to the other

pit-loom Double-heddle apparatus with Asian antecedents, whereby the weaver sits on the edge of a pit

Rasht work Contrast-colour appliquéd textile used as furnishing fabric, made in the port town of Rasht, Iran

r'da Long wraparound robe worn in Tunisia

resist dyeing Technique whereby a dye-resistant substance is used to retain undyed areas in a design

Safavid empire 1501–1736, based in Iran

salvar Baggy trousers with drawstring waist, worn in many parts of the Islamic world

samite Heavy silk fabric of a twill-type weave, often including gold or silver thread

satin stitch Long, straight stitch that appears the same on both sides of the cloth

selvedge Edge of a woven fabric, where the weft begins its return run

shed Opening between warps, through which the weft can be passed while weaving

single-heddle loom Simple loom whereby shed and counter-shed are made by manipulating a single heddle rod

songket Malay brocaded prestige textile woven with silk and metal thread

sprang Method of creating a fabric by manipulating warp threads only; no weft is introduced

stitched resist Technique whereby a resist is formed by stitching into a cloth, compressing the cloth and pulling the thread tight so no dye can penetrate

strip-woven cloth Fabric made up by sewing narrow strips of cloth together, selvedge to selvedge; found throughout West Africa

suzani Large Central Asian hanging, embroidered with flowers and vines

tablet weaving Technique whereby warps are threaded through tablets of card, wood or bone

talli Hand-made metallic thread trims, made using bobbins and a cushion throughout southern Arabia and on the Iranian coast of the Gulf

tapestry weave Technique whereby a discontinuous weft is used to make coloured blocks of pattern

tapis Sarong, usually patterned, Indonesia

tekatan **work** Malay form of gold-thread embroidery, worked on velvet backed with starched cotton

thobe Woman's long garment, traditionally worn in the Arabian Peninsula and Egypt

tie dye Technique whereby small bunches are tied into a fabric before dyeing so these areas remain undyed

tiraz Official state-owned workshops in the Islamic world, producing cloth or clothing

tritik Indonesian term for stitched resist

Umayyad dynasty 661–750, based in Damascus

vertical loom Weaving apparatus on which the warps are stretched vertically rather than horizontally

warp Fixed vertical elements stretching the length of a woven fabric

warp-faced fabric Weave in which the weft has been obscured by the warp threads, and any pattern – most commonly, longitudinal stripes – is carried by the warps

warp ikat Resist-dyeing process applied only to warp threads to give them a pattern prior to weaving

weft Fixed horizontal elements stretching the width of a woven fabric

weft-faced fabric Weave in which the wefts are more densely packed than the warp, or are of a heavier weight, so the warp threads are obscured and dominated by the wefts

whitework Combination of sewing and embroidery techniques using white thread on a white ground

zardozi Costly, high-status, metal-thread-embroidered textiles made in the Indian sub-continent and Iran

Further Reading

Agrawal, Yashodara, *Silk Brocades*, 2003
Allsen, Thomas T., *Commodity and Exchange in the Mongol Empire: A Cultural History of Islamic Textiles*, 2008
Andrews, Mügül and Peter, *Turkmen Needlework: Dressmaking and Embroidery among the Turkmen of Iran*, 1976
Askari, Nasreen, and Rosemary Crill, *Colours of the Indus: Costume and Textiles of Pakistan*, 1997
Askari, Nasreen, Liz Arthur, and Valerie Reilly, *Uncut Cloth: Saris, Shawls and Sashes*, 1999
Atasoy, Nurhan, Walter B. Denny, Louise W. Mackie, and Hülya Tezcan, *Ipek: The Crescent and the Rose. Imperial Ottoman Silks and Velvets*, 2001
Baker, Patricia L., *Islamic Textiles*, 1995
Balfour-Paul, Jenny, *Indigo in the Arab World*, 1997
—, *Indigo*, 1998
Barnes, Ruth, *Indian Block-Printed Cotton Fragments in the Kelsey Museum*, 1993
Belkaïd, Leyla, *Algéroises: Histoire d'un costume méditerranéen*, 1998
—, *Costumes d'Algérie*, 2003
Besancenot, Jean, *Costumes of Morocco*, 1990
Bier, Carol (ed.), *Woven from the Soul, Spun from the Heart: Textile Arts of Safavid and Qajar Iran. 16th–19th Centuries*, 1987
Bilgrami, Noorjehan, *Sindh jo Ajrak*, 1998
Black, David, *Embroidered Flowers from Thrace to Tartary*, 1981
Black, David, and Clive Loveless, *Iselmeler: Ottoman Domestic Embroideries*, 1978
Bonnenfant, Paul, *Zabid au Yémen: Archéologie du vivant*, 2004
Boucher, Jeff W., *Baluchi Woven Treasures*, 1996
Bühler, Alfred, *Ikat, Batik, Plangi*, 1972
Burnham, Dorothy K., *A Textile Terminology: Warp and Weft*, 1981
Campbell Cole, Barbie, and Peri M. Klemm, 'Historical Threads: An Overview of Women's Dresses in Harar', in *Archiv für Völkerkunde* 53: 63–72, 2003
Chaudhuri, K. N., *Trade and Civilization in the Indian Ocean: An Economic History from the Rise of Islam to 1750*, 1985
Chenciner, Robert, *Kaitag: The Textile Art of Daghestan*, 1994
Colyer Ross, Heather, *The Art of Arabian Costume*, 1981
Cooper, Ilay, John Gillow, and Barry Dawson, *Arts and Crafts of India*, 1996
Crichton, Anne-Rhona, *Al Sadu: The Techniques of Bedouin Weaving*, 1998
Crill, Rosemary, *Indian Ikat Textiles*, 1998
Crocker Jones, Gigi, *Spinning and Weaving in the Sultanate of Oman*, 1989

De Guise, Lucian (ed.), *The Message and the Monsoon: Islamic Art of South-East Asia*, 2005
Denamur, Isabelle, *Moroccan Textile Embroidery*, 2003
Dhamija, Jasleen, *Living Tradition of Iran's Crafts*, 1979
Dickson, H. R. P., *Kuwait and her Neighbours*, 1956
Dolyáni, Anna, *Stickereien für 1001 Nacht*, 1989
Dupaigne, Bernard, *Afghan Embroidery*, 1993
Ecker, Heather, *Caliphs and Kings: The Art and Influence of Islamic Spain*, 2004
El Jisr, Bassem, *Mémoire de soie: Costumes et parures de Palestine at de Jordanie: coll. Widad Kamel Kawar*, 1988
Ellis, Marianne, *Embroideries and Samplers from Islamic Egypt*, 2001
Ellis, Marianne, and Jennifer Wearden, *Ottoman Embroidery*, 2001
Fakhry, Ahmed, *Siwa Oasis*, 1973
Ferrier, R. W., *The Arts of Persia*, 1990
Fitzgibbon, Kate, and Andrew Hale, *Ikats: The Rau Collection*, 1988
—, *Ikat: The Guido Goldman Collection*, 1997
—, *Uzbek Embroidery in the Nomadic Tradition*, 2007
Fraser-Lu, Sylvia, *Handwoven Textiles of South East Asia*, 1988
Fullerton, Arlene, and Geza Fehervari, *Kuwait: Arts and Architecture*, 1995
Gargouri-Sethom, Samira, *Les arts populaires en Tunisie*, 1994
Gervers, Veronika, *The Influence of Ottoman Turkish Textiles and Costume in Eastern Europe*, 1982
Gillow, John, *African Textiles*, 2002
—, (foreword by Zahra Freeth), *From Desert to Town: Traditional Weavings of Kuwait*, 2009
Gillow, John, and Nicholas Barnard, *Traditional Indian Textiles*, 1991
—, *Indian Textiles*, 2008
Gillow, John, and Barry Dawson, *Traditional Indonesian Textiles*, 1992
Gillow, John, and Bryan Sentance, *World Textiles*, 1999
Gluck, J. and S. H. (eds), *A Survey of Persian Handicraft*, 1977
Goodwin, Geoffrey, *The Private World of Ottoman Women*, 2006
Goswamy, B. N., *Patkas: Indian Costumes in the Collection of the Calico Museum of Textiles*, 2000
—, *Patkas: A Costume Accessory in the Collection of the Calico Museum of Textiles*, 2002
Grammet, Ivo, and Min De Meersman (eds), *Splendeurs du Maroc*, 1998
Green, Gillian, *Traditional Textiles of Cambodia: Cultural Threads and Material Heritage*, 2003

Grube, Ernst J., *Keshte: Central Asian Embroideries. The Marshall and Marilyn R. Wolf Collection*, 2003
Gürsu, Nevber, *The Art of Turkish Weaving: Design Through the Ages*, 1988
Hamilton, Roy W., *From the Rainbow's Varied Hue: Textiles of the Southern Philippines*, 1998
Harvey, Janet, *Traditional Textiles of Central Asia*, 1996
Hatanaka, Kokyo, and Zahid Sardar, *Textile Arts of India*, 1993
Heathcote, David, *The Arts of the Hausa*, 1976
Hecht, Ann, *The Art of the Loom: Weaving, Spinning and Dyeing across the World*, 1989
Heringa, Rens, and Harmen C. Veldhuisen, *Fabric of Enchantment: Batik from the North Coast of Java*, 1996
Hitchcock, Michael, *Indonesian Textile Techniques*, 1985
—, *Indonesian Textiles*, 1991
Inalcik, Halil, *The Ottoman Empire: The Classical Age, 1300–1600*, 1973
Irwin, John, *The Kashmir Shawl*, 1974
Iwatate, Hiroko, *Desert Village, Life and Crafts, Gujarat, Rajasthan*, 1989
—, *Textiles: The Soul of India*, 2007
Jereb, James F., *Arts and Crafts of Morocco*, 1995
Johnstone, Pauline, *Turkish Embroidery*, 1985
Kalashnikova, Natalia, and Galina Plushnikova, *National Costumes of the Soviet Peoples*, 1990
Kalter, Johannes, *The Arts and Crafts of Turkestan*, 1984
—, *The Arts and Crafts of the Swat Valley*, 1991
Kalter, Johannes (ed.), *The Arts and Crafts of Syria*, 1992
Kalter, Johannes, and Margareta Pavaloi, *Uzbekistan: Heirs to the Silk Road*, 1997
Kay, Shirley, *The Bedouin*, 1978
Keohane, Alan, *Bedouin: Nomads of the Desert*, 1994
Klimova, Nina T., *Folk Embroidery of the USSR*, 1981
Krody, Sumru Belger, *Flowers of Silk and Gold: Four Centuries of Ottoman Embroidery*, 2000
Lamb, Venice, and Judy Holmes, *Nigerian Weaving*, 1980
Lamb, Venice, and Alastair Lamb, *Au Cameroun: Weaving–Tissage*, 1981
Lemaistre, Joëlle, and Marie-France Vivier, *De soie et d'or*, 1996
Lynton, Linda, and Sanjay K. Singh, *The Sari: Styles, Patterns, History, Techniques*, 1995
Maurières, Arnaud, Philippe Chambon, and Éric Ossart, *Reines de Saba: Itinéraires textiles au Yémen*, 2003
Maxwell, Robyn, *Textiles of South East Asia*, 1990

May, Florence Lewis, *Silk Textiles of Spain: Eighth to Fifteenth Century*, 1957
Medjitova, Elmira, *Turkmen Folk Arts*, 1990
Meiselas, Susan, *Kurdistan: In the Shadow of History*, 2008
Musée des Arts d'Afrique et d'Océanie, *Noces tissées, noces brodées*, 1995
Nabholz-Kartaschoff, Marie-Louise, and Axel Langer, *Pfauen, Blüten und Zypressen*, 2006
Namati, Parviz, *Shawls of the East: From Kerman to Kashmir*, 2003
Paine, Sheila, *Chikan Embroidery*, 1989
—, *Embroidery from Afghanistan*, 2006
—, *Embroidered Textiles: A World Guide to Traditional Patterns*, 2008
Pastor-Roces, Marian, *Sinaunang Habi: Philippine Ancestral Weave*, 1991
Paydar, Niloo Imami, and Ivo Grammet (eds), *The Fabric of Moroccan Life*, 2002
Pinner, Robert, and Murray L. Eiland, *Between the Black Desert and the Red: Turkmen Carpets from the Wiedersperg Collection*, 1999
Piotrovsky, Mikhail, *On Islamic Art*, 2001
Rabaté, Marie-Rose, and Frieda Sorber, *Berber Costumes of Morocco: Traditional Patterns*, 2007
Rajab, Jehan, *Palestinian Costume*, 1989
—, *Costumes from the Arab World*, 2002
Rau, Pip, *Ikats: Woven Silks from Central Asia*, 1988
Rehman, Sherry, and Naheed Jafri, *The Kashmiri Shawl: From Jamawar to Paisley*, 2006
Reswick, Irmtraud, *Traditional Textiles of Tunisia*, 1985
Richardson, Neil, and Marcia Dorr, *The Craft Heritage of Oman*, 2003
Rodgers, Susan, Anne Summerfield, and John Summerfield, *Gold Cloths of Sumatra: Indonesia's Songkets from Ceremony to Commodity*, 2007
Rogers, Clive, *Early Islamic Textiles*, 1983
Scarce, Jennifer M., *Middle Eastern Costume from the Tribes and Cities of Iran and Turkey*, 1981
—, *Domestic Culture in the Middle East*, 1996
Scott, Philippa, *The Book of Silk*, 1993
Searight, Sarah, *Yemen: Land and People*, 2002
Serjeant, R. B., *Islamic Textiles: Material for a History up to the Mongol Conquest*, 1972
Sidorenko, A. I., A. R. Artykov, and R. R. Radjabov, *Gold Embroidery of Bukhara*, 1981
Skinner, Margarita, and Widad Kamel Kawar, *Palestinian Embroidery Motifs: A Treasury of Stitches, 1850–1950*, 2007
Spring, Christopher, and Julie Hudson, *North African Textiles*, 1995
Start, Laura E., *The Durham Collection of Garments and Embroideries from Albania and Yugoslavia*, 1977
Stillman, Yedida Kalfon, *Palestinian Costume and Jewelry*, 1979
Stone, Caroline, *The Embroideries of North Africa*, 1985
Taube, Jakob, and Ignazio Vok, *Suzani: A Textile Art from Central Asia*, 1994
—, *Suzani 2: A Textile Art from Central Asia*, 2006
Taylor, Roderick, *Ottoman Embroidery*, 1993
Topham, John, *Traditional Crafts of Saudi Arabia*, 1982
Valeeva-Suleimanova, Guzel, and Rozalina Shageeva, *The Decorative Applied Arts of the Kazan Tatars*, 1990
Vivier, Marie-France, *Broderies marocaines*, 1991
Volbach, W. Fritz, *Early Decorative Textiles*, 1969
Von Falke, Otto, *Decorative Silks*, 1936
Von Folsach, Kjeld, and Anne-Marie Keblow Bernsted, *Woven Treasures: Textiles from the World of Islam*, 1993
Wace, A. J. B., *Mediterranean and Near Eastern Embroideries*, 1935
Wearden, Jennifer, *Persian Printed Cottons*, 1989
Weir, Shelagh, *Spinning and Weaving in Palestine*, 1970
—, *The Bedouin*, 1976
—, *Palestinian Costume*, 1990
—, *Embroidery from Palestine*, 2006
Weir, Shelagh, and Serene Shahid, *Palestinian Embroidery*, 2006
Wong, How Man, and Adel A. Dajani, *Islamic Frontiers of China: Silk Road Images*, 1990
Woodthorpe Browne, Clare, *Ikats*, 1989
Wutt, Karl, *Pashai*, 1981
Yacopino, Feliccia, *Threadlines Pakistan*, 1987

Museum Collections

Museums are listed in alphabetical order by country, then by town or city. Where possible, websites have been included.

ABU DHABI
Al Ain National Museum
near Sultan Fort (Eastern Fort)
Al Ain
www.aam.gov.ae

ALBANIA
National Historical Museum
Skanderbeg Square
Tirana

AUSTRALIA
National Gallery of Australia
Parkes Place
Parkes
Canberra, ACT 2600
http://nga.gov.au

AZERBAIJAN
Azerbaijan Carpet and Applied Arts State Museum
123a Neftchilar Avenue
Baku 370000

Azerbaijan State Museum of Art
31 Istiglaliyat St
Baku 370001

BAHRAIN
Bahrain National Museum
Al Fatih Highway
Manama
www.moci.gov.bh/en/
CultureNationalHeritage/
BahrainNationalMuseum

BANGLADESH
Bangla Academy Folklore Museum
Bangla Academy
Dhaka

Bangladesh National Museum
Shahbag
Dhaka
www.bangladeshmuseum.gov.bd

BENIN
Musée Ethnographique Alexandre Sènou Adandé
BP: 299
Porto Novo

BRUNEI
Muzium Brunei Darussalam
Jalan Kota Batu
Bandar Seri Begawan BB4310
http://www.museums.gov.bn/
bangunan.htm

CAMEROON
National Museum
Yaoundé

CANADA
Royal Ontario Museum
100 Queens Park
Toronto
Ontario M5S 2C6
www.rom.on.ca

Textile Museum of Canada
55 Centre Avenue
Toronto
Ontario M5G 2H5
www.textilemuseum.ca

CHINA
Museum of the Cultural Palace of National Minorities
Chang'an St
Beijing

Yunnan Provincial Museum
2 May 1 Rd
Kunming City
www.chinamuseums.com/yunnan.htm

Xinjiang Uighur Autonomous Region Museum
132 Xibei Rd
Ürümchi
www.chinamuseums.com/xinjiang.htm

DENMARK
Davids Samling [The David Collection]
Kronprinsessegade 30
Copenhagen 1306
www.davidmus.dk

EGYPT
Ethnological Museum
Geographical Society Building
109 Qasr al-Ayni St
Cairo

Folklore Museum
19 Borsa al-Tawfiqiya St
Cairo

Museum of Islamic Art
Ahmed Maher Square
Bab Al-Khalq
Cairo

ETHIOPIA
Ethnographic Museum
Addis Ababa University
Yekatit 12 Square
Addis Ababa

National Museum
Sudan St
Addis Ababa

FRANCE
Musée des Tissus et des Arts Décoratifs
34, rue de la Charité
69002 Lyon
www.musee-des-tissus.com

Musée du Quai Branly
37 Quai Branly
75007 Paris
www.quaibranly.fr

Musée National des Arts Asiatiques Guimet
6, place d'Iéna
75116 Paris
www.guimet.fr

GERMANY
Museum für Völkerkunde
Arnimallee 27
14195 Berlin
www.smb.museum/smb/
sammlungen/details

Rautenstrauch-Joest Museum für Völkerkunde der Stadt Köln
Ubierring 45
50678 Cologne
www.rjmkoeln.de

Linden-Museum-Stuttgart
Staatliches Museum für Völkerkunde
Hegelplatz 1
70174 Stuttgart
www.lindenmuseum.de

GREECE
Benaki Museum
22 Ag. Asomaton & 12 Dipilou St
Benaki
www.benaki.gr/

INDIA
Calico Museum of Textiles
Shahibagh
Ahmedabad 380004
www.calicomuseum.com/

Crafts Museum
Pragati Maidan
Bhairon Rd
New Delhi 110001
http://nationalcraftsmuseum.nic.in

INDONESIA
Museum Tekstil
Jl. K. Satsuit Tubun No. 2-4
Jakarta
Java

Museum Batik
3 Jetayu St
Pekalongan
Java
www.museumronggowarsito.
org/english/jtg/jtg.asp?isi=
pekalongan_batik

IRAN
National Museum of Kashan
Bagh-e Fin
Amir Kabir Ave
Kashan

Rasht Museum
99 Bisotoon St
Taleghani Ave
Rasht

Tabriz Museum
Masjed-e Kabud
Imam Khomenei Ave
Tabriz

Carpet Museum of Iran
Dr Fatemi Ave and Kargar Intersection
Tehran 14154
www.carpetmuseum.ir/home.htm

National Museum of Iran
30 Tir St
Imam Khomeini Ave
Tehran
www.nationalmuseumofiran.ir

IRAQ
Baghdad Museum
Sahat Al-Risafi
Baghdad

Iraq Museum
Karkh Museum Square
Salhiya
Baghdad

Mosul Museum
Dawassa
Mosul

ISRAEL
Islamic Museum
Al-Haram Al-Sharif
Jerusalem

L. A. Mayer Museum for Islamic Art
2 Hapalmach St
Jerusalem
www.islamicart.co.il/en

IVORY COAST
Musée National du Costume
BP 311 Grand-Bassam
www.abidjan-info.com/mapage6/index.html

JAPAN
Museum of Textiles
5-102 Tomobuchi- Cho
1-Chome, Miyakojima-Ku
Osaka

Bunka Gakuen Costume Museum
Shinjuku Bunka Quint Building
3-22-7 Yoyogi
Shibuya-ku
Tokyo 151
www.bunka.ac.jp/museum/text/english.html

Iwatate Folk Textile Museum
25-13 Jiyugaoka-1
Meguroku
Tokyo 152
http://iwatate-hiroko.com

JORDAN
Folklore Museum
Roman Theatre
Amman

KUWAIT
Tareq Rajab Museum
Jabrieh, Area 12, Street 5
Hawelli
www.trmkt.com

Al-Sadu House
Arabian Gulf St
Kuwait City

Kuwait National Museum
Arabian Gulf St
Kuwait City

KYRGYZSTAN
Kyrgyz State Museum of Fine Arts
ul Pervomaiskaja 90
Biskek 720000

LEBANON
Musée National de Beyrouth
rue de Damas
Beirut
www.beirutnationalmuseum.com

LIBYA
Ethnography Museum
Department of Antiquities
Assaraya al-Hamra
Tripoli

MALAYSIA
Sabah Museum
Jalan Muzium
88000 Kota Kinabalu

International Handicraft Museum
9 Jalan Conlay
50450 Kuala Lumpur

Islamic Arts Museum Malaysia
Jalan Lembah Perdana
50480 Kuala Lumpur
www.iamm.org.my

Malay Ethnographic Museum
Department of Malay Studies
University of Malaya
59100 Kuala Lumpur

Sarawak Museum
Tun Abang Haji Openg Rd
93566 Kuching
www.museum.sarawak.gov.my/indexeng.htm

Textile Museum
The Pavilion
Kuching
www.museum.sarawak.gov.my/textilemu.htm

MALI
Musée National du Mali
rue du Général Leclerc
BP 159 Bamako

MOROCCO
Musée Ethnographique
Kasbah Outa Hammam
Chefchaouen

Maison Tiskiwin / Musée Bert Flint
8, rue de la Bahia
Marrakech

Musée d'Archéologique, d'Arts et d' Folklorique de Tanger
Place de la Kasbah
Tangier

Musée Ethnographique
Zankat Skala
65 Bab El Okla
Tetouan

NETHERLANDS
Tropenmuseum
Linnaeusstraat 2
1092 CK Amsterdam
http://collectie.tropenmuseum.nl

Stichting Rijksmuseum Voor Volkenkunde
Steenstraat 1
2312 BS Leiden
www.rmv.nl

NIGER
Musée National du Niger
BP 248 Niamey
www.usenghor-francophonie.org/enseig/pc/inforoutes/niger/musee.htm

NIGERIA
National Museum Kaduna
Ali Akilu Rd
Ungwan Sarki
Kaduna
http://tourismkaduna.org/tourist_centres_details.php?recordID=6

National Museum
Onikan
Lagos

OMAN
Museum of Omani Heritage
Al Alam St
Muscat
www.omanet.om/english/tourism/entert/museums.asp?cat=tour&subcat=entert1

National Museum
A'Noor St
Ruwi
www.omanet.om/english/tourism/entert/museums.asp?cat=tour&subcat=entert1

PAKISTAN
Mohatta Palace Museum
7 Hatim Alvi Rd
Clifton
Karachi
www.mohattapalacemuseum.com

National Museum of Pakistan
Burns Gardens
Karachi

PHILIPPINES
Sulu Ethnological Museum
Notre Dame of Jolo College
Jolo 7901

Metropolitan Museum of Manila
Bangko Sentral ng Pilipinas Complex
Roxas Blvd
Manila 2801
www.metmuseum.ph

Museum of Anthropology
3/F Palma Hall
University of the Philippines
Quezon City 1101

Tawi-Tawi Ethnological Museum
Sulu College of Technology and Oceanography
San Jose Road
Tawi-Tawi 7602

QATAR
Museum of Islamic Art
Corniche
Doha
www.mia.org.qa/english/index.html

RUSSIA
State Museum of Oriental Art
Nikitskij Blvd, 12a
Moscow
www.orientmuseum.ru/en

Peter the Great Museum of
Anthropology and Ethnology
Universitetskaya 3
St Petersburg
www.kunstkamera.ru/en/

Russian Museum of Ethnography
ul. Inzenernaya 4–1
St Petersburg
http://eng.ethnomuseum.ru

SAUDI ARABIA
Oriental Museum for Carpets
Riyadh

Riyadh Museum for History and
Archaeology
Riyadh

Mansoojat Foundation
Online museum of Saudi Arabian
costume: www.mansoojat.org

SIERRA LEONE
Sierra Leone National Museum
Pademba Rd
Freetown

SINGAPORE
National Museum of Singapore
93 Stamford Rd
Singapore 178897
www.nationalmuseum.sg

SWITZERLAND
Museum der Kulturen Basel
www.mkb.ch/en/home.html

SYRIA
National Museum of Aleppo
Baron St
Aleppo

National Museum
Syrian University St
Damascus

Hama Museum
Beit Al-Azem
rue Abdul Fida
Hama

Homs Museum
Cultural Centre
Tripoli St
Homs

TANZANIA
Zanzibar National Museum
of History and Culture
Sokoku Street
Stone Town
Zanzibar

TUNISIA
Musée Régional Le Bardo
rue Mohamed Badra
Djerba 4180

Musée National d'Art Islamique
Raqqâda
Kairouan
www.patrimoinedetunisie.com.tn/eng/musees/raqqada.php

Musée de Mahdia
Mahdia 5100
www.patrimoinedetunisie.com.tn/eng/musees/mahdia.php

Musée de Moknine
Moknine 5050
www.patrimoinedetunisie.com.tn/eng/musees/moknine.php

Musée National du Bardo
Le Bardo 2000
Tunis
www.patrimoinedetunisie.com.tn/eng/musees/bardo.php

TURKEY
Ulumay Museum of Ottoman
Folk Costumes and Jewellery
İkincimurat Caddesi
Muradiye
Bursa

Museum of Turkish and Islamic
Arts
Hippodrome 46
Sultanahmet Square
Istanbul

Topkapi Palace Museum
Sultanahmet
Istanbul

TURKMENISTAN
National Museum of History and
Ethnography
ul Shevchenko 1
Ashkhabad 744000

UNITED KINGDOM
Cartwright Hall Art Gallery
Lister Park
Bradford BD9 4NS
www.bradfordmuseums.org/cartwrighthall/

National Museum of Scotland
Chambers St
Edinburgh EH1 1JF
www.nms.ac.uk/our_museums/national_museum.aspx

Bankfield Museum
Akroyd Park
Boothtown Rd
Halifax HX3 6HG
www.calderdale.gov.uk/leisure/museums-galleries/bankfield-museum/index.html

New Walk Museum & Art Gallery
53 New Walk
Leicester LE1 7EA
www.leicester.gov.uk/your-council-services/lcleicester-city-museums/museums/nwm-art-gallery

British Museum
Great Russell St
London WC1B 3DG
www.britishmuseum.org

Horniman Museum
100 London Rd
Forest Hill
London SE23 3PQ
www.horniman.ac.uk

Victoria & Albert Museum
Cromwell Rd
London SW7 2RL
www.vam.ac.uk

Whitworth Art Gallery
Whitworth Park
University of Manchester
Oxford Rd
Manchester M15 6ER
www.whitworth.manchester.ac.uk

Pitt Rivers Museum
South Parks Rd
Oxford OX1 3PP
www.prm.ox.ac.uk

UNITED STATES
The Field Museum
1400 S. Lake Shore Drive
Chicago, IL 60605
www.fieldmuseum.org

Indianapolis Museum of Art
4000 Michigan Rd
Indianapolis, IN 46208
www.imamuseum.org

Fowler Museum at UCLA
308 Charles E. Young Dr. North
Los Angeles, CA 90095
www.fowler.ucla.edu/incEngine

Newark Museum
49 Washington St
Newark, NJ 07102
www.newarkmuseum.org

Brooklyn Museum
200 Eastern Parkway
Brooklyn
New York, NY 11238
www.brooklynmuseum.org

Metropolitan Museum of Art
1000 Fifth Avenue
New York, NY 10028
www.metmuseum.org

Philadelphia Museum of Art
26th St and Benjamin Franklin
Parkway
Philadelphia, PA 19130
www.philamuseum.org

Mingei International Museum
1439 El Prado
San Diego, CA 92101
www.mingei.org

Fine Arts Museums of San
Francisco de Young
Golden Gate Park
50 Hagiwara Tea Garden Drive
San Francisco, CA 94118
www.famsf.org

Museum of International Folk Art
706 Camino Lejo
Santa Fe, NM 87505
www.moifa.org

Textile Museum
2320 S Street Northwest
Washington, DC 20008
www.textilemuseum.org

UZBEKISTAN
Karakalpak Museum of Arts
Old Museum: Karakalpakstan St, 2
New Museum: K. Rzaev St
Nukus 230100
www.savitskycollection.org/

Museum of Applied Art of
Uzbekistan
Rakatboshi St, 15
Tashkent 100031
www.artmuseum.uz/en/index.html

YEMEN
Crater Folk Museum
Tawila
Aden

Ethnographical Museum
Garden, near Tanks
Aden

Yemen National Museum
Dar as-Sa'd
Tahrir Sq
Sana'a

Taiz Museum
Taiz

Zafar Museum
Zafar

Picture Credits

All photography by Luke Gillow and Tamsin Beedle except:

Elizabeth Andrews p. 234
James Austin pp. 60, 61 right, 64, 82 below, 97, 98 above right, 100, 104 top, 105 left, 109 below, 111, 140 above, 144 top left, 145 above, 146 above, 186, 207 right, 215, 221 above left, above centre and below, 229 centre, 236 above left, 241 above right, 246 left, 256 left and right, 257 below, 258 left, 262, 270 below, 278 second from top, 280 top and centre, 281, 282 above and below, 283 right, 286 above, 291, 292 below, 297, 298 above and below, 299 above and below, 302, 303 above, below and right, 304 above and below, 305 right, 306, 307 centre and below
Jenny Balfour-Paul pp. 98 above left, 137 below, 138, 147 above
Rosie Bose p. 316
Sian Davies pp. 235, 236 above right, 246 right, 259 below
John Gillow pp. 65 above and below, 71 below left and right, 83 below, 137 above, 156 above left, 157 right, 173 above left, above right and below, 174, 202 below left and right, 218, 239, 259 above, 271 below, 307 top left
Mike Glad p. 147 below
Suleiman Haider pp. 128, 130 right
Courtesy of The Hispanic Society of America, New York p. 51
Angelo Hornak p. 1
Hiroko Iwatate p. 260
Ralph Koch p. 13
Longevity Studio, London pp. 9, 10, 11, 12, 16, 52, 52–53, 55, 67, 153 right, 191
Moggy pp. 122, 124 left, centre and right, 125 left, centre and right, 127 above left and right, below left and right
Barbara R. Molloy p. 274 left and right
Andres Moraga p. 13
David and Sue Richardson p. 202 above
Sarawak Museum p. 272
Hitomo Takahashi pp. 261, 262
Eileen Tweedy (engraving by W. Wallis, after drawing by David Roberts) p. 50
Sue Ubagu p. 300
Mark Williams p. 129

Acknowledgments

There are so many to thank for all the help extended over many years. First, thanks to Sheikha Altaf Al-Sabah, who so generously took me to Kuwait and introduced me to Bedouin and urban weaving there. Thanks also to Hamida Ali Reza and Mona Khashoggi and all at the Mansoojat Foundation, who in the same spirit gave me such free access to their unique collection of Saudi Arabian costume.

For the use of photographs, thanks to Elizabeth Andrews, James Austin, Jenny Balfour-Paul, Sian Davies, Mike Glad, Suleiman Haider, the Hispanic Society of America, Hiroko Iwatate, Longevity Studio, Moggy, Barbara R. Molloy, Andres Moraga, the Permanent Collection of Bedouin Weavings and Textiles of the Kuwait Al Sadu Society, David and Sue Richardson, Hitomo Takahashi, Sue Ubagu, Mark Williams, and especially Clive Loveless and Roddy Taylor.

For access to her charming collection of vintage postcards, thanks to Carolyn Dallas.

For access to their collections I'm also deeply indebted to Giambattista D'Alessio, Esther FitzGerald, Dr and Mrs Harry Greenberg, Molly Hogg, Robert Kime, Neville Kingston, Ulrike Montigel, Sheila Paine, Pip Rau, Barbie Rich and Toshio Okamura, Clive Rogers, Caroline Stone, Roddy Taylor, The Textile Gallery (London), Karun Thakar and Roy Short, and Junnaa and Thomi Wroblewski.

For their help in researching the book, thank you to Sara Baghai (to whom I am indebted for information on Iran), Barbie Campbell Cole (Harar and Turkish raw materials), Robert Chenciner (Daghestan), Nick Fielding (Kyrgyzstan), Paul Lunde (Arabia), Shahira Mehrez (Egypt), Sheila Paine (Turkmenistan), David and Sue Richardson (the Karakalpak), Mohammad Abbas Selim of the Museum of Islamic Art, Cairo (Egypt), Ron Stewart (Iraq) and Roddy Taylor (Turkey). I also freely acknowledge my debt to all Shelagh Weir's published works on Palestinian textiles.

For their help with textiles and information over many years, thanks to Janet Anderson, Tim and Ferelith Ashfield, Jim Bishop, Barbie Campbell Cole, Duncan Clarke, Robert Clyne, the late Peter Collingwood, Ilay Cooper, Mary Cooper, Caroline Crabtree, Anna Crutchley, Joyce Doel, Nick Fielding, Ernst Grube and Eleanor Sims, Janet Harvey, Sally Hirons, Alastair Hull, Trudi Kaldschmidt, Leicester Museum, Rosie McMurray, Chander Maheshwari, Michael Maitland, Marion Maule, Jane May, the late Karen Needham, Chantale Noël, Jennie Parry, Tim Price, Merrill Randol, David Reisbord, Victoria Rivers, Judy Rudoe and Antony Griffiths, Masha Stanyukovitch, Charles Vernon-Hunt, Hannah Whyman and Hilary Williams.

For their most generous hospitality, thank you to the Faramazi family of Tehran, Joan and John Fisher, Steve Grossfield, the Mako family of Peshawar, Sara and Tim Price, Foudil Rerizani and family of Cambridge and Algiers, Goodie Vohra, and Yusuf Zacharia and family of Karachi.

And for all their help and constant encouragement, thank you to Clive Rogers and Rosie Bose.

Finally, thanks to all the nameless textile practitioners all over the Muslim world who produced the magnificent textiles that illustrate this book.

Haji Mako, Afghan merchant of Peshawar.

Index

Numbers in *italics* refer to illustrations

A

Abbasids 10, 13, 89, 118, 268

Afghanistan 10, 17, 154, 190, 196, 203, 212, 214, 215, 218–31, 247, 249, 253; *218, 219, 220, 221, 222, 223, 224, 225, 226, 227, 228, 229, 230, 231*

ajarakh print 258; *247, 258*

Akcha (Afghanistan) 221; *221*

Albania 33, 42, 44, 46, 91; *43, 44, 45*

Aleppo (Syria) 17, 18, 36, 91, 96, 98, 99, 103, 104, 106, 110, 138; *98, 99, 101, 102, 104, 106*

Algeria 66–71; *66, 67, 68, 69, 70, 71*

Algiers (Algeria) 66, 67, 68, 70; *67, 68, 71*

Anatolia 11, 17, 22, 24, 25, 26, 31, 33, 36, 39, 41, 44, 174; *24, 31, 32, 36, 39, 40, 41*

Andalusia 10, 13, 50, 53, 58, 61, 72

Andkhui (Afghanistan) 221; *221*

appliqué 91, 116, 126, 153, 161, 229, 240, 257, 274, 279; *91, 93, 107, 161, 257*

Arabs 10, 11, 17, 50, 84, 86, 94–147, 150, 212, 247, 268, 276, 278, 289, 293, 296

Armenia 31, 36, 41, 152

Assyut (Egypt) 99

Azerbaijan 150, 157, 169, 174, 177, 180, 238; *15, 175, 176, 177, 178, 179, 181*

B

Baghdad (Iran) 10, 13, 14, 17, 22, 89, 118; *118*

Bahrain 124, 130

Bajau people 274; *274*

Bakhtiari people 150, 159; *159, 164, 170*

Baku (Azerbaijan) 174; *178*

Balkans 11, 22, 26, 42–47, 104, 174; *42*

Baluch people 131, 133, 157, 247, 249, 253, 259; *221, 249, 250, 252*

Bangladesh 132, 237, 260–65; *260, 261, 262, 263, 264, 265*

batik 15, 98, 169, 174, 214, 221, 246, 272, 275, 278, 287, 289; *213, 272, 277, 286, 287, 289*

beadwork 33, 44, 92, 125; *33, 45, 106*

Bedouin people 84, 96, 110, 112, 116, 122, 124, 128, 129, 130, 131, 133, 136, 137, 146; *84, 86, 88, 96, 102, 118, 121, 129, 130, 132, 146*

beetle's wing embroidery 256

Benares (India) 18, 236, 237; *236*

Bengal 18, 234, 237, 247, 251, 263

Benin *307*

Berbers 50, 61, 64, 66, 70, 72, 74, 79, 80, 84, 91, 92; *61, 80, 85*

Bethlehem 110, 116; *110, 111, 115, 117*

block printing 106, 164, 167, 174, 193, 221, 244, 259; *34, 107, 108, 109, 194, 210, 244, 246, 247, 258*

Bokhara (Uzbekistan) 18, 184, 186, 189, 192, 193, 195, 196, 212, 251; *2, 192, 196, 198, 199, 200, 202*

Borneo 272

Bosnia 42, 46; *45*

Bursa (Turkey) 17, 22, 26, 36, 44; *10, 29, 33, 34, 38, 58*

Brunei 272

Byzantines 8, 10, 11, 15, 22, 72, 84, 86, 89, 96

C

camel hair 24, 124, 130, 157, 203, 270; *102*

Cameroon 8, 306; *307*

Cairo (Egypt) 10, 13, 89, 90, 91, 122, 244; *89, 91, 93*

Caucasus 41, 174–81; *174, 175, 176, 177, 178, 179, 180, 181*

Central Asia 10, 13, 14, 18, 22, 86, 152, 154, 182–231, 251, 271

Chad 305

Chakwal (Pakistan) 247, 249, 251

Chefchaouen (Morocco) 54, 58, 61, 64; *16, 55, 62, 64*

chikan work 240

China 8, 11, 14, 15, 52, 79, 90, 118, 131, 133, 150, 184, 186, 212, 216, 268–71, 272, 276, 279, 282, 289, 290, 293, 298; *268, 269, 270, 271*

Chitral (Pakistan) 251, 253

Constantinople, *see* Istanbul

crochet 103; *103*

D

Daghestan 174, 180, 181; *12, 174, 180*

Damascus (Syria) 10, 11, 13, 18, 36, 89, 96, 98, 99, 104, 105, 106, 109, 110, 122, 238; *100, 104, 105, 106, 107, 108, 109*

E

Egypt 10, 11, 13, 17, 18, 25, 52, 61, 68, 86–93, 99, 103, 110, 112, 128, 298; *6, 13, 86, 87, 88, 89, 90, 91, 92, 93*

Eritrea *297*

Ethiopia 126, 244, 296; *298*

F

Fatimids 10, 13, 89, 152

felt 24, 39, 41, 42, 207, 211, 215, 216, 217; *39, 45, 207, 216*

Ferghana (Uzbekistan) 15, 189, 192, 193, 195, 202, 212, 215; *193, 196, 199*

Fez (Morocco) 18, 53, 54, 58, 61; *52, 52–3, 59, 60, 61, 271*

G

Galilee 103, 110, 116

Gaza 110, 116; *113*

Gaziantep (Turkey) 36; *37, 38*

Ghana *307*

Ghazni (Afghanistan) 218, 221, 225

Granada 18, 50, 52, 53, 61, 72; *51*

Greece 26, 31, 41, 42, 84, 86

Gujarat (India) 18, 140, 234, 236, 237, 244, 246, 278, 279

H

Hadhramaut (Yemen) 133, 138, 146; *139, 146*

Hama (Syria) 96, 98, 104, 110; *97, 98, 101*

Harar (Ethiopia) 296, 298, 299; *298*

Hausa people 303, 305; *296, 304*

Hazar-Booz people 220; *220, 230*

Hazara district (Pakistan) 249, 251, 252; *253, 254, 256*

Hazara people 218, 220, 225; *224, 225*

henna 64, 65, 80; *81, 83*

Herat (Afghanistan) 220, 222, 225; *184, 218, 221, 222*

Hijaz (Saudi Arabia) 124, 125, 126, 128; *124, 127*

Hui people 268, 271

I

ikat 15, 36, 98, 138, 154, 184, 195, 196, 200, 202, 204, 214, 221, 272, 274, 275, 276, 278, 279, 282, 290, 293; *34, 109, 156, 184, 195, 276, 281, 292*; *see also* velvet ikat

Ilanun people 274

India 13, 17, 18, 25, 26, 33, 36, 90, 124, 126, 128, 131, 133, 138, 140, 167, 186, 193, 200, 234–46, 272, 275, 276, 278, 279, 282, 287, 296, 298, 305; *33, 96, 127, 133, 134, 135, 139, 145, 147, 167, 168, 173, 234, 235, 236, 237, 238, 239, 240, 241, 242, 243, 244, 245, 246, 288*

indigo 15, 17, 18, 72, 79, 98, 112, 116, 126, 136,

138, 140, 143, 200, 201, 220, 249, 296, 300, 306; *104, 137, 140, 143, 261, 306, 307*
Indonesia 8, 98, 138, 272, 274, 276–89; *276, 277, 278, 279, 280, 281, 282, 283, 284, 285, 286, 287, 288, 289*
Iran (*also* Persia) 10, 11, 13, 15, 17, 18, 22, 26, 36, 50, 67, 86, 89, 98, 99, 120, 124, 130, 138, 150–73, 174, 177, 193, 196, 203, 211, 212, 237, 249, 251, 270, 305; *150, 151, 152–53, 153, 154, 155, 156, 157, 158, 159, 160, 161, 162, 163, 164, 165, 166, 167, 168, 169, 170, 171, 172, 173*
Iraq 17, 96, 98, 99, 118–21, 128, 130, 157; *14, 118, 119, 120, 121*
Isfahan (Iran) 152, 157, 161, 177; *154, 155, 159, 162, 163, 165, 166, 168, 170, 172, 173*
Istanbul (*also* Constantinople) 6, 11, 13, 17, 22, 26, 33, 36, 67, 106, 200, 202, 211; *23, 27, 31, 34*

J
jamdani weave 260; *260, 262*
Java 15, 118, 138, 272, 276, 282, 287, 289, 293; *276, 277, 286, 287, 289*
Jews 13, 31, 72, 74, 84, 85, 96, 110, 138, 147, 152, 186; *141*
Jordan 96, 99, 106

K
Kabul (Afghanistan) 17, 220; *225*
Kaitag embroidery 174, 180; *12*
Kandahar (Afghanistan) 220, 225
Kano (Nigeria) 15, 303, 306; *306*
kantha quilts 260, 264; *263, 264, 265*
Karakalpak people 201; *195, 200, 201*
Kashan (Iran) 152, 153, 154; *152–53, 177*
Kashmir 99, 157, 161, 174, 237, 238, 240, 251; *24, 158, 179, 235, 237, 238, 240, 246*
Katawaz people 225; *231*
Kenya 299
Kerman (Iran) 99, 157, 159, 160, 161, 169, 174; *157, 158, 159, 160, 163*
Khojent (Tajikistan) 193, 196, 214, 215; *214*
Khorasan 10, 14, 150, 203
Khorezm (Uzbekistan) 201; *201*
knitting 39
Konya (Turkey) 11, 39; *39*
Koochi people 231; *226, 231*
Kosovo 42; *44, 47*
Kungrat people 190
Kurds 41, 118, 120; *7, 106, 120, 122*
Kuwait 124, 128–30, 157; *128, 129, 130*
Kyrgyzstan 212, 215–17, 271; *215, 216, 217, 269*

L
Lakhai people 190, 230; *190, 191, 230*
lampas weave 17, 18, 22, 52, 53, 58–61; *23, 51, 60, 172*
Lebanon 99, 103, 105, 106, 110, 112; *96*

Libya 61, 74, 84–85, 91, 92; *84, 85*

M
Malaysia 272–75; *272, 273, 274, 275*
Mali 70, 303; *303*
Mamluks 10, 13, 89, 90
Maranao (Philippines) 290; *291, 292*
Margellan (Uzbekistan) 189, 196, 202; *202*
mashru fabric 36, 99, 109, 143, 236, 296; *37, 38, 44, 109, 298*
Mauritania *18*
Mecca 122, 124, 125, 126
Minangkabau (Indonesia) 278, 279, 287; *277, 278, 279, 289*
Mindanao (Philippines) 274, 290
Mongols 10, 11, 14, 118, 152, 203, 268, 270; *270*
Morocco 8, 18, 22, 54–65, 71; *7, 11, 14, 16, 54, 55, 56, 57, 58, 59, 60, 61, 62, 63, 64, 65*
Mughals 11, 13, 17, 18, 26, 164, 232–65
Mukur (Afghanistan) 225; *227, 228*
Multan (Pakistan) 220, 247, 249, 251, 256
Mzab (Algeria) 70; *71*

N
Na'in (Iran) 157; *157*
Najaf (Iraq) 120, 130
nakshe embroidery 161; *162*
Niger *303*
Nigeria 300; *300, 304, 305, 306, 307*

O
Oman 70, 131–37, 143; *96, 131, 132, 133, 134, 135, 136, 137*
Ottomans 6, 11, 13, 17, 18, 20–47, 54, 58, 67, 72, 84, 90, 91, 96, 99, 104, 105, 109, 116, 118, 122, 124, 126, 138, 143, 174, 177, 180, 279; *1, 9, 10, 22, 23, 25, 27, 30, 41, 68, 102*
oya needlework 33

P
Pakistan 131, 133, 214, 215, 218, 229, 231, 243, 247–59, 264; *247, 248, 249, 250, 251, 252, 253, 254, 255, 256, 257, 258, 259*
Palestine 11, 89, 99, 103, 109, 110–17, 125; *15, 110, 111, 112, 113, 114, 115, 116, 117*
Pashai people 229; *229*
pashmina 237, 238
pateh embroidery 161; *160*
Persia, *see* Iran
Philippines 132, 274, 290–93; *290, 291, 292, 293*
pit-looms 110, 124, 129, 130, 131, 137, 154, 157, 298
Punjab (Pakistan) 247, 249, 251, 252; *249, 251, 258*
Pushtun people 218, 225, 231, 249, 252; *226, 227, 228*

Q
Qashqai people 150, 169
quilting 106, 257; *106, 158*

R
Ramallah (Palestine) 110, 112, 116, 117; *112, 117*
Rasht (Iran) 160; *161, 162*
Russia 8, 17, 26, 41, 110, 152, 157, 169, 184, 212, 215, 238; *151, 155, 172*

S
Sabah (Malaysia) 272, 274; *274*
Safavids 11, 13, 17–18, 26, 152, 164, 236
Samarkand (Uzbekistan) 184, 189, 193, 195, 200, 212; *186, 195, 196, 197, 199, 200*
Sana'a (Yemen) 138, 140, 143; *138, 140, 141, 143, 144, 146*
Sasanians 13, 15, 150
Saudi Arabia 13, 18, 96, 99, 122–27, 128, 130, 157; *122, 123, 124, 125, 126, 127*
Seljuk Turks 11, 22
Shahsavan (Iran) 150, 169
Shakhrisabz (Uzbekistan) 184, 186, 189, 196; *189*
Shinn people 252; *255, 256*
Sierra Leone *301*
Sinai 110, 112; *86, 88*
Sindh (Pakistan) 225, 247, 249, 251, 253, 257, 259; *247, 249, 250, 257, 258, 259*
Siwa oasis (Egypt) 61, 91, 92; *92*
songket brocade 272, 274, 275, 276, 278, 282, 287; *273, 275*
Spain 10, 13, 17, 18, 50–53, 54, 61, 72, 118; *50, 51*
sprang 54, 72; *258*
stitched resist 276, 282; *282, 283*
Sulawesi (Indonesia) 282, 287
Sulu (Philippines) *293*
Sumatra (Indonesia) 276; *278, 280, 287, 288, 289*
Sumbawa (Indonesia) *283, 284, 285*
Surat (India) 243
suzani embroidery 184, 186, 189, 212, 216, 218; *185, 186, 187*
Swahili people 132, 296, 299; *296*
Swat (Pakistan) 249, 251, 252
Syria 8, 10, 13, 14, 17, 22, 33, 36, 50, 67, 89, 91, 96–109, 110, 112, 116, 117, 120, 125, 128, 130, 138, 140, 150, 157, 174.193, 237, 282; *17, 96, 97, 98, 99, 100, 101, 102, 103, 104, 105, 106, 107, 108, 109, 120, 156, 158*

T
Tabaristan 15, 150
tablet-weaving 103, 159; *103*
Tajikistan 184, 189, 190, 193, 196, 212–14, 215, 216, 230, 271; *212, 213, 214, 230*

talli work 132, 143; *144*

Tashkent (Uzbekistan) 184, 189, 192, 193, 202, 214; *187*

Tekke Turkmen 203, 204, 207, 211; *184, 204, 205, 206, 208, 209*

termeh weaving 154, 161

tie and dye 36, 70, 72, 79, 80, 82, 84, 96, 125, 214, 221, 246, 259, 276, 282, 289; *18, 85, 98, 145, 146*

Tihama (Yemen) 125, 140, 143, 147; *142, 147*

Timurids 11, 14

tiraz system 11, 13, 17, 50, 89, 138

Tuareg people 303; *302, 303*

Tulunids 89

Tunisia 10, 53, 71, 72–83, 85; *13, 52, 52–53, 72, 73, 74, 75, 76, 77, 78, 79, 80, 81, 82, 83*

Turkey 13, 22–41, 68, 98, 99, 120, 193, 211, 215, 237, 305; *7, 10, 22, 23, 24, 25, 26, 27, 28, 29, 30, 31, 32, 33, 34, 35, 36, 37, 38, 39, 40, 41, 58*

Turkmenistan 10, 196, 201, 203–11; *203, 204, 205, 206, 207, 208, 209, 210, 211*

U

Uighurs 271; *268, 270, 271*

Umayyads 10, 11, 50

Urgut (Uzbekistan) 189; *185, 186*

Uzbekistan 10, 184–202, 203, 211, 212, 215, 216, 220, 221, 230; *184, 185, 186, 187, 188, 189, 190, 191, 192, 193, 194, 195, 196, 197, 198, 199, 200, 201, 202, 219, 221, 230*

V

velvet ikat 152, 202, 204; *152–53, 153*

W

Wahaybah (Yemen) 133, 136; *133, 136*

Waziristan (Pakistan) 251; *250*

X

Xinjiang (China) 215, 237; *268, 269, 270, 271*

Y

Yazd (Iran) 152, 173; *153, 155, 156, 168, 170, 177*

Yemen 15, 17, 50, 125, 126, 133, 138–47, 244, 282; *138, 139, 140, 141, 142, 143, 144, 145, 146, 147*

Yomut Turkmen 203, 204, 207, 211; *208, 210, 211*

Z

Zabid (Yemen) 138, 143; *143*

Zanzibar 131, 132, 296, 298, 299; *299*

Zemmour (Morocco) 61; *56*

For Kay Brooks and Irene Feesey

ABOUT THE AUTHOR
John Gillow has spent over thirty years studying, collecting and lecturing on textiles. His books include *Indian Textiles* (with Nicholas Barnard), *African Textiles*, *Traditional Indonesian Textiles* and *World Textiles* (with Bryan Sentance).

READER'S NOTE
In this book, historical names and variants – for example, Calcutta in place of Kolkata; Dacca in place of Dhaka; Persia in place of Iran – have been preferred, where appropriate, in order to give historical context.

ON THE COVER
Seventeenth-century Ottoman embroidered textile. Private collection, New York. Photo courtesy Clive Loveless, London.

PAGE 1
Ottoman embroidered cover, *c.* 1830. This floral style was perhaps an inspiration for certain Central Asian *suzani*.

PAGE 2
Finely embroidered early nineteenth-century *suzani*, Bokhara.

Copyright © 2010 Thames & Hudson Ltd, London

All Rights Reserved. No part of this publication may be reproduced or transmitted in any form or by any means, electronic or mechanical, including photocopy, recording or any other information storage and retrieval system, without prior permission in writing from the publisher.

First published in 2010 in hardcover in the United States of America by Thames & Hudson Inc., 500 Fifth Avenue, New York, New York 10110

thamesandhudsonusa.com

First paperback edition 2013

Library of Congress Catalog Card Number 2010923315

ISBN 978-0-500-29083-5

Printed and bound in China by C&C Offset Printing Co., Ltd